Absolutely Every*
BED & BREAKFAST
in
NORTHERN CALIFORNIA
*almost

TONI KNAPP, EDITOR

Special Contributors:

TRAVIS ILSE

KAREN THORSEN BUTTLES

THE ROCKY MOUNTAIN SERIES

FIRST EDITION

TRAVIS ILSE
PUBLISHERS

POST OFFICE BOX 583
NIWOT, COLORADO 80544

COVER PHOTOGRAPH
© Rhoda Stewart
Napa, California

MAP BY
Trudi Peek
Seattle, Washington

PRODUCTION BY
Alan Bernhard
Argent Associates, Boulder, Colorado

PRINTED BY
Versa Press
East Peoria, Illinois

Library of Congress Cataloging-in-Publication Data

Knapp, Toni.
    Absolutely every° bed & breakfast in northern California (°almost) /
        Toni Knapp, editor ; special contributor, Travis Ilse.
    p. cm. — (The Rocky Mountain series)
    Includes index.
    ISBN 1-882092-13-9
    1. Bed and breakfast accommodations—California, Northern—
    Guidebooks. 2. California, Northern—Guidebooks. I. Isle, Travis,
    1946- . II. Title. III. Title: Absolutely every°
    bed and breakfast in northern California (°almost) IV. Series.
    TX907.3.C22N675 1994   94-37134
                                                                CIP

Printed in the United States of America

A B C D E F 0 5 4 3 2 1

Distributed to the trade by
PUBLISHERS GROUP WEST

To Karen

You saved our
butt on this one.

Northern California

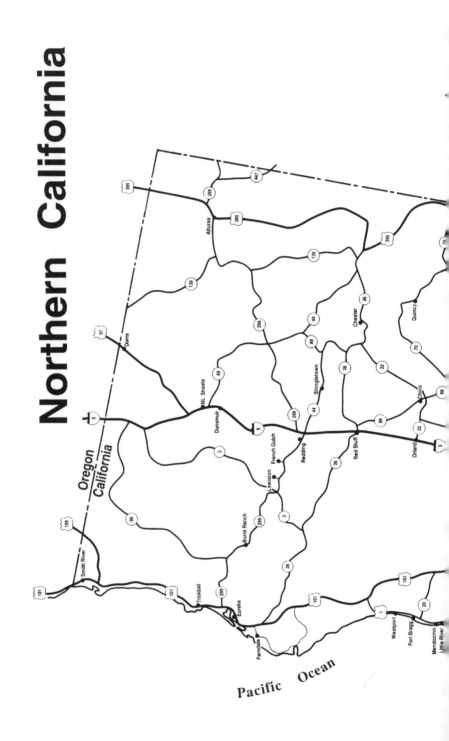

Pacific Ocean

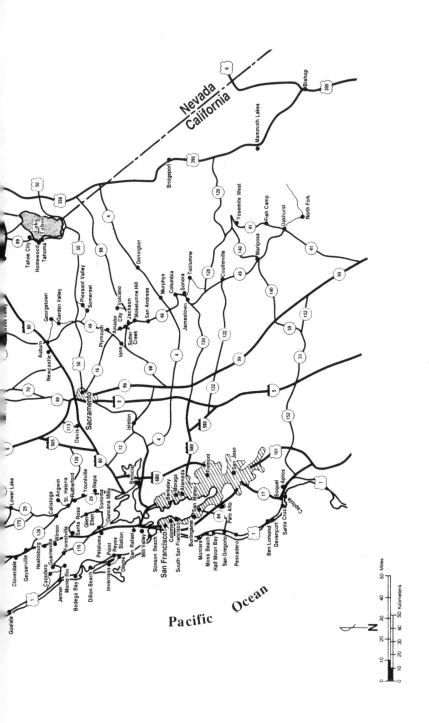

CONTENTS

INTRODUCTION

Northern California is simply a place unlike anyplace else in the world. Within three or four hours of San Francisco a traveler can wander among redwoods, or stand on a mountain top; watch the surf crash against the headlands or cruise through the wine country. But to see this vast array of places you need to take a break from daily life. It happens like this:

It's Monday night, late. Two people are sitting on the couch debriefing. You know the drill. It's almost like they don't have to say anything. He adds an item, she adds an item, several items are dropped, several are tabled and occasionally one is argued with great intensity.

The conversation goes something like this:

"The housecleaners are coming tomorrow so we need make sure the place is picked up before we leave tomorrow morning, "he says.

"Did you get the laundry after work? "she asks. "My boss wants us to come to dinner Saturday after next "she continues.

"Thank God we don't have to serve on the dog committee of the community association anymore, "he says and she nods in agreement.

"I mailed the package to your sister this afternoon, "he says.

"Do we really want to go to your parent's for Thanksgiving again? Why not have them over here? "she asks.

"I found my yellow wind jacket in the trash again. I just hate it when you throw away my stuff, "he says

"Makes you look like a street person, like you got your clothes out of a dumpster, "she says. "It's like wearing wing-tip shoes or a pocket protector, like telling the whole world 'I am not vice presidential material.' "

"Says you, "he says and the argument rages for a bit, she promises never to toss out the yellow wind jacket but has her fingers crossed. He catches the crossed fingers, stomps off and returns wearing a raggedy yellow jacket. She takes a debating stand but bursts into laughter when he sticks out his tongue at her.

"We need out of here for a couple days, "he says. "What say if we find a B&B up the coast and just hang out for the weekend, just you and me and no phone, FAX, modem or beady-eye computer dumping spreadsheets from a smoking printer?"

Somewhere you find this B&B book, you pick a town and then you start reading the entries. So many choices, but remember you must decide right now . . . you can't wait . . . don't hesitate . . . no excuses . . . life is short . . . Northern California is waiting for you.

NORTHERN CALIFORNIA BED & BREAKFASTS

Absolutely Every° Bed & Breakfast in Northern California (°Almost) offers you a choice of 481 B&Bs in 136 cities, towns, villages and wide places in the road. This is the sixth book in our *Absolutely Every° Bed & Breakfast* series that includes individual books on Arizona, California (Monterey to San Diego), Colorado, New Mexico and Texas. There is ordering information in the back of the book.

We build our books by checking telephone directories, chambers of commerce, B&B associations, other books and tourism brochures until we have developed a relatively large list of what may or may not be B&Bs. In the case of *Absolutely Every° Bed & Breakfast in Northern California (°Almost)* we had an initial list just under 800 B&Bs from Half Moon Bay to the Oregon border.

After compiling the list, we mailed a four-page survey to the innkeepers, followed up 45 days later with a reminder post card. When the survey came back we entered the information into our databaase from which we published the book. These surveys are signed by the innkeeper and kept on file with the publisher.

We received about 350 responses and from those surveys wrote 326 full entries. Then we started working the phone making about 700 phone calls to confirm or delete those B&Bs who did not respond to the survey or the reminder post card. Admittedly, our method of confirmation was arbitrary, we did not leave messages on answering machines, we called back later in the day and deleted the B&B if we got the answering machine a second time. If an innkeeper was rude or suspicious, we deleted them. If they hesitated, when we asked if at the minimum, a Continental breakfast was included in the price of the room, we deleted them, and obviously, if the phone was disconnected or if there was no answer after two tries we deleted them. All in all, we made at least four attempts to contact B&Bs, i.e., survey, reminder post card and two telephone calls.

We make an extreme effort to have the most accurate, timely and complete information in our book at press time. If we have missed a B&B let us apologize here and now, it will get into the next edition if we get a note or letter with an address on it. In fact, we love to get letters and appreciate any comments on our books or on B&Bs. Our address is Travis Ilse Publishers, PO Box 583, Niwot, CO 80544.

This gets to the reason for *(°Almost)* in our title. Given that we tentatively identified just under 800 B&Bs and could confirm less than 500, we have fallen short on our goal of *Absolutely Every°*. But, our decision will always be to get accurate information to our readers. If we don't have a fairly high confidence level in the existence and efficacy of a B&B, we simply don't put it in the book.

But there are other reasons for the (*Almost): Innkeepers are busy people who forget to return their survey forms with the information that gets them listed, even after a reminder or two. Innkeepers are also independent folks who may not want to be listed in any book in general, or our book in particular. Fine, be that way.

Some Reservation Service Organizations (RSOs) don't want their B&Bs listed with information that could allow the traveler to call the B&B directly, thus endangering the RSO's commission; kind of small-time thinking, but ours is not to wonder why.

Some homestays are located in areas that are zoned for residential use only. These homestays are frowned on by the local bureaucrats (and sometimes neighbors). To have information widely disseminated by a book might cause legal problems for these homestay innkeepers.

And then there is the "Goathead Factor "where someone has been rude or arrogant on the phone. If they are rude to us, there's a chance that they'll be rude to you. Here we exercise our right under the First Amendment to take them off the list and out of the databaase.

CAVEATS

(1) Because of the breadth of coverage of our books, we depend on the honesty of the innkeepers. We know as a fact that these are some of the most hard working, interesting and nicest people in the world. We deeply admire their work. But there is always the exception. Please write us if an innkeeper has treated you badly or misrepresented their inn.

(2) No one at Travis Ilse Publishers benefits in any way from the B&Bs in this book. We don't accept free rooms or request or receive payment for entries in the book. This book is a service to our readers, not the Northern California bed and breakfast industry; *no Innkeeper ever pays anything to be listed in the book.*

(3) The bed and breakfast industry is volatile; openings, closings and changes in prices and ownership occur regularly. That is why it is always advisable to call ahead and ask questions before you make reservations. Dropping in is chancy and seldom welcome.

(4) We wish to make it perfectly clear that the editor, contributors and Travis Ilse Publishers make no warranty, implied or specific, about operations or policies of bed and breakfast establishments, or trade associations mentioned in this book.

Bed & Breakfast Definitions

Our guide is essentially an annotated database of small and medium-sized bed and breakfast inns, hotels and host homes that include a proper breakfast in the price of the room. However, we have exercised our right as editors, writers and data entry clerks to be inconsistent by including a few "grand "inns with more than 50 rooms (our maximum) because we felt their location and quality warranted inclusion. Though neither absolutely concise nor agreed upon by everyone in the industry, the following definitions may help you determine differences between types of establishments in order of size.

Host Home (or Homestay): The original B&B. Here the resident owner rents from one to three spare bedrooms, typically with shared bathroom, although private bathrooms are becoming more common. With professionalism and competition on the rise, host homes can offer the best of all worlds in terms of rates, services and personal touches.

Guesthouse: A separate unit - cabin, carriage house, etc. Breakfast is either served in the main house or delivered to the guest house. Sometimes B&Bs have a guesthouse in addition to rooms in the main building. Clearly, these are the most private of B&B accommodations.

Inn: The largest and fastest growing category in the B&B industry - five to fifteen rooms, generally with private bathrooms, larger staff and outstanding hospitality.

Country Inn: Usually located in the "country"—rural areas far from the maddening crowd. Rooms number between five and twenty-five and a restaurant or dining hall serves other meals besides breakfast.

Hotel: Usually small or historic hotels between twenty-five and fifty rooms, that have been renovated to preserve their historic past and charm.

Lodge or Working Ranch: A country inn located in a resort or remote area. While breakfast is always included in the price of the room, often, complete meal packages are offered.

Our Guidebook Definitions

Our guide is organized in a clear, friendly format that avoids codes, symbols and endless narrative. Our goal is provide you with more information than you need to make an informed decision about a B&B and ask the right questions when you call for reservations. Each town for which there are complete B&B listings is covered with a thumbnail sketch of information on sights, festivals and strange, little-known facts followed by brief instructions on how to get there.

In addition to 326 survey-based listings, there are 160 short listings that include the B&B name, address, telephone number, innkeeper's name and sometimes a KUDO/COMMENT. These listings are based on a telephone conversation where the person answering the p hone confirmed that the number called was a functioning B&B and that breakfast is included in the price of the meal. For these short listings, no one signed a survey warranting that all the information was correct. We assume honesty on the part of the innkeepers; but *always call first*.

The B&B name is set in large type followed by the address, telephone number, toll-free number, fax number, and names of the innkeepers and languages other than English spoken by the staff. Note that there are some towns in Northern California where the post office does not deliver to street addresses. Always ask the innkeeper for a mailing address; never assume that mailing to an address in the book will get your deposit to the B&B.

Digression #1 . . . 800 numbers followed with cute words, e.g., 800-INN-FOOL. One of the worst marketing ideas ever, because it is inconvenient to look for all those letters on the key pad. In fact, wasn't it the THE TELEPHONE COMPANY in the 50s that changed all the old word exchanges to numbers for just that reason. Dumb, stupid, a waste of time and inconvenient for B&B guests. By the way, there are digressions throughout the book that are always marked by ellipses (...TI). Most of these come from Travis himself on the final edit, but a good number come from the editor, the data entry clerk, or the production type.

LOCATION: Where the B&B actually is relative to the town or area it is in (i.e., directions and miles from the center of town, a highway exit or nearest landmark). It's a good idea to carry the book along with you or keep the B&B telephone number in your daybook just in case you are direction-impaired.

OPEN: Most B&Bs in Northern California are open all year, but there are some seasonal B&Bs, particularly in the mountains and backcountry. Note that some B&Bs close for a week or two randomly when the Innkeeper decides that someplace else like Aspen or Abaco sounds like a pretty good idea.

DESCRIPTION: On our survey form that the Innkeeper competes for this book, we ask when a building was built, the architectural style, type of furnishing and whether it is on the California or National Historic Registers. With this book we have let some notes on landscaping and surroundings slip in here. Tell us if this helps in your decision.

NUMBER OF ROOMS: This is a notation of the rooms with private bathrooms and with shared bathrooms. Also noted here are the availability of suites and guesthouses that are assumed to have private bathrooms, *but always ask*. We also ask the innkeepers to name a favorite room. While it is not surprising that the room named is often the most expensive room in the house, it is usually a very special room with extra amenities, such as a tub for two and a terrific view.

RATES: This may be the most confusing section of our book, simply because there is no standard in the B&B industry for setting rates. We have simply tried to reprint the innkeeper's range of rates that vary by private or shared bathroom, season and rooms. Use the rates in the book as a guideline only. Ask the innkeeper for a specific rate for a specific room. Ask about lower mid-week rates, extended stay rates, seniors' rates. There are some very good deals out there.

BREAKFAST: The second most important reason (think about it) for staying in a B&B is the breakfast that is *always* included in the price of the room. So we ask the innkeepers for an accurate description of their morning fare: a *full breakfast* ranges from the familiar eggs, pancakes, meats, fruits and beverages to three courses formally served, to a full buffet. *Continental* is usually fresh coffee, fruit, fresh juices and assorted baked goodies, usually homemade; *Continental Plus* is somewhere in between, more than Continental and less than a full breakfast.

CREDIT CARDS: Whether or not credit cards are accepted is listed here. But be prepared - bring a checkbook or travelers checks. Some B&Bs do not accept credit cards because the local bank is run by morons or because of the added expense to the innkeeper. Note also that some innkeepers will accept credit cards for a reservation conformation only but not for payment when you check-out.

AMENITIES: All the "extras "that make a B&B vastly different from other accommodations. These may include: a hot tub, fireplaces, afternoon wine and cheese, nature trails, a llama petting zoo. . . .

RESTRICTIONS: Things that you can't do or bring to a B&B that usually involve smoking, children and pets.

Most B&Bs do not allow smoking inside the establishment, although a good number have outside smoking areas.

Children are problematical. While some B&Bs welcome them, others do not; and most set an age limit although in California it is apparently illegal to say "no children "in any advertising or media. Be considerate. If you take your children to a B&B make sure that they are under voice command. One Colorado Innkeeper said it best, "Children of responsible parents are always welcome."

A good number of B&Bs have resident pets and would rather not have dog fights every time a guest rolls up with a pack of Irish Wolfhounds in the back of his Land Cruiser; so leave you best friend at the kennel. We also list the names of resident pets because we believe that pets are an integral part of a home away from home and good fun to have around. Not to worry if you are allergic to pets as most Innkeepers do not allow their pets in the guestrooms. *A good rule is to always ask about restrictions when you call for a reservation.*

AWARDS: Any awards given an inn that are recognized and significant to the hospitality industry or historic preservation organizations.

REVIEWED: Books in which a B&B has been reviewed. We have made an effort to include only those B&B books that are truly "review "publications where the writer and publisher receive no compensation of any kind (including free rooms and meals) for their review.

Digression #2. Fee-based bed & breakfast books . . . while no one really cares about the standards of another industry, there is a clear distinction in book publishing between the author and publisher who assume all risks for a book and the author or publisher who solicit a fee for including a B&B in a book, the former is called publishing, the latter is called advertising.

RATED: Indicates whether a B&B has been rated by the American Automobile Association, American Bed & Breakfast Association or Mobil Travel Guides. These ratings are a good indication of the quality of a B&B, *but* because a B&B is not rated is meaningless. There are many great B&Bs that are not rated.

MEMBER: Membership in professional associations recognized by the hospitality industry.

KUDOS/COMMENTS: These are comments solicited from Innkeepers and inveterate B&B guests. We welcome your comments too; write us at Travis Ilse Publishers, PO Box 583, Niwot, CO 80544.

OTHER B&B GUIDEBOOKS

The following are some good guidebooks in which we think the writers have tried to be objective.

Without any doubt, the best all-around guidebook to Northern California is *Northern California Best Places* by Rebecca Poole Foree and Stephanie Irving, Sasquatch Books, Seattle, Washington. It is simply without competition.

For superb descriptions of the high end B&Bs buy, *America's Wonderful Little Hotels and Inns* by Sandra Soule, St. Martins Press, New York. Wonderful writing and accurate information.

Don't miss Karen Brown's *California Country Inns & Itineraries*, The Globe Pequot Press, Old Saybrook, Connecticut. It's a beautiful book filled with beautiful inns. Karen Brown was nice enough to write a letter wishing us good luck when we first started this book. Thank you, Karen.

Bed & Breakfast in California by Kathy Strong is also published by Globe Pequot. There should be a B&B book for every state that is as good as this one.

BED & BREAKFAST ASSOCIATIONS

Trade associations are not reservations services, although many do make direct reservations. Normally, a true trade association is a non-profit organization whose principal purpose is help promote its member B&Bs.

NATIONAL BED & BREAKFAST ASSOCIATIONS

American Bed & Breakfast Association
1407 Huguenot Road
Midlothian, VA 23113
804-379-2222

Association of American Historic Inns
PO Box 336
Dana Point, CA 92629
714-496-6953

National Bed & Breakfast Association
PO Box 332
Norwalk, CT 06851
203-847-6196

Professional Association of Innkeepers International
PO Box 90710
Santa Barbara, CA 93190
805-965-0707

Tourist House Association
RD 2, Box 355A
Greentown, PA 18426
717-857-0856

Formal Rating Systems

American Automobile Association
1000 AAA Drive
Heathrow, FL 32746

American Bed & Breakfast Association
1407 Huguenot Road
Midlothian, VA 23113

Mobil Travel Guides
PO Box 7600
Chicago, IL 60680

Dear Traveler:

As you visit B&Bs you leave with opinions, particularly from the great B&Bs where the room was perfect, the innkeepers wonderful and the food beyond description.

We'd like to hear your thoughts on any B&B that you visit. Just copy the form on the following page and fold a bunch of them into the book so that they'll be handy when you travel. If you give us permission to use some or all of your comments in the next edition of this book, we'll send you a free copy of this or any other books in the series (AZ, CA, Northern CA, NM, TX).

Let us know what you think. Write to us at Travis Ilse Publishers, PO Box 583, Niwot, CO 80544. We love to get letters.

—Travis Ilse

—Toni Knapp

B&B GUEST COMMENT CARD

B&B VISITED: _____

LOCATION: _____

DATES VISITED: _____

COMMENTS, KUDOS, QUIBBLES: _____

_____

_____

_____

_____

❑ I/we grant Travis Ilse Publishers permission to incorporate some or all of our comments in future editions of this book.

❑ I/we prefer not to be quoted, but here are our comments anyway.

NAME_____ DATE _____

ADDRESS (CITY, STATE, ZIP)_____

_____ PHONE _____

Please mail to: Travis Ilse (CAN), PO Box 583, Niwot, CO 80544

B&B GUEST COMMENT CARD

B&B VISITED: _____

LOCATION: _____

DATES VISITED: _____

COMMENTS, KUDOS, QUIBBLES: _____

_____

_____

_____

_____

❑ I/we grant Travis Ilse Publishers permission to incorporate some or all of our comments in future editions of this book.

❑ I/we prefer not to be quoted, but here are our comments anyway.

NAME_____ DATE _____

ADDRESS (CITY, STATE, ZIP)_____

_____ PHONE _____

Please mail to: Travis Ilse (CAN), PO Box 583, Niwot, CO 80544

ALAMEDA
(OAKLAND)

If you love Islands and airplanes, you'll love it here. West of Oakland in San Francisco Bay, this once-thriving resort community is now home to Alameda Naval Air Station. During fall and winter, watch for loons, grebes and other birds at Robert C. Crown Memorial Beach. The Crab Cove shoreline is a designated estuarine marine reserve with great exhibits of undersea creatures. The town is handy to all the goodies in Oakland.

GARRATT MANSION

900 Union, Alameda, CA 94501   510-521-4779
Royce & Betty Gladden, Resident Owners   FAX 510-521-6796

LOCATION	From Highway 880 take the High Street/Alameda exit. Go west on High Street five blocks, then turn right on Central Avenue. Go 1.5 miles and turn left on Union Street and go four blocks to the inn on the corner of Clinton and Union.
OPEN	All year
DESCRIPTION	A three-story 1893 Colonial Revival mansion with antique furnishings.
NO. OF ROOMS	Five rooms with privatre bathrooms and two rooms share two bathrooms.
RATES	Year round rates are $95 for a single or double with a private bathroom and $75 for a single or double with a shared bathroom. The suite is $125. There is no minimum stay and cancellation requires three days notice.
CREDIT CARDS	Amex, MC, Visa
BREAKFAST	Full breakfast served in the dining room changes daily and may include cheese blintz souffle with fresh strawberries, chicken and apple sausage, fresh squeezed orange juice and beverages.
AMENITIES	Robes, telephones, fresh flowers in every room. TV room with old movies and popcorn, chocolate chip cookies, Califonia grown pistachios, hot and cold drinks and area maps and menus.
RESTRICTIONS	No smoking in the house, no pets.
REVIEWED	*Bed & Breakfast California, Northern California Best Places*
MEMBER	California Association of Bed & Breakfast Inns, Professional Association of Innkeepers International, American Bed & Breakfast Association
KUDOS/COMMENTS	An innkeeper writes, "Betty Gladden thinks of every little detail - I stole a bunch of ideas from her. Beautiful house."

WEBSTER HOUSE

1238 Versailles Avenue, Alameda, CA 94501   510-523-9697
Susan McCormack, Resident Owner

ALBION

Nestled on the Mendocino Coast and Albion River, and famous for its salmon and crab fishing. This is the perfect place for divine eating, not to mention its location. Not to be missed is Van Damme State Park, next door near Little River—it's a gem. Between Fort Bragg and Point Arena on Hwy. 1.

ALBION RIVER INN

3790 North Highway 1, Albion, CA 95410   707-937-1919
Peter Wells & Flurry Healy, Resident Owners   800-479-7944 *(N. CA only)*
Some Spanish spoken.   FAX 707-937-2604

LOCATION	Three miles north of the intersection of Highway 128 and Highway 1. Just 1/8 mile north of the Albion Bridge.
OPEN	All year
DESCRIPTION	Two-story 1983 New England Clapboard and cottages with "country comfortable" furnishings on ten clifftop acres overlooking the Pacific and Albion River Cove.
NO. OF ROOMS	Twenty rooms with private bathrooms. Linda the manager suggests room #20.
RATES	Year round rates are $160 to $250 for a single or a double with a private bathroom. There is a two night minimum stay when Saturday is involved and cancellation requires seven days notice.
CREDIT CARDS	Amex, MC, Visa
BREAKFAST	Full breakfast is served in the dining room and is an "all you can eat, full menu". Dinner is available in the gourmet restaurant.
AMENITIES	Bathrobes, complimentary local wines, fireplaces, binoculars or telescopes in room, all rooms have private garden entrances, 18 rooms have decks, no TVs in rooms, piano in restaurant, handicapped access, weddings and receptions catered. Headland hiking trails.
RESTRICTIONS	No smoking, no pets. The resident cat is called Albion and "loves left-overs from dinner."
REVIEWED	*50 Romantic Getaways, Best Places to Kiss in Northern California, Karen Brown's California Country Inns & Itineraries.*
MEMBER	California Lodging Industry Association
RATED	AAA 3 Diamonds, Mobil 3 Stars

FENSALDEN INN

38810 Navarro Ridge Road, Albion, CA 95410
Scott & Frances Brazil, Resident Owners

707-937-4042
800-959-3850
FAX 707-937-2416

LOCATION	Seven miles south of Mendocino and 1/4 mile east of Highway 1.
OPEN	All year
DESCRIPTION	An 1860 stagecoach way station with antique furnishings.
NO. OF ROOMS	Nine rooms with private bathrooms. The Captain's Walk is the best room.
RATES	High season, May through December, rates are $75 to $95 for a single or double with private bathroom, $105 to $130 for a suite, $115 to $125 for the guest house and $785 to $865 for the entire inn. Low season, January through April, rates are $10 less. There is a minimum stay on weekends and holidays and cancellation requires seven days notice.
CREDIT CARDS	MC, Visa
BREAKFAST	Full breakfast is served in the dining room includes a baked entree, fresh baked bread, baked or marinated fruit and beverages.
AMENITIES	Guest telephone, wine and hors d'oeuvres in evening, meeting rooms, handicapped accomodations, grand piano, telescope and books.
RESTRICTIONS	No smoking, no pets, children over nine are welcome. The resident cats are called Bobbie and Thunder.
REVIEWED	*Country Inns of the Far West, Historic Country Inns of California, The Official Guide to American Historic Bed & Breakfast Inns and Guesthouses, Havens, Retreats and Hidaways North of San Francisco*
KUDOS/COMMENTS	"Peaceful, genteel, with a view ... decompression come easily here."

THE WOOL LOFT

32751 Navarro Ridge Road, Albion, CA 95410   707-937-0377
Jan Tarr & Sid Spring, Resident Owners

LOCATION	From Albion, one mile south on Highway 1, turn left and go 1.2 miles. Mail box 32751 on the right side has a couple of white sheep on it.
OPEN	All year except for an occasional vacation.
DESCRIPTION	A contemporary host home overlooking the Navarro River with contemporary furnishings, "not a fancy place, just comfortable and homey."
NO. OF ROOMS	Four rooms with private bathrooms. Jan suggests the Eweview as the best room.
RATES	Year round rates are $65 to $85 for a single or double with a private bathroom. There is a minimum stay on weekends and holidays, cancellation requires seven days notice.
CREDIT CARDS	No
BREAKFAST	Full breakfast served in the sunroom "with a view of the ocean" and includes juice, fresh fruit, sausage or bacon, eggs from the henhouse, pancakes, veggies from the garden, beverages, "Depends on how I feel, nobody leaves hungry."
AMENITIES	Wool loft, vegetable garden, strawberry and raspberry patches, bee hives, fresh honey and lambs.
RESTRICTIONS	No smoking, no pets, the inn is not suitable for children. The resident critters are sheep, hens and quail.
REVIEWED	*Bed & Breakfast Homes Directory*
KUDOS/COMMENTS	"Great river view, fun hosts, nice accomodations."

ALLEGHANY

This is deep in the northernmost reaches of Gold Country in the Sierra Nevada. There's good skiing and maybe fishing in Kaneka Creek. Take Highway 49 northeast of Sacramento and have a good map.

KENTON MINE LODGE

#2 Footes Crossing Road, Alleghany, CA 95910   916-287-3212
William Geary, Manager

LOCATION	Take Highway 49 from Nevada City to North San Juan. Left turn two miles out of North San Juan on the Ridge Road. Alleghany is 19 miles, turn left before town on rock/gravel road, go three miles.
OPEN	All year
DESCRIPTION	1930s lodge and cabin in restored gold mining camp on Kanaka Creek. Furnished with antiques and mining memorabilia.
NO. OF ROOMS	Six cabins with private bathrooms, nine lodge rooms with shared bathrooms. Pick cabin #4.
RATES	Year round rates for a single or double cabin with private bathroom are $40 to $55, and $35 to $50 for a single or double boarding house room with shared bathroom. Seven day cancellation policy.
CREDIT CARDS	MC, Visa
BREAKFAST	Continental breakfast includes homemade sweets, fruit and beverages served family style. Lunch and dinner also available.
AMENITIES	Gold panning, fishing, library
RESTRICTIONS	Smoking in designated areas, pets limited to cabins. A Chow and a Hound, Cory and Nugget, will share your visit.
REVIEWED	*Historic Country Inns of California, The Califonias B & B Inns*

ALTURAS

Set in a semi-arid landscape between Modoc National Forest and the South Warner Wilderness, the Modoc county seat is the marketing center for local livestock, potatoes and prime alfalfa. The geology of this area is fascinating; rockhounds should keep an eye out for quartz crystals, jasper, obsidian, and perlite. There's good birdwatching in Modoc National Wildlife Refuge on the shores of Dorris Reservoir, as well as abundant fish and few people at Goose Lake. In town, do the historic tour and County Museum, and remember that on Saturday nights the cowboys come into town! At the northeast corner of the state, and a short zip into Oregon. The Pitt River runs through it.

DORRIS HOUSE B&B

County Road 57, Alturas, CA 96101   916-233-3786
Karoe & Mary Woodward, Resident Owners

LOCATION	Four miles east of Alturas on Country Road 56 & 57.
OPEN	All year
DESCRIPTION	A two-story 1912 ranch furnished with family heirlooms and antiques on Dorris Lake.
NO. OF ROOMS	Four rooms share two bathrooms. Mary recommends Kathy's room.
RATES	Year round rates are $40 to $45 for a single or double with shared bathroom. There is no minimum stay and cancellation requires ten days notice with a $5.00 cancellation fee.
CREDIT CARDS	No
BREAKFAST	Continental Plus is served in the dining room or on the deck and includes homemade muffins, banana bread, all available fruit, homemade jams and homegrown strawberries and raspberries in season.
AMENITIES	Wine available at cocktail hour, located on a lake with bass and catfish fishing, bird watching and horse pasture, parlor with piano and large deck.
RESTRICTIONS	No pets, children over 12 are welcome.
REVIEWED	*Northern California Best Places*

AMADOR CITY

Once the "saddle on the Mother Lode," the state's smallest incorporated city is only one block long. Browsing the block is pretty much the main event, or wander out into the Gold Country. North of Sutter Creek on Hwy. 49.

IMPERIAL HOTEL

14202 Highway 49, Amador City, CA 95601   209-267-9172
Bruce Sherrill & Dale Martin, Resident Owners   FAX 209-267-9249

LOCATION	Northwest corner of Highway 49 and Water Street.
OPEN	All year except Christmas Eve.
DESCRIPTION	A two-story gothic brick hotel with Victorian furnishings, veranda, fountains and a waterfall.
NO. OF ROOMS	Six rooms with private bathrooms.
RATES	Year round rates are $55 to $90 for a single or double with private bathroom. There is a two night minimum stay when Saturday is involved and cancellation requires seven days notice and there is a $10 cancellation fee.
CREDIT CARDS	Amex, Carte Blanche, Diners Club, Discover, MC, Visa
BREAKFAST	Continental Plus is served in the dining room, guest rooms, patio or balcony and includes eggs, fresh fruit, homemade breads and beverages. Dinner and Sunday brunch is available.
AMENITIES	Flowers, morning paper, hair dryers, room service, bar, air conditioning, meeting space and AV equipment available.
RESTRICTIONS	No smoking, no pets. There are four "adopted" resident cats: Carla, Perl, Jose and Hose-B.
REVIEWED	*Best Places to Kiss in Northern California, Recommended Romantic Inns of North America, American and Canadian B&Bs, Best Places to Stay in California, The Definitive California Bed & Breakfast Touring Guide, Northern California Best Places, America's Wonderful Little Hotels & Inns*
MEMBER	California Association of Bed & Breakfast Inns, Amador B&B Association
KUDOS/COMMENTS	"An excellent opportunity to spend a night in an 1800's vintage hotel."

MINE HOUSE INN

14125 HIghway 49, Amador City CA 95601   209-267-5900
Allen and Rose Mendy, Resident Owners   800-646-3473
Fluent Spanish, some German and French

LOCATION	Five miles north of Jackson on Highway 49
OPEN	All year, closed December 24 and 25.
DESCRIPTION	1879 Federal style Victorian inn, built in 1879, is on the California State Historic Register. Victorian antiques from 1800's furnish all rooms, each with a separate entrance.
NO. OF ROOMS	Seven rooms with private bathrooms. The Vault room is recommended.
RATES	Year round rates for a single or a double are $65 to $105. The entire inn rents for $590. There is a minimum two night stay on weekends and cancellation requires seven days notice and a $10 fee.
CREDIT CARDS	MC, Visa
BREAKFAST	Continental breakfast served in guestroom includes juices, fresh fruit, baskets of bread and pastries, yogurt and coffee and tea.
AMENITIES	Outdoor swimming pool and patio overlooks hillside and Amador City.
RESTRICTIONS	No pets, children over the age of 12 are welcome, children under 12 limited to one room availability. The resident Maltese is known as, Killer Snowball...and is sometimes confused about his/her name...TI
MEMBER	Professional Association of Innkeepers International, Amador County Bed and Breakfast Association

ANGWIN

It's in Wine Country, but wine is not welcome here (no coffee, tea, meat or cigarettes are sold in the local store, either). The Seventh-day Adventist Pacific Union College is here, and most of the populace belongs to the church. But it is in Napa Valley and away from the madness of Hwy. 29's wine spine. Check out the Newton Observatory nearby and Los Posadas State Forest. In the hills just east of St. Helena, via Deer Park and Howell Mountain roads.

FOREST MANOR

415 Cold Springs Road, Angwin, CA 94508   707-965-3538
Corlene & Harold Lambeth, Resident Owners   800-788-0364
Spanish spoken   FAX 707-965-3303

LOCATION	North through St. Helena on Highway 29 one mile. Turn right (east) on Deer Park Road and proceed 6 miles. Turn right on Cold Spring Road.
OPEN	All year
DESCRIPTION	A three-story 1982 English Tudor estate furnished with English antiques surrounded by 20 acres of extensive landscaping. The building features hand hewn beams, vaulted ceilings and verandas.
NO. OF ROOMS	Three rooms with private bathrooms. The Somerset Room is the best in the house.
RATES	High season, August through November, rates for a single or double with private bathroom are $139 to $239, and $99 to $219, December through February, except holidays. Seven day cancellation notice required with $10 fee.
CREDIT CARDS	Amex, MC, Visa
BREAKFAST	Full breakfast served in the dining room, guestroom or veranda includes egg entree, fruit, homemade muffins, pastry and beverages.
AMENITIES	Swimming pool, spa, billard room, robes, roses in season, phone and VCR on request, some fireplaces and private spas, in room refrigerators and coffee-makers, down comforters and pillows, oversized beds, afternoon cookies and tea.
RESTRICTIONS	No smoking inside, no pets, children over 12 years old are welcome. The outside pets are Felicia, a kitty who "entertains the guests." Dinch the German Shepherd and the ranch Ostriches.
REVIEWED	*Bed & Breakfast California, America's Wonderful Little Hotels and Inns, The B & B Traveler, AAA Bed & Breakfast Guide—Northern and Central California*
MEMBER	California Association of Bed & Breakfast Inns

NAPA VALLEY BED & BREAKFAST

630 Linda Falls Terrace, Angwin, CA 94508   *707-965-2440*
Thea Hanson, Resident Owner
Dutch and German spoken

LOCATION	After St. Helena go north on Highway 29, immediately past the Krug Winery make a right turn on Deer park Road. Cross Silverado Trail at the flashing red light and continue up the hill toward Angwin. Linda Falls Terrace is 4.5 miles from the flashing light.
OPEN	All year
DESCRIPTION	A two-story host home with eclectic Victorian furnishings.
NO. OF ROOMS	One room with a private bathroom.
RATES	High season, March through October and the Christmas holidays, rates are $125 for a single or a double with a private bathroom. Off season rates are $100. There is a two day minimum stay during high season and cancellation requires seven days notice and a $10 fee.
CREDIT CARDS	No
BREAKFAST	Continental Plus breakfast is served in the guest room and includes croissants, bagels, apple crisp, gingerbread, cinammon rolls, crepes, fresh fruit, waffles, beverages and an assortment of cereals.
AMENITIES	Robes, slippers, TV in room, videos, CD, telephone, kitchenette, double Jacuzzi, private patio, wine, cheese & crackers, fruit basket, games, king brass bed, fireplace and handicapped access.
RESTRICTIONS	No smoking, no pets, the inn is not suitable for children. The resident Schnauzer is called Sparky.

APTOS

A southern suburb of Santa Cruz at the upper reaches of Monterey Bay, on the east side of Hwy. 1. This is the entrance into Nature Conservancy's Forest of Nisine Marks State Park, an oasis of pristine solitude and a hiker's dream (also epicenter of the 1989 earthquake). Cabrillo College, art galleries and craft shops gallore are here, as well as the World's Shortest Parade (usually) on July 4th weekend. Handy to Seacliff State Beach and coastal redwoods.

BAYVIEW HOTEL

8041 Soquel Drive, Aptos, CA 95003
Barry Hooper, Manager

408-688-8654
800-229-8439
FAX 408-688-5128

LOCATION	Approximately eight miles south of Santa Cruz, just off Highway 1. Take Seacliff Beach/Aptos exit, turn right on Soquel Drive, hotel is 1.25 miles up the drive.
OPEN	All year
DESCRIPTION	Late 1800s, three-story hotel.
NO. OF ROOMS	Eleven rooms with private bathrooms. Rooms 12 and 14 have fireplaces and oversized tubs.
RATES	Year round rates for a double with a private bathroom are $80 to $150 (weekends and holidays), $140 to $150 for suites. Mid-week rates are $80 for a double with private bathroom, $140 for suites. Two night minimum stay required over Saturday night, cancellation policy requires five days notice and $15 charge per night.
CREDIT CARDS	Amex, MC, Visa
BREAKFAST	Full breakfast served in the dining room includes fruit, cereals, egg dish, pastries and beverages.
AMENITIES	Fresh flowers, phones, veranda, four star restaurant on premises.
RESTRICTIONS	No smoking, no pets. Meow Mix is the resident cat...Good name...we are thinking of calling our next cat, Feed Me...TI
REVIEWED	*Best Places to Kiss in Northern California*
MEMBER	American Bed and Breakfast Association, California Association of Bed and Breakfast Inns
RATED	ABBA 2 Crowns

Mangels House

570 Aptos Creek Road, Aptos, CA 95003   408-688-7982
Jacqueline Fisher, Resident Owner
Spanish and French spoken

LOCATION	From Highway 1 take the Seacliff Beach exit. Take Soquel Drive south to Aptos Creek Road east. The inn is one mile from the exit.
OPEN	All year except December 24 through 27.
DESCRIPTION	An 1886 Italianate Victorian on four acres with eclectic interior furnishings.
NO. OF ROOMS	Six rooms with private bathrooms. Jacqueline thinks the guest room is her best room.
RATES	Year round rates are $105 to $135 for a single or a double with private bathroom. For mid-week, or three days or seniors there is a 10% discount. There is a minimum stay over Saturday and cancellation requires seven days notice with a $10 processing fee.
CREDIT CARDS	Amex, MC, Visa
BREAKFAST	Full breakfast served in the dining room includes beverages, egg dish, homemade scones, muffins or coffee cake, French bread, butter and jams.
AMENITIES	Large formal gardens, fresh flowers, robes in some rooms, sherry and shortbread in the afternoon, table tennis, darts and croquet on the porch and lawn.
RESTRICTIONS	No smoking in the bedrooms, no pets, children over 12 years of age are welcome. The resident Rotweiller/Alsatian is called Dieter and is very friendly. The cat has no name.
REVIEWED	*National Trust Guide to Historic B&Bs, Karen Brown's Bed & Breakfasts of the West Coast, Best Places to Kiss in Northern California*
MEMBER	California Association of Bed & Breakfast Inns, Bed & Breakfast Innkeepers of Santa Cruz, American Bed & Breakfast Association

Arcata

The Lady Anne

902 14th Street, Arcata, CA 95521   707-822-2797
Sam Pennisi, Resident Owner

ARNOLD

LODGE AT MANUEL MILL

PO Box 998, Arnold, CA 95223   209-795-2622
Anne Saunders, Manager

AUBURN

This was one of the first towns in the gold country. Still small with an old-fashioned downtown and Victorian homes, it's fast giving way to encroaching suburban sprawl. Check out the many fine museums, or head out to the Auburn State Recreation Area. Also fairly handy to the Folsom State Recreation Area. Interesting doings: April's Pro-Rodeo; Western States Gold Fair and Panning Championships in July; and the hilarious Funk Soap Box Derby Nationals in August. For a more hair-raising thrill, cross over the Foresthill Bridge. Northeast of Sacramento via I-80 and Hwy. 49.

LINCOLN HOUSE BED & BREAKFAST

191 Lincoln Way, Auburn, CA 95603   916-885-8880
Leslie & Stan Fronczak, Resident Owners

KUDOS/COMMENTS   "A 1920s house with a view of the American River Canyon, clean, orderly, nice breakfast, friendly and informative hostess."

POWER'S MANSION INN

164 Cleveland Avenue, Auburn, CA 95603   916-885-1166
Anthony & Tina Verhaart and Jean & Arno Lejnieks, Resident Owners
Dutch, German, Mandarin Chinese spoken   FAX 916-885-1386

LOCATION	Take Elm exit in Auburn, turn left, first traffic light turn right, next traffic light turn left.
OPEN	All year
DESCRIPTION	A two-story 1885 Victorian inn with Victorian furnishings, listed on the California Historic Register
NO. OF ROOMS	Eleven rooms with private bathrooms. The best room in the house is the honeymoon suite.
RATES	Year round rates are $69 to $149 for a single or a double with a private bathroom. The suite is $149 and the entire B&B rents for $939. There is no minimum stay and cancellation requires 72 hours.
CREDIT CARDS	Amex, MC, Visa
BREAKFAST	Full breakfast is served family style in the dining room.
AMENITIES	Robes, telephones, TV, heart-shaped Jacuzzi in honeymoon suite. Wedding and meeting facilities.
RESTRICTIONS	No smoking

BEN LOMOND

Reached via scenic Hwy. 9 and about 16 miles north of Santa Cruz, along the San Lorenzo River. From here it's a short drive to Big Basin Redwoods State Park, the first of the state's park system. For sandy beaches and good swimming, try Highlands County Park, and old estate transformed, and Ben Lomond County Park.

CHATEAU DES FLEURS

7995 Highway 9, Ben Lomond, CA 95005   *408-336-8943*
Lee and Laura Jonas, Resident Owners
German spoken

LOCATION	From Highway 17 take Mt. Vernon Road turnoff, through Scott's Valley to Felton. Turn right at Graham Hill Road, after one block turn right on Highway 9. Two miles to Chateau, directly across from Andersen Jewelry.
OPEN	All year
DESCRIPTION	An 1879 Country French Victorian with Country French antiques.
NO. OF ROOMS	Three rooms with private bathrooms. The Orchid room is the best in the house.
RATES	Year round rates for a single or double with private bathroom are $95 to $105. Two night minimum stay on all holiday weekends and UCSC graduation. Five days notice required for cancellation.
CREDIT CARDS	Amex, MC, Visa, Discover
BREAKFAST	Full breakfast served in the dining room includes fresh fruit, pastry, hot entree such as quiche, blintzes, French custard toast or cheese souffle and beverages.
AMENITIES	Wine and hors d'oeuvres, phone available, meeting rooms for 30 or less.
RESTRICTIONS	No smoking, no pets, children over 16 years old welcome. The resident cats are La Pouf, La Mousse and Nakima...wish I'd thought of one of those names for my cat...La Pouf, indeed...TI
REVIEWED	*AAA Bed & Breakfast Guide—Central and Northern California, Bed and Breakfast California, Bed and Breakfast in California, The Painted Ladies Guide to Bed and Breakfast Inns*
MEMBER	California Association of Bed and Breakfast Inns, Bed and Breakfast Association of Santa Cruz County

FAIRVIEW MANOR

245 Fairview Avenue, Ben Lomond, CA 95005   *408-336-3355*
Nancy Glasson, Resident Owner

LOCATION	Exit from Highway 17 onto Mt. Herman/Glen Canyon. Stay on Mt. Herman exactly four miles to Felton. Go right, north on Highway 9 three miles to Ben Lomond. Go left on Fillmore off Highway 9, turn left to Fairview Avenue, the inn is a 100 yards on the left.
OPEN	All year
DESCRIPTION	A mid-1920s country redwood inn on the San Lorenzo River, with country English furnishings.
NO. OF ROOMS	Five rooms with private bathrooms.
RATES	Year round rates are $109 for a single or a double with a private bathroom. The entire inn rents for $500 a night. There is no minimum stay.
CREDIT CARDS	MC, Visa
BREAKFAST	Full breakfast served in the dining room includes fruit, juice, muffins, egg dish, meat and potaotes.
AMENITIES	Soft drinks/coffee and tea available at all time. Wine and hors d'oeuvres. Gazebo, walking paths, deck overlooking the river great room with stone fireplace, and meeting facilities.
RESTRICTIONS	No smoking, no pets, children over 12 are welcome.
REVIEWED	*Recommended Country Inns—West Coast, Bed, Breakfast & Bike Northern California, Cooking and Traveling Inn Style, Bed & Breakfast California.*
MEMBER	California Association of Bed & Breakfast Inns, Bed & Breakfast Innkeepers of Santa Cruz County

BENICIA

This splendid little town had a short reign as the state capital between 1853–1854. Set along the northern edge of Suisun Bay, it's now experiencing overall revitalization and art-community boom. The town's an historic charmer, with lots of architecture worth looking at; especially St. Paul's Episcopal Church, and Benicia Capital State Historic Park. Benicia State Recreation Area along the strait is for outdoor fun, and it's a short drive to Marine World/Africa U.S.A. Pick your route northeast of Oakland.

CAPTAIN WALSH HOUSE

235 East L Street, Benicia, CA 94510   707-747-5653
Reed and Steve Robbins, Resident Owners

LOCATION	From San Francisco, go north on Highway 80 to East 780, take Central Benicia/East Second Street exit. Turn left onto East Second Street, go to L Street, turn left, inn is the third building on the left.
OPEN	All year
DESCRIPTION	An 1849 two-story Gothic inn restored in 1989 listed on the California State Historic Register.
NO. OF ROOMS	Five rooms with private bathrooms. Sample the Epiphania Room.
RATES	Year round rates for a double with private bathroom are $110 to $125. Reservation must be secured with a credit card, seven day cancellation notice required.
CREDIT CARDS	Amex, Visa
BREAKFAST	Full gourmet breakfast served in the dining room. Lunches, dinners, weddings and special meals on request.
AMENITIES	Hors d'ourves and wine, snacks, phone, flowers, grand piano, harp, wedding receptions and business meetings, early morning coffee served in guestroom.
RESTRICTIONS	No smoking, no pets. Bill, the Clumber Spaniel, has graced the cover of "Dog World" magazine and has his own pet cat! ...My dog Sam has graced the covers of some magazines too...TI
REVIEWED	*Northern California Best Places, National Trust Guide to Historic Bed and Breakfasts, Painted Ladies Guide to Victorian Bed and Breakfasts, Here Comes the Guide, Perfect Places*

THE PAINTED LADY BED & BREAKFAST

141 East F Street, Benicia, CA 94510   707-746-1646
Sally Watson, Resident Owner

LOCATION	Located in historic downtown Benicia.
OPEN	All year
DESCRIPTION	An 1896 Victorian cottage with Victorian and Country furnishings and surrounded by an old fashioned garden.
NO. OF ROOMS	Two rooms with private bathrooms. Daisy's room has a large bathroom with whirlpool tub.
RATES	Year round rates for a single or double with private bathroom are $78 to $88. Entire cottage rents for $161. No minimum stay, four day notice for cancellation with full refund.
CREDIT CARDS	MC, Visa
BREAKFAST	Full breakfast is served in the dining room or on the patio and might include breakfast breads, waffles, pancakes, omelettes, fruits and beverages "depending on what's in season and the cook's whim." Will cater luncheons and small parties.
AMENITIES	Robes, wine in room, books, tape player, games.
RESTRICTIONS	No smoking in the house, pets OK with prior arrangement, children welcome if guests rent both rooms. Outdoor cats, Miss Kitty and Beau, are affectionate hosts.
MEMBER	California Lodging Industry Association, California Association of Bed and Breakfast Inns

Union Hotel & Gardens

401 First Street, Benicia, CA 94510　　　　　　　707-746-0100
Eric Wolf, Manager　　　　　　　　　　　　　　800-544-2278
Spanish, Dutch, Hebrew, Flemish spoken　　　　FAX 707-746-6458

LOCATION	From San Francisco take Highway 101 to I-80 across the Carquinez Bridge to I-780. Take 2nd Street exit, left to first light, turn right on Military to 1st Street then go eight blocks.
OPEN	All year
DESCRIPTION	Historic 1882 three-story bordello and restaurant that was renovated in 1982 with individually decorated rooms.
NO. OF ROOMS	Twenty rooms with private bathrooms.
RATES	Year round rates are $75 to $135 for a single or a double. There is no minimum stay and cancellation requires 48 hours.
CREDIT CARDS	Amex, Diner's Club, Discover, MC, Visa
BREAKFAST	Continental breakfast is served in the dining room. Lunch and dinner are available.
AMENITIES	Queen or king sized beds, TV, Jacuzzi bathtubs, atrium & gazebo for weddings and parties, meeting room, live music five nights a week, parking on premises
RESTRICTIONS	No pets
RATED	AAA 2 Diamonds

BERKELEY

Everything here seems to radiate out from the campus of the University of California, where the '60s really took root. There's no denying or ignoring its power and presence. But once you have done the magnificent campus, the city has endless offerings including excellent repertory theatre, museums, book stores, and restaurants—check out the Gourmet Ghetto area. Or leave it all and opt for the outdoors at Tilden and Wildcat Canyon Regional Parks, or Claremont Canyon Regional Preserve. Of course, there's always The Bay!

BANCROFT CLUB HOTEL

2680 Bancroft Way, Berkeley, CA 94704   *510-549-1000*
Mark Flaherty, Manager   *800-549-1002*
      FAX 510-549-1070

ELMWOOD HOUSE

2609 College Avenue, Berkeley, CA 94704   *510-540-5123*
John Ekdahl & Steve Hyske, Resident Owners   *FAX 510-540-5123*
French & German spoken

LOCATION	From the west on Highway 24 exit on Clairmont Avenue, then left to College Avenue. From the east on Highway 24 exit on College Avenue and go right.
OPEN	All year except for two week vacation period that varies.
DESCRIPTION	A two-story Berkeley Bay Tradition turn-of-the-century host home with redwood trimmed interior.
NO. OF ROOMS	Two rooms have private bathrooms and two rooms share two bathrooms. John recommends the Maybeck room.
RATES	Year round rates for a single or double with a private bathroom are $65 to $100. A single or double with a shared bathroom ranges from $55 to $85. There is no minimum stay but add $10 for a single night's stay. Cancellation requires seven days notice.
CREDIT CARDS	Amex, MC, Visa
BREAKFAST	Continental breakfast
AMENITIES	Private line phone in each room.
RESTRICTIONS	No smoking, no pets. The resident cats are called Ruby and Bebe.
MEMBER	American Bed & Breakfast Association, California Association of Bed & Breakfast Innkeepers
RATED	ABBA B+

GRAMMA'S

2740 Telegraph Avenue, Berkeley, CA 94705   510-549-2145
Barry Cleveland & Kathy Kuhner, resident Owner

HILLEGASS HOUSE

2834 Hillegass Avenue, Berkeley, CA 94705   510-548-5517
Richard Warren, Resident Manager

BISHOP

At the southeastern edge of the Sierras, this is the gateway into the Inyo National Forest—the place to stop, refresh and outfit up and continue on with fishing gear and skis in hand. From here it's a straight shot into Mammoth Lakes area for diehard pursuit of trout. In March, the Early Sierra Trout Derby sets the mood. Then there's Mule Days Celebration over Memorial Day; Wild West Rodeo over Labor Day; and Millpond Blue Grass Festival in September.

THE CHALFANT HOUSE

213 Academy Street, Bishop, CA 93514   619-872-1790
Fred & Sally Manecke, Resident Owners

LOCATION	One block off of Highway 395 in the center of Bishop on the corner of Academy and Warren.
OPEN	All year
DESCRIPTION	An 1898 country inn with Victorian furnishings.
NO. OF ROOMS	Seven rooms with private bathrooms. Try the Blanche Room.
RATES	Year round rates are $50 to $90 for a single or a double with a private bathroom. There is no minimum stay and cancellation require seven days notice and a $15 fee.
CREDIT CARDS	Amex, MC, Visa
BREAKFAST	Full breakfast served in the dining room on china and silver includes fruit, juice, main entree such as peach and cream French toast, breakfast meat and homemade bread.
AMENITIES	Handmade quilt and flowers in the rooms, old time ice cream sundaes every night from 8 to 9 p.m., afternoon orange frosty drink, iced tea and in the winter, hot apple cider.
RESTRICTIONS	No smoking, children over eight are welcome.
REVIEWED	AAA Bed & Breakfast Guide—Southern California, Mobil Travel Guide—California and the West, The Definitive California Bed & Breakfast Touring Guide, Non-Smoker Guide to Bed & Breakfasts
RATED	AAA 3 Diamonds, Mobil 3 Stars

THE MATLICK HOUSE

1313 Rowan Lane, Bishop, CA 93514   *619-873-3133*
Ray and Barbara Showalter, Resident Owners   *800-898-3133*

LOCATION	One mile north of Bishop on Highway 395. Entrance to Matlick House is 200 feet east of the corner of Highway 395 and Rocking West Drive.
OPEN	All year
DESCRIPTION	Two-story 1906 ranch house wraparound verandas and "informal" antique furnishings.
NO. OF ROOMS	Five rooms with private bathrooms. Favorite room for Barbara is Lenna's suite.
RATES	Please call for latest rates. Cancellation policy includes seven day prior notice and $15 fee.
CREDIT CARDS	Amex, MC, Diners, Visa, Discover
BREAKFAST	Full breakfast includes juice, fresh fruit, meat and egg dishes, breads, coffee and tea. Lunch and dinner are also available.
AMENITIES	Common area with fireplace and TV. Wine and hors d'oeuvres served in the evening.
RESTRICTIONS	No smoking, children over 15 years old are welcome. ZaZa is the resident cat.
REVIEWED	*AAA Bed and Breakfast—Southern California, Directory of American B&Bs*
MEMBER	Professional Association of Innkeepers International, California Association of Bed and Breakfast Inns

BODEGA

A little jewel to be savored, but especially in the fall when the crowds go home. But anytime is fine to explore the headlands, beachcomb, tidepool, and whalewatch. This is a working fishing village first, and the seafood is to dream about. Do a walking tour of settings from "The Birds," and plan to be here for the Fishermans' Festival and Blessing of the Fleet in April. On the Sonoma Coast, north of San Francisco on Hwy. 1.

BODEGA ESTERO BED AND BREAKFAST

17699 Highway 1, Bodega, CA 94922   *707-876-3300*
Edgar A. Furlong and C. Michael O'Brien, Resident Owners   *800-422-6321*

LOCATION	Located on Highway 1, 1,000 feet from the turnoff into Bodega.
OPEN	All year
DESCRIPTION	A 1984 contemporary Geodesic dome with 50 foot ceilings and country antique furnishings.
NO. OF ROOMS	Four rooms with private bathrooms.
RATES	High season rates, March through November, for a single or double room with private bathroom are $75 to $90, and $55 to $90 for a single or double room with private bathroom during the off season, December thorugh February. Two night minimum stay required on Saturdays, seven day cancellation notice required.
CREDIT CARDS	MC, Visa
BREAKFAST	Continental Plus breakfast served in the dining room includes fresh fruit salad, homemade scones, muffins, quiche, hot dessert such as Apple Betty and beverages.
AMENITIES	Goose down comforters, fireplace, wine and desserts in the evening, handicapped access.
RESTRICTIONS	No smoking, no pets. Resident pets and farm animals includes goats, sheep, llama, exotic birds, a potbelly pig Piggy Lee, Baby the Siamese cat, the dog, a Komondor named Phoebe.

BODEGA HARBOR INN

1345 Bodega Avenue, Bodega CA 94923   707-875-3594
Bill & Elda Stevens, Resident Owners

LOCATION	On the Bluffs off the east side of Highway 1 at the north end of Bodega Bay. Turn east on Bodega Avenue.
OPEN	All year
DESCRIPTION	1950 cottage bungalow style. Attached cottage rooms, a water tower, and a vintage home divided into two suites on the main premises. Furnished with country-motif antiques.
NO. OF ROOMS	Thirteen rooms have private bathrooms.
RATES	All weekends and holidays, and high season weekdays March through November: singles and doubles $48 to $75; suites $85 to $100; guesthouses $90 to $185. Low season weekdays December through February: singles & doubles $40 to $65; suites $75 to $90; guesthouses $80 to $150. Minimum stay of two nights on weekends during the high season and three-day weekends all year round. Reservation/cancellation policy: 48 hours; three weeks for holidays.
CREDIT CARDS	MC, Visa
BREAKFAST	Continental breakfast of juice, coffee, tea, and blueberry muffins served holidays and weekends year round and on weekdays June through October.
AMENITIES	TV in rooms, courtesy phone for guests. Views of Bodega Harbor and the surrounding fishing village.
RESTRICTIONS	No pets.

BOLINAS

Down at the far south end of the Point Reyes Peninsula, this is a prime ocean spot. So good the locals' unofficial Bolinas Border Patrol like to keep outsiders ou;by removing the road signs. We hope the B&Bs fare well in spite of this. From San Francisco, it's a short drive north on Hwy. 1. Once in town, the Bolinas Lagoon, surrounded by a crescent-moon sandspit, is serene and perfect.

ONE FIFTY-FIVE PINE

PO Box 62, Bolinas, CA 94924   415-868-0263
Bill and Karen Arthur, Resident Owners

ROSE GARDEN COTTAGE

PO Box 845, Bolinas, CA 94924   415-868-2209

THOMAS' WHITE HOUSE INN

118 Kale Road, Bolinas, CA 94924   415-868-0279
Jackie Thomas, Resident Owner

LOCATION	Twenty seven miles north of San Francisco off Highway 1 in West Marin.
OPEN	All year
DESCRIPTION	Two-story 1979 New England inn with an observation tower, on a bluff overlooking San Francisco.
NO. OF ROOMS	Two rooms with a shared bathroom.
RATES	Year round rates for a double room with shared bathroom are $85 to $95. Minimum stay required on weekends, 10 day cancellation notice required.
CREDIT CARDS	No
BREAKFAST	Continental Plus breakfast served in the dining room includes fresh fruit, pastries and beverages.
AMENITIES	TV, VCR, phone, fireplace in common room, views, gardens.
RESTRICTIONS	No pets. Two cats Misha and Nicholas and 20 Zebra Finches in residence.
REVIEWED	*Northern California Best Places*

BOONVILLE

ANDERSON CREEK INN

12050 Anderson Valley Way, Boonville, CA 95415   707-895-3091
Rod & Nancy Graham, Resident Owner

KUDOS/COMMENTS   "Delightful, peaceful retreat on Anderson Creek, beautifully decorated and impecably clean; charming innkeepers."

THE BOONVILLE HOTEL

Highway 128 and Lambert Lane, Boonville, CA 95415   707-895-2210
John Schmitt & Jeanne Eliades, Resident Owners

BRIDGEPORT

Surrounded by Toiyabe National Forest in the eastern Sierras, this is an exceedingly good place to stop before heading further into the wilderness. While here, check out Big Hot Warm Springs, and good trout fishing in Twin Lakes southwest of town (with trailhead access into the Hoover Wilderness). Be warned: the western U.S. chapter of Harley Davidson motorcyclists convenes here the last weekend in June. On scenic Hwy. 395 between Lake Tahoe and Bishop, just off the Nevada border.

THE CAIN HOUSE

340 Main Street, Bridgeport, CA 93517   619-932-7040
Chris & Marachal Gohlich, Resident Owners   800-488-2246
                                         FAX 619-932-7419

LOCATION	Center of town.
OPEN	Seasonal from May 1 through November 1.
DESCRIPTION	A 1920s two-story western inn with English country furnishings.
NO. OF ROOMS	Seven rooms with private bathrooms. The best room is called Masonic.
RATES	Seasonal rates are $80 to $135 for a single or double with private bathroom. There is a minimum stay on the last weekend in June and July 3-4, cancellation requires 48 hours notice.
CREDIT CARDS	Amex, Diners Club, Discover, MC, Visa
BREAKFAST	Full breakfast is served in the dining room, guestrooms or outside and includes blackberry and lemon pancakes, Tennesse sausage, herbed potatoes, fresh fruit and beverages.
AMENITIES	Fresh flowers, robes, television, air conditioning, wine and cheese in the evening and full front porch with swing.
RESTRICTIONS	No smoking, no pets, only two people per room, no matter what age. The resident cat is called Amadeus.
REVIEWED	*Best Places in Northern California, Mobil Guide*
MEMBER	Professional Association of Innkeepers International, California Association of Bed & Breakfast Inns, American Bed & Breakfast Association.
RATED	AAA 3 Diamonds, ABBA 3 Crowns, Mobil 3 Stars

BURLINGAME

A very nice upscale, country club community on the windswept, often foggy, always gorgeous, south San Francisco Bayshore. Check out Coyote Point Park, Museum, and (live) Wildlife Habitats Hall. Thirteen miles farther south on Hwy. 101 leads to San Francisco Bay National Wildlife Refuge.

BURLINGAME BED & BREAKFAST

1021 Balboa Avenue, Burlingame, CA 94010   *415-344-5815*
Joe and Elenora Fernandez, Resident Owners
Spanish, Italian, some French spoken

LOCATION	Three miles south San Francisco on Highway 101 toward San Jose. After three miles, exit at Broadway. Cross over the railroad tracks and go about 8 blocks, turn left onto Balboa Avenue, house is 1.5 blocks up on the right.
OPEN	All year
DESCRIPTION	A 1940s English stucco bungalow.
NO. OF ROOMS	One room has a private bathroom.
RATES	Year round rate for a single or double with private bathroom is $40 to $50. No minimum stay, one week advance notice required for cancellation.
CREDIT CARDS	No
BREAKFAST	Continental Breakfast served in the breakfast area includes fresh croissants, coffee cake, English muffins, and beverages.
AMENITIES	Flowers, cable TV, clock radio
RESTRICTIONS	No smoking
REVIEWED	*Bed and Breakfast USA, Great Affordable Bed and Breakfast Getaways*

BURNT RANCH

Named after the torching of farmhouses during an Indian raid in 1853. This is an isolated little hamlet at the western edge of the Shasta-Trinity National Forest, on the Trinity River and scenic Hwy. 299, east of Arcata/Eureka. Watch for Bigfoot.

MADRONE LANE B&B

HCR #34, Burnt Ranch, CA 95527   *916-629-3642*
Jane & Roger Cinnamond, Resident Owners

LOCATION	Twelve miles east of Willow Creek on Highway 299. Take Denny Road from Hawkins Bar, tuen left at large Trinity Village sign. Turn on Hawkins Bar Road to Big Oak, right to N-14 Madrone Lane.
OPEN	All year
DESCRIPTION	A 1977 Shaker Barn host home in a hardwood forest with year round creek. The interior is heavy beam construction and white walls.
NO. OF ROOMS	Two rooms with private bathrooms. The studio is the best room.
RATES	Year round rates are $65 to $75 for a single or a double with private bathroom. There is a three day minimum stay on major holidays and no cancellation policy.
CREDIT CARDS	No
BREAKFAST	Continental Plus is served in the guestrooms and includes fresh fruit, bakery goods, juice, hard boiled eggs, coffee and smoked salmon in season.
AMENITIES	Refrigerator in room stocked with beer, wine, cheese, soda and mineral water.
RESTRICTIONS	No smoking. The local cat is called Philly.
REVIEWED	*Best Places in Northern California*

CALISTOGA

"In the cauldron boil and bake," said the witches in Macbeth. You can do it here, too. The town is built on a simmering underground river, making this a spa heaven of mud and mineral baths. Do this before hitting the wineries. From here, a 10-miles drive up Mt. St. Helena gets you to Robert Louis Stevenson State Park where he honeymooned and wrote a lot. At the northernmost end of the Napa Valley, northeast of San Francisco via Hwy. 29.

BRANNAN COTTAGE INN

109 Wapoo Avenue, Calistoga, CA 94515   707-942-4200
Dieter Back, Resident Owner
German spoken

LOCATION	From Highway 29 go east on Lincoln Avenue for a quarter mile into town, Wapoo Avenue angles off on your left where you will see the white and green inn.
OPEN	All year
DESCRIPTION	An 1863 Victorian cottage with 11 foot ceilings, oak floors, stencils and antiques. On the National Historic Register.
NO. OF ROOMS	Six rooms with private bathrooms.
RATES	High season rates, April through October, are $100 to $140 for a single or double with a private bathroom. Low season rates, November through March, are $80 to $125 for a single or a double with a private bathroom. There is a two night minimum stay on the weekend and cancellation requires seven days notice with a $15 cancellation fee.
CREDIT CARDS	MC, Visa
BREAKFAST	Full breakfast is served buffet style in the parlor or garden.
AMENITIES	Down quilts, flowers, decanter of wine, NO TV and offstreet parking.
RESTRICTIONS	No smoking, no pets, children over 12 are welcome.
REVIEWED	*AAA Bed & Breakfast Guide—Northern and Central California*
MEMBER	Napa Valley B&B Association

CALISTOGA COUNTRY LODGE

2883 Foothill Boulevard, Calistoga, CA 94515   707-942-5555
Rae Ellen Felds, Resident Owner

CALISTOGA WAYSIDE INN

1523 Foothill Boulevard, Calistoga, CA 94515   707-942-0645
Pat O'Neil, Innkeeper

KUDOS/COMMENTS   "Small but very helpful and nice."

CALISTOGA WISHING WELL INN

2653 Foothill Boulevard, Calistoga, CA 94515   707-942-5534
Marina & Keith Dinsmoor, Resident Owners   FAX 707-942-4485
Russian spoken

LOCATION	Northwest one mile from the center of town on Highway 128.
OPEN	All year
DESCRIPTION	A 1930s three-story farmhouse and cottage furnished with period antiques.
NO. OF ROOMS	Three rooms with private bathrooms. Marina recommends the St. Helena Cottage.
RATES	Year round rates for a single or double with private bathroom are $110 to $150. Two night stay required over Saturday, seven days cancellation notice.
CREDIT CARDS	Amex, MC, Visa
BREAKFAST	Full breakfast served in the dining room includes fruit, entree, meat, potatoes, pastry and beverages.
AMENITIES	Swimming pool and spa, flowers, robes, hot tub, wine and hors d'oeuvres, ping pong, vineyard, croquet, parlor with fireplace and piano.
RESTRICTIONS	No smoking inside, no pets. Outside cats are Oscar and Half-Nose...the most original cat name in all the B&Bs in Northern California...TI
MEMBER	Bed and Breakfast Inns of Napa Valley

CHRISTOPHER'S INN

1010 Foothill Boulevard, Calistoga, CA 94515   707-942-5755
Christopher Layton, Resident Owner

THE ELMS BED & BREAKFAST

1300 Cedar Street, Calistoga, CA 94515   707-942-9476
Stephen & Karla Wyle, Resident Owners   800-235-4316
Spanish, Italian, German, French, and Flemish spoken   FAX 707-942-9479

LOCATION	North on Highway 29 to flashing light at Lincoln Avenue. Turn right on Lincoln, two blocks to Cedar Street, and then left to B&B.
OPEN	All year
DESCRIPTION	An 1871 French Victorian Inn on the National Historic Register with Victorian and French furnishings and enormous elm trees in front.
NO. OF ROOMS	All rooms have private bathrooms with the "La Chambre" room being the innkeeper's favorite.
RATES	Year round rates are: Sunday through Thursday $100 to $150; Fridays and Saturdays $120 to $170. Minimum stay of two days on weekends and three days on some holidays. Reservation/cancellation policy: seven days in advance with $20 processing charge.
CREDIT CARDS	MC, Visa
BREAKFAST	Full three-course gourmet breakfast served in the dining room, with menu changing daily.
AMENITIES	Robes, coffeemakers, and Port wine in rooms. Telephone room, air conditioning, and chocolates, TV, and fireplaces in rooms. Wine and cheese served in the afternoon. Full concierge service.
RESTRICTIONS	The Inn is not suitable for young children. No smoking, no pets. One resident golden retriever, Ivory.
MEMBER	California Association of Bed & Breakfast Inns

FALCON'S NEST

471 Kortum Canyon Road, Calistoga, CA 94515   707-942-0758
Michael & Yvonne Rich, Resident Owners

FANNY'S

1206 Spring Street, Calistoga, CA 94515   707-942-9491
Deanna Higgins, Resident Owner

LOCATION	Follow Highway 29 north into Calistoga. Continue through the blinking light 2 blocks, turn right at Spring Street, one block down, to the big red house on the right.
OPEN	All year
DESCRIPTION	A 1915 two-story Craftsman cottage with a big front porch, rockers, and a porch swing.
NO. OF ROOMS	All rooms have private bathrooms.
RATES	Year round rate for a double or single with private bathroom is $75. Two night minimum stay required on weekends, July through October.
CREDIT CARDS	No
BREAKFAST	Continental breakfast served in the dining room includes fresh fruit, fresh baked breakfast breads and beverages.
AMENITIES	Fireplace in the living room, large common area upstairs.
RESTRICTIONS	No smoking, no pets, children over 12 years old welcome. The resident pets include a Dandy Dinmont, Muttley, Max the Dachshund and three cats: Shy, O'Brian and Elizabeth.

FOOTHILL HOUSE BED & BREAKFAST

3037 Foothill Boulevard, Calistoga, CA 94515   *707-942-6933*
Gus and Doris Beckert, Resident Owners   *800-942-6933*
          FAX 707-942-5692

LOCATION	Where highway 29 becomes Highway 128/Foothill Boulevard at the intersection of Lincoln Boulevard, continue north 1.5 miles, Foothill House will be on the left.
OPEN	All year, except Thanksgiving and Christmas day.
DESCRIPTION	An 1893 farmhouse and cottage with country antique furnishings and landscaped gardens, including waterfalls and fresh water ponds.
NO. OF ROOMS	All three rooms have private bathrooms. Gus and Doris recommend the Quail's Roost, a cottage.
RATES	Year round rates are $115 to $220. Two day minimum over Saturday night. Seven day cancellation includes $10 fee.
CREDIT CARDS	Amex, MC, Visa, checks accepted.
BREAKFAST	Full breakfast served in the dining room, guestroom, gazebo or patio includes fresh fruit, croissants, muffins, baked souffles and coffee.Willing to work around food allergies.
AMENITIES	Evening wine and hor d'oeuvres, fresh flowers, robes, wood burning stoves or fireplaces in all rooms, TV, phones, in-room tape decks with tapes, air conditioning/ceiling fans, turn-down service includes sherry and cookies.
RESTRICTIONS	No smoking, no pets, children over 12 years old welcome in selected rooms. There are Koi fish in the pond, Grizzie is "a 'fraidy cat that came with the inn."
REVIEWED	*Bed and Breakfast—A Select Guide, Best Places to Kiss in Northern California, Best Places to Stay in Northern California, Bed and Breakfast American Style, American's Wonderful Little Hotels and Inns, Northern California Best Places*
MEMBER	Professional Association of Innkeepers International, California Association of Bed and Breakfast Inns
RATED	ABBA 3 Crowns, Mobil 3 Stars

LA CHAUMIERE, A COUNTRY INN

1301 Cedar Street, Calistoga, CA 94515   707-942-5139
Gary Venturi, Resident Manager   800-474-6800
                                                  FAX 707-942-5199

LOCATION	Greater downtown Calistoga
OPEN	All year
DESCRIPTION	A 1910 English Cotswald country inn with French interior.
NO. OF ROOMS	All rooms have private bathrooms. Gary recommends the Cottage.
RATES	Year round rates are $125 to $135 for a double with private bathroom and $150 to $175 for the guesthouse. There is a two night minimum stay on the weekend; a seven day cancellation policy and a $20 cancellation fee.
CREDIT CARDS	Amex, MC and Visa
BREAKFAST	Full breakfast served in the dining room includes fruit platter, sausage frittata with home fries and croissant, coffee and orange juice.
AMENITIES	Wine & cheese in the afternoon, in-house massage in tree house under huge Redwood tree, hot tub, port and fresh flowers in the room.
RESTRICTIONS	No smoking, no pets, the inn is not suitable for children.

LARKMEAD COUNTRY INN

1103 Larkmead Lane, Calistoga, CA 94515   707-942-5360
Gene & Joan Garbarino, Resident Owners

MEADOWLARK COUNTRY HOUSE

601 Petrified Forest Road, Calistoga, CA 94515   707-942-5651
Jane Fuschak, Manager
German and Spanish spoken

LOCATION	From Calistoga follow Highway 128 for a mile to Petrified Forest Road.
OPEN	All year
DESCRIPTION	A two-story 1886 California country inn with country antique and contemporary furnishings, on 20 acres.
NO. OF ROOMS	Four rooms with private bathrooms.
RATES	High season, April through November, rates are $95 to $140 for a double with a private bathroom. Low season, December through March, rates are $95 to $125 for a double with a private bathroom. There is a two night minimum stay on the weekend and cancellation requires 72 hours notice.
CREDIT CARDS	No
BREAKFAST	Continental Plus is served in the dining room or guest room and includes, fruit, baked goods, eggs, ganola and beverages.
AMENITIES	Complimentary soft drinks, swimming pool and sundeck, secluded sunning area past the pool.
RESTRICTIONS	No smoking, pets are allowed with prior arrangement. The resident cat is called Miss Kitty and the peacocks are called Fritz, Frida and Greta and two thoroughbred horse roam the pasture.
REVIEWED	*California Country Inns and Itineraries, Hidden California— San Francisco and North*
MEMBER	California Association of Bed & Breakfast Inns, Bed & Breakfasts of Napa Valley, Bed & Breakfasts of Calistoga
KUDOS/COMMENTS	...We booked this place by mistake...the best mistake we made."

MOUNTAIN HOME RANCH

3400 Mountain Home Ranch Road, Calistoga, CA 94515   707-942-6616
Kimo Fouts, Resident Owner
Spanish spoken   FAX 707-942-9091

LOCATION	Five miles southeast of Calistoga. Mountain Home Ranch Road is off of Petrified Forest Road. The lodge is at the end of the road.
OPEN	All year
DESCRIPTION	A 1953 lodge and cabins with modern furnishings.
NO. OF ROOMS	Thirteen rooms with private bathrooms, six rooms share one bathroom and Kimo likes the Willows room.
RATES	High season, June through August, rates are $88 to $145 for a single or double with private bathroom, $49 to $79 for a single or double with shared bathroom and $165 for the suite. Off season, September through May, rates are $45 to $109 for a single or double with private bathroom, $30 to $50 for a single or double with shared bathroom and $115 for the suite. There is no minimum stay and cancelation requires three days notice.
CREDIT CARDS	MC, Visa
BREAKFAST	Either Continental of full menu with table service served in the dining room. Dinner and special meals are available.
AMENITIES	Tennis, fishing, five miles of hiking trails, "blah-blah"...thank you for your input Kimo, we sometimes think the same thing when we are sitting here inputing this information...TI, sulphur springs, facilities for meetings, retreats, weddings and large BBQs.
RESTRICTIONS	None. The resident "lazy dog"is a Lab called Kupua

PINE STREET INN

1202 Pine Street, Calistoga, CA 94515   707-942-6829
Tom Lunney, Resident Owner

THE PINK MANSION

1415 Foothill Boulevard, Calistoga, CA 94515   707-942-0558
Bob Segfried, Resident Owner   800-238-7465
Spanish spoken   FAX 707-942-0554

LOCATION	In Calistoga from Highway 29, at the stop light, go one block and the inn is on the right.
OPEN	All year
DESCRIPTION	A two-story 1875 Victorian with antique furnishings.
NO. OF ROOMS	Six rooms with private bathrooms. Bob says the rose suite is his best room.
RATES	High season, April through November, rates are $105 for a single or a double with a private bathroom and $145 to $165 for a suite. Low season, December through March, rates are $85 for a single or a double with a priovate bathroom and $145 to $160 for a suite. There is a two night minimum stay on weekends and cancellation requires seven days notice.
CREDIT CARDS	Amex, MC, Visa
BREAKFAST	Full breakfast served in the dining room or guest room and is a "full gourmet breakfast with many interesting recipes."
AMENITIES	Flowers in the room, hot tub and indoor pool, air conditioning, handicapped access and wine and cheese in the afternoon, some rooms have TV and fireplaces.
RESTRICTIONS	No smoking. The resident 16-year-old German Shepard is called Tang.
MEMBER	California Association of Bed & Breakfast Inns

QUAIL MOUNTAIN B&B COUNTRY INN

4455 North St.reet, Helena Highway, Calistoga, CA 94515   707-942-0316
Don & Alma Swiers, Resident Owners

LOCATION	Two miles south of Calistoga, on Quail Mountain Lane off Highway 29, (St. Helena Highway)
OPEN	All year
DESCRIPTION	1984 two story contemporary estate on 26 acres and a Cabernet vineyard
NO. OF ROOMS	Three rooms with private bathrooms. Try the Fern Room for a treat.
RATES	Year round rates for a single with private bathroom are $90 to $115, double with private bathroom are $100 to $125. Two night minimum stay on weekends and holidays and five day cancellation policy with 10% cancellation fee.
CREDIT CARDS	MC, Visa
BREAKFAST	Full hot breakfast served in the dining room includes juice, fruit, hot entree with meat, fresh baked goods, coffee and tea.
AMENITIES	Pool and hot tub, robes, fresh flowers. Wine and hors d'oeuvres before dinner.
RESTRICTIONS	No smoking, no pets, the inn is not suitable for children. Guard cat and huntress, Gypsy, will keep you safe from harm.
REVIEWED	*Karen Brown's California Country Inns & Itineraries, America's Wonderful Little Hotels and Inns, Northern California Best Places*
MEMBER	Professional Association of Innkeepers International, California Association of Bed and Breakfast Inns
KUDOS/COMMENTS	"Excellent!"

SCARLETT'S COUNTRY INN

3918 Silverado Trail, Calistoga, CA 94515   707-942-6669
Scarlett Dwyer, Resident Owner

KUDOS/COMMENTS	"Peaceful, quiet, attention to detail, comfy, cozy, wonderful hostess."

SCOTT COURTYARD

1443 Second Street, Calistoga, CA 94515   707-942-0948
Joe and Lauren Scott, Resident Owners   800-942-1515
                                                          FAX 707-942-5102

LOCATION	Two blocks from downtown Calistoga. From Highway 29 north, turn left on Fairway and drive two blocks to Second Street. Office is at poolside.
OPEN	All year
DESCRIPTION	A 1920s Mediterranean Villa and Bungalows with tropical Art Deco interior.
NO. OF ROOMS	Six rooms with private bathrooms.
RATES	High season, May through November, rates for a single or double with a private bathroom are $125 to $135, low season, December through April, rates for a single or double with a private bathroom are $110 to $125. Weekends require a two night minimum stay, seven day cancellation policy with 10% fee.
CREDIT CARDS	Amex, MC, Visa
BREAKFAST	Full buffet breakfast served in the dining room includes cereals, fresh breads, eggs, pancakes or French toast, meat, fresh fruit and beverages.
AMENITIES	Court yard and swimming pool, flowers, robes, TV room, art studio, rose garden, library, cheese and drinks served each evening.
RESTRICTIONS	No smoking, children welcome in the bungalows, one per parental unit. Resident Maltese, Spike and Jake "love people and children."
REVIEWED	*Wine Country Access, Best Places to Kiss in Northern California, Country Inns and Back Roads*
MEMBER	Professional Association of Innkeepers International, California Association of Bed and Breakfast Inns, California Lodging Industry Association

SILVER ROSE INN

351 Rosedale Road, Calistoga, CA 94515 707-942-9581
Sally & J. Paul & Derrick Dumont, Resident Owners 800-995-9381
FAX 707-942-0841

LOCATION	From Calistoga, just off the Silverado Trail.
OPEN	All year
DESCRIPTION	A three-story 1984 lodge with "elegant" western furnishings.
NO. OF ROOMS	Nine rooms with private bathrooms.
RATES	Year round rates are $115 to $135 for a single or double with a private bathroom, suites are $150 to $190. There is a minimum stay on the weekend and cancellation requires seven days notice.
CREDIT CARDS	Amex, Discover, MC, Visa
BREAKFAST	Continental Plus is served just about anywhere and includes a fresh fruit plate, homemade breads and muffins,
AMENITIES	Hot springs pool and spa, telephones in rooms, mineral water, wine and cheese each afternoon.
RESTRICTIONS	No smoking, no pets, children over 16 are welcome. There are three outdoors cats, Patches, Blue Eyes and Pumpkin.
REVIEWED	*Karen Brown's California Country Inns & Itineraries, Northern California Wine Country Access, The Best Places to Kiss in Northern California, Best Places to Stay in California, Country Inns & Back Raods—California, America's Wonderful Little Hotels & Inns*
MEMBER	Professional Association of Innkeepers International, Caslifornia Association of Bed & Breakfast Inns.
RATED	Mobil 3 Stars
KUDOS/COMMENTS	"Beautifully maintained, excellent location, spacious rooms and pool."

WASHINGTON STREET LODGING

1605 Washington Street, Calistoga, CA 94515   707-942-6968
Joan Ranieri, Resident Owner

LOCATION	Head north on Main Street, turn left at the one and only stop light at Washington Strteet. The inn is between 4th and Lake Streets.
OPEN	All year
DESCRIPTION	An 1873 country farm home with five cottages decorated with country furnishings and down comforters.
NO. OF ROOMS	Five rooms with private bathrooms. Joan suggest that you try cottage #3.
RATES	Year round rates are $80 to $90 for a single or double with a private bathroom. There is a two night minimum stay on weekends and holidays and cancellation requires 48 hours with a $5 cancellation fee.
CREDIT CARDS	No
BREAKFAST	Continental breakfast is served in the cottages.
AMENITIES	Three cottages are on the Napa River and two cottage have decks, fresh flowers in each cottage, all cottages have kitchens.
RESTRICTIONS	None. The resident Bassett Hound is called Willy and the cat goes by Sampson.
REVIEWED	*AAA Bed & Breakfast Guide—Northern and Central California*

WINE WAY INN

1019 Foothill Boulevard, Calistoga, CA 94515   707-942-0680
Moye & Cecil Stephens, Resident Owners   800-572-0679

LOCATION	On Highway 29, one block south of Lincoln Avenue (Calistoga's main street).
OPEN	All year except for December 21 through December 25.
DESCRIPTION	A two-story 1915 craftsman with antique furnishings.
NO. OF ROOMS	Six rooms with private bathrooms. Cecil suggests the Calistoga room.
RATES	High season, April through November, rates are $70 to $130 for a single or a double with a private bathroom. Weekday and low season, December through March, rates are $60 to $120 for a single or a double with private bathroom. There is a minimum stay on high season weekends and cancellation requires five days notice with a $10 cancellation fee.
CREDIT CARDS	Amex, MC, Visa
BREAKFAST	Full breakfast served in the dining room includes frittatas or omeletts or French toast, fruits, orange juice, pastries or breads and beverages.
AMENITIES	Wine and hors d'oeuvres, robes, sherry in parlor, full service spa, three-level deck.
RESTRICTIONS	No smoking, no pets. The resident dog is a "ShepaDor" by the name of George who does tricks.
REVIEWED	*Wine Country Access, America's Wonderful Little Hotels & Inns*
RATED	Mobil 1 Star

WISTERIA GARDEN BED & BREAKFAST

1508 Fair Way, Calistoga, CA 94515   707-942-5358
Carmen Marb, Resident Owner

LOCATION	From Main Street in Calistoga take Lincoln Avenue one block to Fair Way.
OPEN	All year
DESCRIPTION	A 1916 Victorian under a 150 year old oak tree.
NO. OF ROOMS	Two rooms with private bathrooms, pick the Cottage.
RATES	High season, March through December, rates are $100 to $110 for a single or a double with private bathroom, low season, January and February, rates are $50 to $65. There is no minimum stay and cancellation requires 48 hours notice.
CREDIT CARDS	MC, Visa
BREAKFAST	Continental breakfast is served in guestroom and includes pastries, fruit platter and beverages.
AMENITIES	Cable TV, fresh flowers, microwave, refrigerator and coffee makers.
RESTRICTIONS	Smoking outside the rooms only please. The resident Fox Terrier is called Buffy.

ZINFANDEL HOUSE

1253 Summit Drive, Calistoga, CA 94515   707-942-0733
Bette & George Starke, Resident Owners   FAX 707-942-4618

LOCATION	Halfway between St. Helena and Calistoga. Private road off of Highway 29. Call for directions.
OPEN	All year
DESCRIPTION	A 1980 hillside Redwood host home with a mixture of traditional and antique furnishings.
NO. OF ROOMS	Two rooms with private bathrooms and two rooms share one bathroom. Ask for the room with the king-sized bed.
RATES	Year round rates are $75 to $100 for a single or a double with a private bathroom. There is a two-night minimum stay on weekends and cancellation requires five days notice.
CREDIT CARDS	No
BREAKFAST	A full breakfast is served in the dining room.
AMENITIES	Fresh flowers in the rooms and house, robes, telephones available for all rooms, complimmentary wine and snacks, food and wine library, hot tub on deck.
RESTRICTIONS	No smoking, no pets. Due to steps, the house is not convenient for children or handicapped.
MEMBER	California Association of Bed & Breakfast Inns

CAMINO

Apples and all things divinely delectable can be had here, especially in late summer and fall. Don't miss the Fall Harvest Festival or the rest of summer's pickings either. Check out the Apple Hill Visitors Center and local wineries. East of Sacramento and Placerville off Hwy. 50. Skip weekends, the traffic's insane.

CAMINO HOTEL SEVEN MILE HOUSE

4103 Carson Road, Camino, CA 95709   916-644-7740
Paula Nobert & John Eddy, Resident Owners   800-200-7740
FAX 916-644-7740

LOCATION	From Highway 50 take the Camino exit and turn right on Carson Road, hotel is 1.2 miles up on the left.
OPEN	All year
DESCRIPTION	Turn-of-the-century two-story restored Country boarding house surrounded by a large front porch with swing.
NO. OF ROOMS	Three rooms with private bathrooms, six rooms share two bathrooms. The E. J. Barrett room is the best in the house.
RATES	Year round rates for a single or double with private bathroom are $85 to $95, and $75 to $85 for single or double room with shared bathroom. Entire hotel rents for $745 per night. Minimum three night stay required weekends in September and October, seven days cancellation notice required for full refund.
CREDIT CARDS	Amex, MC, Visa, Discover
BREAKFAST	Full breakfast served in the dining room or in guestroom includes juice, fresh fruit, homemade muffins, French toast or apple pancakes and beverages. Other meals available for a minimum of 10 people.
AMENITIES	Robes, fresh flowers, gift basket with local gourmet food items, Big Band CD's in parlor, lots of board games, private phone booth, champagne, wine and hors d'oeuvres available. Meeting facilities, English teas, socials, private parties, reunions and retreats.
RESTRICTIONS	No smoking, no pets.
REVIEWED	*Non-smokers Guide to B&Bs, Breakfast 'N Bed.*
MEMBER	Professional Association of Innkeepers International, American Historic Inns, Dana Point, California, Historic Country Inns of El Dorado County

CAPITOLA

The seaside suburb of Santa Cruz at the northernmost reaches of Monterey Bay is a bonanza of art galleries and craft shops. But it's most famous for its begonias, and the main event here is the Begonia Festival in early September. Anytime, stroll the historic 1857 wharf. Take Highway 1, or course.

THE INN AT DEPOT HILL

250 Monterey Avenue, Capitola, CA 95010   408-462-3376
Suzie Lankes and Dan Floyd, Resident Owners   800-572-2632
French, German, Italian spoken   FAX 408-462-3697

LOCATION	Four miles south of Santa Cruz. On a hill overlooking the village of Capitola-by-the-Sea on the west side of Highway 1.
OPEN	All year
DESCRIPTION	1901 restored two-story railroad depot.
NO. OF ROOMS	Eight rooms with private bathrooms. Suzie recommends the Delft Room.
RATES	Year round rates for a double with a private bathroom are $165 to $250. Two night minimum stay on weekends, ten days notice required for cancellation.
CREDIT CARDS	Amex, MC, Visa
BREAKFAST	Full breakfast including a variety of entrees, served in the dining room or in your guestroom.
AMENITIES	TV, VCR, fireplaces, spas, phones, classic garden, afternoon wine and hors d'oeuvres, evening dessert, port and sherry, one room in handicapped accessible.
RESTRICTIONS	No smoking, no pets.
REVIEWED	*Best Places to Kiss in Northern California, Special Places, California Country Inns and Itineraries*
MEMBER	Professional Association of Innkeepers International, International Innkeepers Association, California Association of Bed and Breakfast Inns, Bed and Breakfast Innkeepers of Santa Cruz County
RATED	AAA 3 Diamonds, Mobil 4 Stars
KUDOS/COMMENTS	"A wonderful getaway, close to beach and dining - the rooms are done to perfection." "My second favorite inn in California."

SUMMER HOUSE

216 Monterey Avenue, Capitola Valley, CA 95010   408-475-8474
Patricia Dolling, Resident Owner

CAZADERO

Bring slicker and umbrella—it rains a lot here, about 80–100 inches a year, but it's greener than anywhere else, too. The town has a lumber mill, general store, and sometimes a restaurant. The Kruse Rhododendron State Reserve is a beauty, about nine miles west. Get gas and directions before going, and do this before the vineyards and wine tasting. About 23 miles north of Bodega Bay via Hwy. One.

CAZANOMA LODGE

1000 Kidd Creek Road, Cazadero, CA 95421   707-632-5255
Randall & Gretchen Neuman, Resident Owners

LOCATION	Three miles off highway 116, turn left on Kidd Creek Road, one mile to lodge.
OPEN	From March 1 through December 7.
DESCRIPTION	A three-story 1926 lodge on 147 acres.
NO. OF ROOMS	Four rooms with private bathrooms and two cabins. Randall picked the canyon view spa as the best room.
RATES	Year round rates are $90 to $110 for a single or a double with a private bathroom and the cabins are $115 to $125. There is a two night minimum with a Saturday stay and cancellation requires four days notice.
CREDIT CARDS	Amex, Discover, MC, Visa
BREAKFAST	Continental Plus is served in the guestroom and includes fresh baked breads, fruit plater, juice, oatmeal and beverages. Dinner and Sunday brunch are available.
AMENITIES	Wine and cheese, fruit basket, firewood for fireplaces.
RESTRICTIONS	No pets in rooms, but okay in cabins. The resident critters are dogs, cats and "wild" raccoons.

CHESTER

In the shadow of Lassen Peak, this little logging town has limited southern access into Lassen Volcanic National Park (a geologic wonderland) via the Chester-Warner Valley Road. It's also on the north shore of absolutely perfect Lake Almanor, a good reason to be here in itself. The Deer Creek foothills south of Lassen is Ishi country, the tribal home of the last Yahi. About 32 miles west of Susanville via Hwy. 35, which continues west in the the Park's main entrance. Get detailed information from Park headquarters.

BIDWELL HOUSE

1 Main Street, Chester, CA 96020　　　　　　　　　916-258-3338
Kim and Ian James, Managers　　　　　　　　　　FAX 916-258-3338

LOCATION	Located on Highway 36 on the east end of Chester. If you are heading east, we are on the left.
OPEN	All year
DESCRIPTION	The Bidwell House is a fully restored farmhouse listed on the California State Historic Register and furnished with antiques throughout.
NO. OF ROOMS	Twelve rooms with private bathrooms, two rooms that share one bathroom.
RATES	Year round rates are $60 to $106. Cancellation policy requires 72 hours notice with no cancellation fee.
CREDIT CARDS	MC, Visa
BREAKFAST	Full breakfast is served in the dining room. Catered dinner parties by special request.
AMENITIES	Patio, flower gardens, coffee and candy in your room, hors d'oeurves and games available in common areas.
RESTRICTIONS	No smoking, no pets.
REVIEWED	*Northern California Best Places, The Complete Northern California Handbook*
MEMBER	Professional Association of Innkeepers International
RATED	AAA 2 Diamonds

CHICO

The town's founders, John and Annie Bidwell, left a legacy of well-laid-out, tree-shaded streets, parks, and a college that is now a California State University campus (they did not include its infamous, recently deceased Pioneer Days festivals). Don't miss Bidwell Mansion State Historic Park (yes, this was the Antebellum house in "Gone With the Wind"), and summer Concerts and Shakespeare in the Park. Diehard beer consumption and brewing are celebrated with gusto during Oktoberfest. At the north end of the great Central Valley. From here, Hwy. 32 leads to Lassen Volcanic National Park.

THE ESPLANADE BED & BREAKFAST

620 The Esplanade, Chico, CA 95926   916-345-8084
Lois I. Kloss, Resident Owner

LOCATION	Two blocks from the center of town, across the street from the Bidwell Mansion, two blocks from CSU Chico.
OPEN	All year
DESCRIPTION	A 1904 two-story Craftsman "comfortable" home.
NO. OF ROOMS	Five rooms with private bathrooms, one room with shared bathroom. Natalie's Room is Lois' choice.
RATES	Year round rates for single or double room with private or shared bathroom are $55 to $75.
CREDIT CARDS	MC, Visa
BREAKFAST	Full breakfast buffet served in the dining room or on the patio includes fresh orange juice, fresh fruit, and a varied menu, and "extra special" homemade apple pie..
AMENITIES	Cable TV in rooms, evening wine.
RESTRICTIONS	None, although smokers usually retire to the patio.
MEMBER	California Association of Bed and Breakfast Inns

JOHNSON'S COUNTRY INN

3935 Morehead Avenue, Chico, CA 95928   916-345-7829
Joan & David Johnson, Resident Owners   FAX 916-345-7829

LOCATION	Turn west at the intersection of Highway 32 and West 5th Street that becomes Chico River Road. Travel one mile to Morehead Avenue, from the intersection of Chico River Road and Morehead Avenue proceed 1/2 mile to the inn.
OPEN	All year
DESCRIPTION	A two-story 1992 Victorian farmhouse with a veranda and traditional interior furnishings.
NO. OF ROOMS	Four rooms with private bathrooms. Joan likes the Harrison room.
RATES	Year round rates for a single with a private bathroom are $80 to $90 and a double with a private bathroom is $125. There is no minimum stay and cancellation requires seven days notice.
CREDIT CARDS	Visa
BREAKFAST	Full breakfast is served in the dining room and includes home baked items, fresh fruit, special egg dishes and beverages.
AMENITIES	Fresh flowers, robes, telephones, wine, hors d' oeuvres, one room with a fireplace and Jucuzzi, coffee, juice or tea delivered to the room before breakfast, one handicapped access room and meeting facilities, parlor with fireplace, game room, horseshoes and badminton.
RESTRICTIONS	No smoking, no pets, children over the age of 10 are welcome. The "Chow Poo" goes by the name of Zackary Taylor.
MEMBER	California Association of Bed & Breakfast Inns

MUSIC EXPRESS INN

1091 El Monte Avenue, Chico, CA 95928   916-345-8376
Irene Cobeen, Resident Owner   FAX 916-893-8521

LOCATION	Three blocks east of the intersection of Highway 99 and Highway 32, close to Bidwell Park and the University.
OPEN	All year
DESCRIPTION	1970/1988 two-story country inn on three acres with country and family antique furnishings
NO. OF ROOMS	Nine rooms with private bathrooms
RATES	Please phone for year round rates
CREDIT CARDS	Amex, MC, Visa, Discover
BREAKFAST	Full breakfast served in the dining room includes fresh juice and fruit, hot entree, breads, cereals, coffee and tea.
AMENITIES	Inn also serves as a music school, so music is part of the atmosphere. Other amenities include Jacuzzi tubs, king size beds, TVs, phones, refrigerators and microwaves in rooms, meeting facilities and handicapped access.
RESTRICTIONS	Smoking in designated areas only. The resident tail-free Manx is Purrfect.
REVIEWED	*AAA Bed & Breakfast Guidebook—California*
MEMBER	Professional Association of Innkeepers International, California Association of Bed and Breakfast Inns

Clio

A tiny hamlet in the eastern Sierra on Highway 89, just south of the interseciton of I-70, halfway between Quincy and Truckee. Continuing northwest will get you into Lassen Volcanic National park, or head south to Lake Tahoe.

White Sulphur Springs Ranch B&B

2200 Highway 89, Clio, CA 96106
Karen & Don Miller, Owners

916-836-2387
800-854-1797
FAX 916-836-2387

LOCATION	Five miles south of Graeagle on Highway 89.`
OPEN	Year round
DESCRIPTION	Originally a stage coach stop, this 1852, two-story Modified Greek Revival inn is furnished with antique and country-rustic furnishings.
NO. OF ROOMS	Two cottages with private bathrooms, five rooms share two bathrooms. Try the Fern Room.
RATES	Year round rates for a single or double room or cottage with private bathroom are $100 to $140, and $85 to $90 for a single or double room with shared bathroom. The inn can accommodate 23 people and rents for $1,000. Minimum stay required on weekends in July, August, and holidays. Seven day cancellation notice required.
CREDIT CARDS	MC, Visa, Discover
BREAKFAST	Full breakfast served in the dining room or delivered to cottages includes a hot entree such as sausage, spinach frittata, and stuffed French toast, homemade breads, home-style spuds, fruit and beverages.
AMENITIES	Robes, Olympic size natural warm springs pool, piano, pump organ, evening treats in rooms, 42 acres to hike.
RESTRICTIONS	No smoking, no pets. Prefer younger children in the cottages. Tucker, a Golden Retriever, "is the official greeter and tour guide of the grounds," and Martha is the cat.
MEMBER	Professional Association of Innkeepers International

CLOVERDALE

The clover has long since been replaced by grapes. This is a charm of a town with lots going on: Fiddle Contest in January; Citrus Fair in February; Russian River Wine Fest in May, and the Annual Grape Festival in September. In winter, whitewater rafting on the Russian is the reason to be here. About 87 miles north of San Francisco and 17 miles north of Healdsburg.

ABRAMS HOUSE INN

314 North Main Street, Cloverdale, CA 95425   707-894-2412
Betsy Fitz-Gerald, Patti and Ray Roberts, Resident Owners   800-764-4466
FAX 707-894-2412

LOCATION	From Highway 101 exit at Citrus Fair Drive. Turn right on Cloverdale Boulevard, go five blocks to Third Street, turn right, turn left on Main Street, three houses down on right.
OPEN	All year
DESCRIPTION	A two-story 1872 Victorian inn furnished with antiques.
NO. OF ROOMS	Two rooms with private bathrooms, two rooms share a bathroom.
RATES	High season rates, June through October and holidays, for a single or double room with private bathroom are $80 to $90, and $80 to $85 for shared bathroom, suites $125. Off season rates are $10 less. Two night stay required on weekends, seven days cancellation notice required with $15 charge.
CREDIT CARDS	Amex, MC, Visa
BREAKFAST	Full breakfast served in the dining room includes fruit cup, meat, eggs, French toast or crepes and beverages. Early morning muffins and beverages in the parlor.
AMENITIES	Afternoon tea and lemonade, evening dessert, flowers, robes, hair dryers in rooms, wine available. Prearranged wine tasting and food sampling for small groups.
RESTRICTIONS	Smoking in designated areas, no pets. Sonoma, a Golden Retriever, will welcome your visit. Tweeters the canary is kept in private quarters.
REVIEWED	*Best Places in Northern California*
MEMBER	Professional Association of Innkeepers International, California Association of Bed and Breakfast Inns, California Lodging Industry Association, California Hotel & Motel Asssociation

VINTAGE TOWERS B&B

302 North Main Street, Cloverdale, CA 95425   707-894-4535
Jane Patton, Resident Owner

YE OLDE SHELFORD HOUSE

29955 River Road, Cloverdale, CA 95425   707-894-5956/5621
Ina and Al Sauder, Resident Owners   800-833-6479

LOCATION	Highway 101 north to Cloverdale, take Citrus Fair Drive exit. Right to Asti Road, left to First Street, right on First Street, one mile to the inn.
OPEN	All year
DESCRIPTION	1885 two-story Country Victorian and carriage house furnished in family antiques.
NO. OF ROOMS	Six rooms with private bathrooms. Try the Elsie Shelford room for a treat.
RATES	Year round rates for a single or double room with private bathroom $85 to $110. Minimum stay required on weekends February through October. Seven day cancellation notice required for full refund.
CREDIT CARDS	MC, Visa, Discover
BREAKFAST	Full breakfast served in the dining room includes fresh seasonal fruit, quiche or egg dish, fresh baked muffins or breads and beverages. Lunch is available by prior arrangement.
AMENITIES	Flowers, homemade quilts, wrap around Victorian porch with swing, cookies in the cookie jar, beverages, hot tub on sun deck, wine barrel gazebo, pool, bikes, recreation room, piano, ping pong, exercise equipment, antique car wine tour with picnic lunch available.
RESTRICTIONS	No smoking indoors, children by prior arrangement. Two nameless cats and a horse are the resident animals
REVIEWED	*Karen Brown's California Country Inns and Itineraries, Country Inns and Back Roads*
MEMBER	Wine Country Inns of Sonoma County

COLOMA

The Gold Rush started here, and the town is now mostly a part of the 240-acre Marshall Gold Discovery State Historic Park. Visit the offerings at Lotus County Park, including the full-size replica of Sutter's Mill, or laze around the American River (watch out for rafters). From Sacramento, east of Hwy. 50, and north on Hwy. 49.

THE COLOMA COUNTRY INN

345 High Street, Coloma, CA 95613   916-622-6919
Alan and Cindi Ehrgott, Resident Owners
Spanish spoken

LOCATION	Located 60 miles east of Sacramento. Take Highway 50 to Placerville. Take Highway 49 north 8 miles. Property corner fronts Highway 49 and Church Street. Go north 1 block to High Street, turn right to the inn.
OPEN	All year
DESCRIPTION	A two-story New England farmhouse built in 1852 surrounded by five acres, large pond, rose gardens and an orchard.
NO. OF ROOMS	Four rooms with private bathrooms, four rooms with shared bathrooms.
RATES	Year round rates for a single or double room with a private bathroom $89 to $99, $74 to $84 for a single or double with shared bathroom. Suites rent for $120, the guesthouse for four people $155. Minimum stay on holidays, 10 day cancellation notice required in writing.
CREDIT CARDS	No
BREAKFAST	Full breakfast includes homemade baked goods, fresh fruit salad, egg dish and beverages. Catered event meals available.
AMENITIES	Fresh flowers, canoeing on the pond, heritage rose garden, gazebo, mountain bikes, afternoon refreshments, inn set in middle of 300 acre historic park.
RESTRICTIONS	No smoking, no pets.
REVIEWED	*California Country Inns and Itineraries, Best Places to Stay in California, Best Places in the Gold Country*
MEMBER	Historic Country Inns of the Motherlode

THE VINEYARD HOUSE

530 Cold Springs Road, Coloma, CA 95613   916-622-2217
Les & Christine Widger, Resident Owners

COLUMBIA

Once one of the largest and most important mining towns in the Mother Lode, its 12-square-block downtown is now a State Historic Park filled with wonderfully preserved buildings. Living History Weekend in June, and the two-weekend Miners Christmas in December are special times to be here. On Highway 49, southeast of Sacramento, and a handy distance from Yosemite.

COLUMBIA CITY HOTEL

Main Street, Columbia, CA 95310   209-532-1479
Tom Bender, Manager   800-446-1333 ex 280
                                                          FAX 209-532-7027

LOCATION	On Main Street in Columbia State Historic Park.
OPEN	All year, except Christmas Eve and Christmas Day.
DESCRIPTION	An 1856 two-story Victorian brick hotel listed on the National and State Historic Registers.
NO. OF ROOMS	Ten rooms with private bathrooms. Room #2 on the balcony is the best in the house.
RATES	Year round rates for a single or double room with private bathroom are $65 to $90. No minimum stay, 72 hour cancellation policy.
CREDIT CARDS	Amex, MC, Visa
BREAKFAST	Full breakfast served in the dining room buffet style includes quiche, cereal, yogurt, breakfast breads, fruit and beverages. Special meals include Sunday Brunch and Winemaker dinners.
AMENITIES	Shower baskets, robes, slippers, fresh fruit and evening sherry in the parlor, balconies, original saloon, dining room.
RESTRICTIONS	No smoking, no pets.
REVIEWED	*Bed and Breakfasts of California, Best of Northern California, California Country Inns and Itineraries, Best Places to Kiss in Northern California*
MEMBER	California Association of Bed and Breakfast Inns, Toulumne County Innkeepers Association

HARLAN HOUSE

22890 School House, Columbia, CA 95310   *209-533-4862*
Samantha O'Brien, Resident Owner

LOCATION	From Sonora, take Highway 49 to Parrot's Ferry Road. Turn right at Columbia Street, right at Pacific Street and follow signs to Historic School. B&B is across the street from the school.
OPEN	All year
DESCRIPTION	A 1900 two-story Victorian furnished with period antiques.
NO. OF ROOMS	Four rooms with private bathrooms. Samantha is most proud of the Wine Cellar Suite which includes a spa.
RATES	Year round rates for a double with private bathroom are $75 to $85, and $130 for suites. No minimum stay, 72 hours cancellation notice required.
CREDIT CARDS	MC, Visa
BREAKFAST	Full breakfast served in the dining room or outside includes hash browns, special eggs, fresh fruit, ham, fresh muffins and beverages.
AMENITIES	Flowers, phone, TV in parlor, sherry.
RESTRICTIONS	No smoking, children over eight years old are welcome. Two resident cats, Tom and Hazel.
REVIEWED	*Best of the Gold Country*
AWARDS	Tuolumne Historical Society, 1993

COULTERVILLE

HOTEL JEFFERY

PO Box 440, Coulterville, CA 95311   *209-878-3471*
Karin Fielding, Resident Owner

CRESCENT MILLS

CRESCENT HOTEL

Highway 89, Crescent Mills, CA 95934   *916-284-9905*
Jack & Barbara Tucker, Resident Owners

DAVENPORT

This quiet and uncrowded seaside town is the perfect stopping place on the way to Ano Nuevo State Preserve, breeding ground and rookery for sea lions and seals. This is a great hot-spot for sailboating, and all-over tans can be had at certain local beaches (in general not recommended). Twelve miles north of Santa Cruz on Hwy. 1.

NEW DAVENPORT BED & BREAKFAST INN

1 Davenport Avenue, Davenport, CA 95017　　　　　　*408-425-1818*
Marcia & Bruce McDougal, Resident Owners　　　　　*800-870-1817*
　　　　　　　　　　　　　　　　　　　　　　　FAX 408-423-1160

LOCATION	Nine Miles North of Santa Cruz on Coast Highway 1.
OPEN	All year
DESCRIPTION	A 1906 cottage and 1978 old west building furnished with crafts and antiques.
NO. OF ROOMS	Twelve rooms with private bathrooms. Bruce likes Captain Davenport's Retreat.
RATES	Year round rates are $65 to $115 for a single or a double with a private bathroom. There is two day minimum stay on three day holiday weekends and cancellation requires four days notice.
CREDIT CARDS	Amex, MC, Visa
BREAKFAST	Continental Plus is served in the sitting room on weekends and in the restaurant on weekdays and includes fresh croissants and muffins from the bakery, fruit, juice and eggs. Lunch and dinner are available at the restaurant.
AMENITIES	Phones, gift shop, bar on premises and limited handicapped access.
RESTRICTIONS	No smoking, no pets, children over three are welcome but only in the family rooms.
REVIEWED	*Best Places to Stay in California, America's Wonderful Little Hotels & Inns, California B&B Guide, Hidden Coast of California, American Historic B&Bs, Inns & Guesthouses*
MEMBER	Bed & Breakfast Innkeepers of Santa Cruz, California Association of Bed & Breakfast Innkeepers
AWARDS	ABBA 2 Crowns

DAVIS

UC Davis is here, one of the top 20 research universities in the U.S., an intellectual oasis among its agricultural roots. The result is a terrific mesh of casual and culture. It's also the self-proclaimed Bicycle Capital of the World. In April, the event of the year is Picnic Day (you have to be here); and in May it's the tortuous Double Duty Bike Tour. But the thing to do here is just hang out. About 15 miles west of Sacramento via I-80.

UNIVERSITY INN BED & BREAKFAST

340 A Street, Davis, CA 95616   916-756-8648
Lynda & Ross Yancher, Resident Owners   800-756-8648
Spanish, French, German and Japanese spoken

LOCATION	Directly adjacent to the University of California at the southeast corner of Fourth and A Streets.
OPEN	All year
DESCRIPTION	A 1925 Spanish inn with country and southwest furnishings.
NO. OF ROOMS	Four rooms with private bathrooms.
RATES	Year round rates are $47.50 to $60 for a single with private bathroom, $52.50 to $65 for a double with private bathroom, $47.50 to $75 for a suite and the entire inn rents for $180 to $250. There is a two day minimum stay during special university events and higher rates. Non-refundable prepayment required to confirm reservations.
CREDIT CARDS	Amex, Diners Club, Discover, MC, Visa
BREAKFAST	Continental Plus is served all over and catered picnic lunches and celebratory hors d'oeuvres platters are available with advanced notice.
AMENITIES	Phones, cable TV, refrigerator, off-street parking, microwave, complimentary tea, chocolates and flowers.
RESTRICTIONS	No smoking, pets are limited.

DILLON BEACH

WINDMIST COTTAGE

524 Oceana Drive, Dillon Beach, CA 94929   707-878-2465
Charlotte Smith, Resident Owner

DORRINGTON

It's not on the map, but it's worth the trip. Here in Calaveras County in the Sierra Nevada Gold Country, the offerings are splendid: Calaveras Big Trees State Park, the first Giant Redwood grove ever discovered by white explorers; Mercer and Moaning Caverns; and winter sports at Cottage Springs and Bear Valley. Check the ongoing festivals and events at Bear Valley and neighboring Arnold. Directly northeast of Stockton and Angel's Camp via very scenic Hwy. 4.

DORRINGTON HOTEL & RESTAURANT

3431 Highway 4, Dorrington, CA 95223   *209-795-5800*
Bonnie & Arden Saville, Resident Owners

LOCATION	Center of town on the north side of Highway 4.
OPEN	All year
DESCRIPTION	A two-story 1852 Motherlode clapboard restored stage stop with country furnishings.
NO. OF ROOMS	Five rooms share two bathrooms. Pick room 2.
RATES	Year round rates are $80 to $85 for a single or double with a shared bathroom. There is no minimum stay and cancellation requires five days notice with a $10 cancellation fee.
CREDIT CARDS	MC, Visa
BREAKFAST	Full breakfast is served in the restaurant downstairs and includes a selection of omelets, eggs benedict, breakfast burritos, waffles and French toast. Lunch and dinner are available.
AMENITIES	Morning coffee and newspaper at the door, robes, fruit and sherry in the rooms, brass beds, armoires, quilts and the ghost of Rebecca Dorrington Gardner, the original owner.
RESTRICTIONS	No smoking, no pets, the inn is not suitable for children.
REVIEWED	*Northern California Best Places, Historic B&B's, Inns and Small Hotels, Historic Inns of California's Gold Country Cookbook and Guide, The National Directory of Haunted Places.*

DORRIS

At the far north central edge of Siskiyou County just short of the Oregon line. This is Mt. Shasta country. From Weed, Hwy. 97 cuts along Klamath National Forest and continues past Dorris to Klamath Falls and Upper Klamath Lake. From town, it's easy access to Lower Klamath National Wildlife Refuge, internationally known for its diverse wildlife and habitats. Or there's Lower Klamath and Meiss Lakes . . . you just have to be here. Northeast of Redding via I-5 and Hwy. 97.

HOSPITALITY INN

200 South California Street, Dorris, CA 96023   916-397-2097
Donna & Jeff Burcher, Resident Owners
A little Spanish spoken

LOCATION	In Dorris, one block off Highway 97, corner of 2nd and California Streets.
OPEN	All year
DESCRIPTION	Two-story turn-of-the-century hospital that has been converted to an inn with French country furnishings.
NO. OF ROOMS	Four rooms share four bathrooms.
RATES	Year round rates are $30 to $42 for a single or double with a shared bathroom. Entire inn rents for $175 a night. There is no minimum stay and cancellation requires 24 hours notice.
CREDIT CARDS	No
BREAKFAST	Continental Plus is served in the dining room and includes fresh juice, coffee, fruit and pastries.
AMENITIES	Sitting room with TV, full basement with 100 year old pool, tandum bike, wine, hor d'oeuvres, homemade beer, and dog boarding.
RESTRICTIONS	None. A Yellow Lab, Brew, a mini-Schnauzer, Molly and Bright Eyes the tabby cat.

DUNCANS MILLS

On the Russian River, once called Slavianka, Little Beauty, by Russian fur traders, this stretch is good for steelhead in winter and floating all summer. The tiny hamlet is surrounded by Redwoods and wine country. Explore Armstrong Redwoods State Reserve, or head down to the Sonoma State Beach. From San Francisco, north on Hwy. 1 and east on Hwy. 116.

THE INN AT DUNCANS MILLS

25233 Steelhead Boulevard, Duncans Mills, CA 95430   707-865-1855
Christina Harrison, Resident Owner
Spatterings of Español

LOCATION	Just off Highway 116 in central Duncans Mills, which is really only a wide spot in the road. Landmark is the Historical Railroad Depot, 4 miles east of Highway 1 on Highway 116, turn south on Moscow Road.
OPEN	All year
DESCRIPTION	1989 contemporary redwood country shingle guesthouse nestled next to the Russian River amidst a redwood forest and furnished with eclectic antiques.
NO. OF ROOMS	Four rooms with private bathrooms. Three bedroom apartment or guesthouse available.
RATES	Year round rate for a double with private bathroom is $95, and $200 for three bedroom apartment with kitchen and private bathroom. Entire facility rents for $800. One day cancellation notice for single room, three months notice for entire facility.
CREDIT CARDS	Amex, MC, Visa
BREAKFAST	Full breakfast served in the community room, kitchen or guestroom is "delicious and bountiful." Additional meals available by prior arrangement.
AMENITIES	Flowers, telephones, wine, appetizers and fruit upon arrival, meeting facilities, catering, croquet, horseshoes, putting green, river access, game room, VCR and videos, handicapped access.
RESTRICTIONS	No smoking, no pets.

THE SUPERINTENDENT'S HOUSE

24951 Highway 116, Duncans Mills, CA 95430   707-865-1572
Phil Dattola, Resident Owner

LOCATION	From the east on Highway 116, go 100 yards past the "Duncans Mills, pop. 20" sign and turn right at windmill. Make an "S" pattern up to red and white Victorian. From the west on Highway 116, go 300 yards past town and turn left at the old metal windmill.
OPEN	All year
DESCRIPTION	An 1880 two-story redwood Victorian roadhouse, listed on the California State Historic Register. Designed with 12 foot ceilings, large windows, hardwood floors and an old fashioned porch.
NO. OF ROOMS	Five rooms share two bathrooms.
RATES	Year round rates for a double room with shared bathroom are $70 to $80.
CREDIT CARDS	No
BREAKFAST	Full breakfast served in the dining room or on the porch includes pastries, fruit salad, coffee cake, breakfast meats, eggs, pancakes or French toast and beverages. Special meals can be arranged.
AMENITIES	Parlor with TV/VCR and video library.
RESTRICTIONS	No pets, no smoking in bedrooms. The resident cats are Bongo and Cow Kitty.
MEMBER	Russian River Region Chamber of Commerce

DUNSMUIR

The Sacramento River runs through this unspoiled old railroad town on the National Historic Register, with scenery that is sublime. Railroad buffs: check out Railroad Park, Archives and Library. Big event (of course) is Railroad Days in June. This is also the gateway into Castle Crags State Park, a heaven for trekkers and serious rock climbers. The Pacific Crest Trail swings through here. Just south of Mt. Shasta.

ABBOTT'S RIVERWALK INN

4300 Stagecoach Road, Dunsmuir, CA 96025   *916-235-4300*
Danny & Terry Jo Abbott, Resident Owners

DUNSMUIR INN

5423 Dunsmuir Avenue, Dunsmuir, CA 96025   *916-235-4543*
Jerry & Julie Iskra, Resident Owners

LOCATION	From I-5 take Central Dunsmuir exit. At stop sign turn left onto Dunsmuir Avenue in a southerly direction and follow 1/2 mile to the inn.
OPEN	All year
DESCRIPTION	A two-story 1925 inn with country furnishings.
NO. OF ROOMS	Four rooms with private bathrooms. The suite is the best room.
RATES	Year round rates are $55 to $60 for a single or a double with a private bathroom, the suite is $65 and the entire inn rents for $200. There is no minimum stay and cancellation requires 72 hours notice and a $10 fee.
CREDIT CARDS	Amex, Diners Club, Discover, MC, Visa
BREAKFAST	Continental Plus is served in the kitchen and includes quiche, fresh cinnamon rolls, fresh fruit cup and beverages. Lunch and vegetarian meals are available.
AMENITIES	Outdoor hot tub, guest kitchen for use throughout the day, snacks and sodas, ice cream parlor.
RESTRICTIONS	No smoking, no pets, all children are welcome. The Corgy X is called Katie and the Lab is called Penny. The pot-belly pig is called Rosie and is housebroken.
KUDOS/COMMENTS	". . .roomy, friendly atmosphere. . .nice sandwich shop and ice cream parlor. . ."

EAST BROTHER ISLAND
(SAN FRANCISCO BAY)

This is one of four rocky islands known as The Sisters and The Brothers, that mark the straits separating San Francisco and San Pablo Bays. The one-acre East Brother Island holds the oldest light station still operating in the Bay. Three miles north of the San Rafael Bridge, I-580. Transportaion is by boat from Point San Pablo Yacht Harbor.

EAST BROTHER LIGHT STATION

---

117 Park Place, Point Richmond, CA 94801 510-233-2385
Pat Diamond, Director

LOCATION	On a small rocky outcropping at the north end of San Francisco Bay. Approximately 45 minutes from San Francisco. From either direction on Interstate 80, take San Rafael exit to Interstate 580 west toward Richmond - San Rafael Bridge. Just before toll plaza, take Point Molate exit to the right. Follow signs to Point San Pablo Yacht Harbor.
OPEN	All year
DESCRIPTION	Built in 1873, this three-story Carpenters Gothic light station is furnished in period antiques and reproductions and surrounded by a white picket fence. On the National Historic Register.
NO. OF ROOMS	Two rooms with private bathrooms, two rooms share two bathrooms.
RATES	Year round rates for a single or double room with private bathroom are $235-$295. Sixty days advance notice of cancellation for full refund, 10% fee if less than 30 days notice.
CREDIT CARDS	No
BREAKFAST	Full breakfast served in the dining room includes homemade waffles, fresh fruit and beverages. Rates also include four-course dinner with wine (vegetarian available on request.)
AMENITIES	Boat transportation to and from the island. Wine and hors d'oeuvres served upon arrival, guide tour of the station with champagne.
RESTRICTIONS	No smoking, no pets, children over 12 years old welcome. Limited access for those not able to climb 10 feet up a ladder.
REVIEWED	*California Country Inns and Itineraries, Romantic Getaways, Non Smokers Guide to B&Bs, America's Wonderful Little Hotels and Inns, By Recommendation Only*
KUDOS/COMMENTS	"Cozy, with a great escape to nature."

ELK

This tiny hamlet perched on the coastal bluffs was once a lumber port. Central to the town is Greenwood Creek State Beach and Park, great for picnics and ocean fishing. Or visit the historic exhibits at the park's visitor center. Halfway between Pt. Arena and Mendocino with handy access to the best of both without the crush.

ELK COVE INN

6300 South Highway 1, Elk, CA 95432   707-877-3321
Elaine Bryant, Resident Owner   800-275-2967
Spanish   FAX 707-877-1808

LOCATION	From Cloverdale, turn west on Highway 128. Elk is located on Highway 1, six miles south of the intersection of Highway 128 and Highway 1. Inn is at the south end of town on the oceanside.
OPEN	All year
DESCRIPTION	This French Victorian inn, built in 1883, is nestled in peaceful seclusion atop a bluff overlooking the ocean.
NO. OF ROOMS	Ten rooms with private bathrooms
RATES	High season rates, March through November, are $78 to $198 for a single or double with private bathroom, oceanfront cottages $125 to $198. Off season rates, December through February are $70 to $150 for a single or a double with private bathroom, and $100 to $175 for oceanfront cottages. Two night minimum stay on weekends and holidays, cancellation seven days in advance, $10 per night cancellation fee.
CREDIT CARDS	Amex, MC, Visa
BREAKFAST	Full breakfast served in the oceanfront dining room includes French toast, eggs, croissants, baked goods, fruit, and Elaine's "famous Southern spoonbread"...Let's have a field report on this spoonbread please...TI
AMENITIES	All rooms have bathrobes, coffeemakers, port and chocolates, fresh flowers, and comfortable chairs for relaxing. Wine and cheese each afternoon gazebo.
RESTRICTIONS	No smoking, children over 14 years old are welcome. Personality range of resident canines runs the gamut from Boomer, the lovable and laid-back German Shepard, to Asta, the fox terrier "in charge of everything"...Boomer would fit better here at the intergalatic headquarters of Travis Ilse Publishers...TI
REVIEWED	*Best Places to Kiss in Northern California*
MEMBER	California Association of Bed and Breakfast Inns, Mendocino Coast Innkeepers Association

GREENWOOD PIER INN

5928 South Highway 1, Elk, CA 95432
Isabel & Kendrick Petty, Resident Owners

707-877-9997

GRIFFIN HOUSE AT GREENWOOD COVE

5910 South Highway 1, Elk, CA 95432
Leslie Griffin Lawson, Resident Owner
Spanish spoken

707-877-3422

LOCATION	Center of "downtown" Elk (pop. 250). On the ocean side of Highway 1, watch for signs.
OPEN	All year
DESCRIPTION	1920 rural Victorian cottages and restaurant.
NO. OF ROOMS	Seven rooms with private bathrooms.
RATES	Year round rates for garden cottages are $57 to $100, and for ocean front cottages $110 to $145. Minimum stay on weekends, 72 hour cancellation policy, no fee if room is resold.
CREDIT CARDS	MC, Visa
BREAKFAST	Full hot breakfast served in guestroom includes cheese and egg souffles, waffles, pancakes, turkey, ham and sausages, fruits and juices. Dinner available seven nights a week in Bridget Dolan's Irish Pub.
AMENITIES	All cottages have woodburning stoves, split of local wine on arrival, and fresh flowers. Several cottages include claw-foot tubs, separate parlors, and ocean front private decks.
RESTRICTIONS	No smoking, no pets. Assorted cats adorn the grounds, Lucky, Rosie and "G Pat the Cat".
REVIEWED	*Karen Brown's California Country Inns and Itineraries, Northern California Best Places, Bed and Breakfast in Northern California*
MEMBER	Professional Association of Innkeepers International, California Lodging Industry Association

HARBOR HOUSE

5600 South Highway 1, Elk, CA 95432   707-877-3203
Dean Turner, Resident Owner

SANDPIPER HOUSE INN

5520 South Highway 1, Elk, CA 95432   707-877-3587
Claire & Richard Melrose, Resident Owners

LOCATION	From Highway 101 north to Cloverdale, take Highway 128 exit west to Highway 1. The Sandpiper is six miles south of the Highway 128/Highway 1 junction.
OPEN	All year
DESCRIPTION	A 1916 two-story California Craftsman with traditional furnishings and European antiques, perennial gardens and private beach.
NO. OF ROOMS	Five rooms with private bathrooms.
RATES	High season rates, April through December, for a single or double room with private bathroom are $100 to $195, $10 less January through March. Two night minimum stay on weekends, seven day cancellation notice required with $10 fee.
CREDIT CARDS	Amex, MC, Visa
BREAKFAST	Full breakfast served in the dining room includes fresh fruit, main course, meats, baked goods and beverages.
AMENITIES	Afternoon tea and fresh baked pastries, sherry, fresh flowers, massage available, private beach access from the garden.
RESTRICTIONS	Children over 10 years old welcome. Three friendly cats in residence are Yoda, Hobo and Rudy.
REVIEWED	*America's Wonderful Little Hotels and Inns, Karen Brown's California's Country Inns and Itineraries.*
MEMBER	Professional Association of Innkeepers International, California Association of Bed and Breakfast Inns

EUREKA

Nothing dispels the fog here on Humboldt Bay. It's part of the landscape of barrier sandbars, islands, peninsulas and sloughs, marine life and seafood without end. The town's seafaring, lumbering and cultural roots are reflected everywhere, especially in the stately Victorians once owned by lumber barons, and sadly, now in the Bay's pulp-mill pollution. Great sights: Old Town; Gothic Carson Mansion; the Samoa Cookhouse and Museum on Samoa Peninsula; and performing arts at the Cultural Center. Don't forget a harbor cruise, or Field's Landing when the big fishing boats come in. Big events: Rhododendron Festival (fog or no fog) in April; Old Town Fourth of July; and in August, Arts Festival, Concerts in the Park, and Tour of the Unknown Coast Bicycle Race. On the far North Coast via Hwy. 101. From here it's the Redwood Highway.

THE CARTER HOUSE

1023 Third Street, Eureka, CA 95501   707-445-1390
Mark and Christi Carter, Resident Owner   800-444-1390
French, Spanish spoken   FAX 707-444-8062

LOCATION	From Highway 101 take L Street exit, turn left, go two blocks to Third Street. Carter House is at the corner of L Street and Third Street, across from the Hotel Carter.
OPEN	All year
DESCRIPTION	A four-story architectural reconstruction of a Victorian home destroyed in the 1910 earthquake, with Victorian and Edwardian furnishings.
NO. OF ROOMS	Seven rooms have private bathrooms. Mark recommends the Burgundy Room.
RATES	High season rates, April through December, for a single or double with private bathroom are $125 to $135, and $225 to $285 for suites. Off season rates, January through March, for a single or double with private bathroom are $95 to $105, and $225 for suites. Business rates are available and the entire inn rents for $1,000. Minimum stay on selected weekends, 72 hour cancellation policy.
CREDIT CARDS	Amex, MC, Diners Club, Visa, Discover, Carte Blanche
BREAKFAST	Full breakfast is served in the dining room and includes fruit, muffins and pastries, poached pears in wine sauce, eggs benedict, expresso and coffee. Special meals available on request.
AMENITIES	Evening social hour, pastries, tea and cordials at turn down, robes, small library, some rooms have spa tubs, fireplaces, harbor views, herb gardens and common area with fireplace..
RESTRICTIONS	No smoking, no pets, children over eight years old are welcome.
REVIEWED	*Special Places, Fifty Romantic Getaways, Unique Northwest Country Inns*
MEMBER	California Association of Bed and Breakfast Inns
RATED	AAA 3 Diamonds, Mobil 3 Stars
AWARDS	Uncle Ben's Inn of the Year Award, 1986, 1993

THE DALY INN

1125 H Street, Eureka, CA 95501   707-445-3638
Sue and Gene Clinesmith, Resident Owners   800-321-9656
                                                    FAX 707-444-3636

LOCATION	Turn east off of Highway 101 onto "H" Street. Continue on "H" Street, inn is located on the corner of 12th Street and "H" Street.
OPEN	All year, except Thanksgiving and Christmas holidays.
DESCRIPTION	A three-story 1905 Colonial Revival with Victorian antiques.
NO. OF ROOMS	Three rooms with private bathrooms, two rooms with a shared bathroom. Try the Garden View Suite for the best views.
RATES	High season, May through October, rates for a single or double with a private bathroom are $80 to $125, and $65 to $85 for a single or double with a shared bathroom. Suites are $125 and the entire inn rents for $500. Off season, November through April, rates for a single or double with a private bathroom are $70 to $100, and $60 to $80 for a single or double with a shared bathroom. Suites are $100 and the entire inn rents for $400. No minimum stay, cancellation required seven days in advance for full refund.
CREDIT CARDS	Amex, MC, Visa, Discover
BREAKFAST	Full breakfast served in the dining room, guest rooms, or breakfast room includes homemade coffee cake or muffins, egg entree, meat, fruit and beverages. "My grandmother's sticky buns are my speciality."...There are people we know who are serious about their sticky buns...may we have a field report please...TI
AMENITIES	Robes, guest telephone, flowers, wine and hors d'oeuvres each evening, chocolate truffles and turn down service, Victorian garden with fish pond and waterfall.
RESTRICTIONS	Smoking outdoors only, no pets, children over 12 years old welcome.
MEMBER	California Association of Bed and Breakfast Inns, Eureka Bed and Breakfast Association
RATED	AAA 3 Diamonds
KUDOS/COMMENTS	"Beautiful, large, well-appointed room. Lovely baths." ... " One of the most outstanding cooks I've met."

AN ELEGANT VICTORIAN MANSION BED & BREAKFAST

1406 C Street, Eureka, CA 95501   707-444-3144
Doug and Lily Vieyra, Resident Owners
French, Dutch, Flemmish, German spoken

LOCATION	Inn is located at the corner of 14th and 'C' Streets in Eureka. From Highway 101 north, turn right at "Denny's" restaurant. From Highway 101 south, turn left at 'C' Street and continue south ten blocks to 14th Street.
OPEN	All year
DESCRIPTION	Constructed entirely of 1000-year-old California Redwood, this 1888 two-story Victorian inn is trimmed in "Gingerbread" woodwork furnished with Victorian pieces and listed on the State and National Historic Registers.
NO. OF ROOMS	Two rooms have private bathrooms, two rooms have shared bathrooms. Doug recommends the Governor's Suite.
RATES	Year round rates for a double with a private bathroom are $135, and $75 to $125 for a double or single with a shared bathroom, and $135 to $145 for suites. Cancellation policy requires seven days notice and $10 cancellation charge.
CREDIT CARDS	MC, Visa
BREAKFAST	Full multi-course French gourmet breakfast served in the dining room includes fresh breads, fresh juice, and fruit, cold cuts, cereals, quiches, Eggs Benedict, cobblers and beverages.
AMENITIES	Complimentary Bay Cruise and Horseless Carriage ride, sauna, croquet, Victorian flower gardens, movies, ice cream sodas, bicycles, tennis courts, valet parking.
RESTRICTIONS	No smoking, no pets. Talented resident birds include Victoria the Ostrich, Victoria the Peacock, and Albert the Parrot. So you won't be confused, the parrot talks and the peacock dances.
REVIEWED	*Fodor's California, America's Wonderful Little Hotels and Inns, Northern California Best Places, Fodor's Bed and Breakfasts and Country Inns—West Coast, Best Places to Stay in Northern California*
MEMBER	Professional Association of Innkeepers International, Bed and Breakfast Innkeepers International, California Association of Bed and Breakfast Inns, Eureka Bed and Breakfast Association
RATED	AAA 3 Diamonds, Mobil 3 Stars
KUDOS/COMMENTS	"Small but elegant Victorian inn, outstanding breakfasts and warm, welcoming innkeepers." ..."Charming Victorian building decor and furnishings, hosts are delightful, lovely gardens."

HEUER'S VICTORIAN INN

1302 E Street, Eureka, CA 95501   *707-443-3034*
Charles & Ausbern Heuer, Resident Owners

LOCATION	From highway 101 North, turn right onto E Street and go seven blocks to the corner of E and Hillsdale Street.
OPEN	All year
DESCRIPTION	An 1894 three-story Queen Ann Victorian restored to its original splendor.
NO. OF ROOMS	One room with private bathroom, two rooms with shared bathroom.
RATES	Year round rates are $75. 48 hour cancellation notice required.
CREDIT CARDS	Amex, Diners Club, Discover, MC, Visa
BREAKFAST	Continental breakfast served in dining room.
AMENITIES	Fresh flowers in rooms. Guests have the full use of the first two stories of the inn.
RESTRICTIONS	No smoking, no pets. Children over 12 years of age are welcome. One resident dog, "Lady."

HOTEL CARTER

301 L Street, Eureka, CA 95501   707-444-8062
Mark and Christi Carter, Resident Owners   800-404-1390
French spoken   FAX 707-444-8062

LOCATION
From Highway 101, turn left onto L Street. Go two blocks to 3rd and L Street (Highway 101 is 5th Street).

OPEN
All year

DESCRIPTION
This three-story hotel is a reconstruction of a Eureka Victorian hotel.

NO. OF ROOMS
All rooms have private bathrooms

RATES
High season rates, April through December, for a single or double with private bathroom are $89 to $95 and $185 to $225 for suites. Off season rates, January through March, for a single or double with private bathroom are $79 to $85 and $165 to $185 for suites. Minimum stay on selected holidays, 72 hour cancellation policy.

CREDIT CARDS
Amex, MC, Diners Club, Visa, Discover, Carte Blanche

BREAKFAST
Full breakfast is served in the dining room and includes changing hot entree, variety of muffins and pastry and beverages. Dinner and special meals available on request.

AMENITIES
Robes, phones, TV, VCR, fireplaces, spa and soaking tubs, featherbeds, CD players, mini bars, wine and hors d'oervres, turn down service, dining room with classical guitarist on weekends.

RESTRICTIONS
No smoking, no pets.

REVIEWED
Best Places to Kiss in Northern California, Fifty Romantic Getaways, Special Places

MEMBER
California Association of Bed and Breafast Inns, Romantique, Special Places, Unique Northwest Country Inns

RATED
AAA 3 Diamonds, Mobil 3 Stars

NAUTICAL NIGHTS BED & BREAKFAST

Woodley Island Marina, Dock D, Slip 5, Eureka, CA 95501   707-443-5172
Marcia & Tony Keeling, Owners

LOCATION	From Highway 101, turn west on "R" Street in Eureka or take Highway 255 and go 1/4 mile to Woodley Island Marina Dock D, Slip 5.
OPEN	All year
DESCRIPTION	A 1980, 45-foot custom Cutter rigged Roberts sloop with teak cabin.
NO. OF ROOMS	One bedroom with shared bathroom.
RATES	Year round rates for a double with shared bathroom $85, additional person $35. Seven days advance notice required for cancellation.
CREDIT CARDS	No
BREAKFAST	Full breakfast served in the main salon includes fresh fruits, Grand Marnier French toast, chicken apple sausage, croissants and beverages.
AMENITIES	Dessert served the night of your arrival, "lounge in the cockpit and enjoy sun tea or freshly brewed coffee."
RESTRICTIONS	No smoking, no pets, children over 12 are welcome.
MEMBER	Humboldt County Bed and Breakfast Association

OLD TOWN BED & BREAKFAST INN

1521 Third Street, Eureka, CA 95501   707-445-3951
Leigh & Diane Benson, Resident Owners   800-331-5098
Spanish & Italian spoken   *FAX 707-445-8346*

LOCATION	Eureka is laid out on a grid of 1-2-3, A-B-C. The inn is located at 3rd and P.
OPEN	All year, closed most of January.
DESCRIPTION	An 1871 two-story Greek Revival Italianate inn furnished with antiques. The Inn is on the California Historic Register.
NO. OF ROOMS	Four rooms with private bathrooms and two rooms share one bathroom. Carlottas is the best room.
RATES	Year round rates are $65 to $125 for a single or a double with a private bathroom and $65 to $75 for a single or a double with a shared bathroom. Ask about a variety of discounts. The entire inn rents for $500. There is a minimum stay during university graduation in mid-May and cancellation requires three days.
CREDIT CARDS	Amex, Diners Club, Discover, MC, Visa
BREAKFAST	Full breakfast served in the dining room includes beverages, nut sweetbreads, biscuits, muffins, homemade jams (for sale), meat, potatoes, eggs and cheeses. Special meals available.
AMENITIES	Teak hot tub, handmade robes, slippers, rubber duckies, flowers, complementary wine and fruit, woodstoves, fireplaces, afternoon tea, massage available.
RESTRICTIONS	No smoking, no pets, no "uncouth persons", children over 10 are welcome. The cats go by Puschka and L'il Bit.
REVIEWED	*Bed & Breakfast California, Country Inns of the West Coast, Hidden Coast of California, The Official Guide to American Historic Inns, Nationa Trust Guide to Historic B&Bs*...and about 20 other books...TI
MEMBER	American Bed & Breakfast Association, California Association of Bed & Brekfast Inns
RATED	ABBA 3 Crowns, Mobil 2 Stars
KUDOS/COMMENTS	"Fun decor and entertaining innkeepers."

SHANNON HOUSE B&B

2154 Spring Street, Eureka, CA 95501   707-443-8130
David & Barbara Shannon
Spanish, French spoken

LOCATION	Heading north turn right on Wabash and right onto Spring Street (off of Broadway). Located about seven miles south of Arcata and two miles southwest of the Old Town district.
OPEN	All year
DESCRIPTION	An 1891 Queen Anne built entirely of redwood with Victorian furnishings, period wallpaper and antiques throughout. Cozy parlor with plenty of natural light.
NO. OF ROOMS	One room with private bathroom; two with shared bathroom.
RATES	Year round rates are $55 to $65 for single with private bathroom and $45 to $55 for single with shared bathroom. Double with private bathroom is $75 and $55 with shared bathroom. Entire B&B available for $185. Reservation/cancellation policy: One week in advance.
CREDIT CARDS	Amex, Discover
BREAKFAST	Full breakfast, served in dining room, usually includes eggs, meat, muffins or pancakes, fruit, coffee or tea, milk, juice and other special dishes.
AMENITIES	Fresh flowers in the rooms, robes and telephones in rooms for business travelers.
RESTRICTIONS	No smoking, no pets. One resident cat, "Kitty."
REVIEWED	*AAA Bed & Breakfasts, Northern and Central California, Nevada.*
MEMBER	Eureka Bed and Breakfast Association
KUDOS/COMMENTS	A Weaver's Inn and Daly Inn — "Both are excellent, gardens for walking or sitting. Innkeepers quite congenial, spacious sitting rooms with fireplaces. The conversation is great!" "Beautifully restored Victorian-every attention paid to guest comfort."

Upstairs at the Waterfront

102 F Street, Eureka, CA 95501   707-443-9190
Diane Smith, Resident Owner

LOCATION	Overlooks Humboldt Bay and Eureka's historic Old Town District.
OPEN	All year
DESCRIPTION	An 1892 Queen Anne Victorian restored to period, including high ceilings with wallpaper freize work. Listed on the National and California State Historic Registers.
NO. OF ROOMS	Two rooms with private bathrooms. Sophie's Suite is the best in the house.
RATES	High season May through September rates for a double or suite with private bathroom are $100 to $150, and $85 to $125 off-season October through April. Entire B & B available for $200 to $250.
CREDIT CARDS	MC, Visa
BREAKFAST	Choose from breakfast menu service provided at the Cafe Waterfront downstairs.
AMENITIES	Fresh flowers, phones, TVs, stereo CDs, washer, dryer, kitchen, horse and carriage pick up.
RESTRICTIONS	No smoking, no pets, children are not encouraged.
AWARDS	Governor's Award for Excellence in Bed and Breakfast Design, 1994.

A Weaver's Inn

1440 B Street, Eureka, CA 95501   707-443-8119
Dorthy & Bob Swendeman, Resident Owners

LOCATION	From Highway 101 north, turn right on B Street and stop at 1440.
OPEN	All year
DESCRIPTION	A two-story 1883 Queen Anne Colonial Revival with Victorian furnishings and weaver's studio.
NO. OF ROOMS	Two rooms with private bathrooms and two rooms share one bathroom. The best room is called Marcia.
RATES	Year round rates for a single or a double with a private bathroom are $60 to $85; for a single or double with shared bathroom, $45 to $65, and the suite is $85 to $100. There is a minimum stay during holidays and graduation and cancellation requires 72 hours notice.
CREDIT CARDS	Amex, MC, Visa, Discover
BREAKFAST	Full breakfast is served in the dining room and includes fruit juice, fruit, entree, breads and pastry.
AMENITIES	Gardens, wood fireplaces, flowers, robes, piano concert and croquet.
RESTRICTIONS	Smoking on porch only.
MEMBER	California Association of Bed & Breakfast Inns

FERNDALE

Ooohh! Sweet butter. . . . . Danish and Portuguese settlers established the town's dairy industry for which it is known. Its perfection as a Victorian village is reflected in the beautifully restored "butterfat palaces" built by the founding fathers. An historic walking tour is a must as are these events: the Portuguese Holy Ghost Festival in May, Scandinavian Festival in June, and the month-long Victorian Christmas with the world's tallest living Christmas tree—125-ft. Silke spruce. On the ocean, just south of Eureka via Hwy. 1.

GINGERBREAD MANSION INN

---

400 Berding Street, Ferndale, CA 95536
Ken Torbert, Resident Owner

707-786-4000
800-952-4136
FAX 707-786-4381

LOCATION	From Highway 101 take Ferndale exit. From north, go to second stop sign and turn right. From south, go to first stop sign and turn left. Continue over bridge into Ferndale, approximately 5 miles. Turn left at Brown Street.
OPEN	All year
DESCRIPTION	An 1899 two-story Queen Anne Victorian Eastlake listed on the California State Historic Register. Surrounded by formal English garden and furnished with Victorian antiques.
NO. OF ROOMS	Nine rooms with private bathrooms. The Fountain Suite is the best in the house.
RATES	High season rates, May through October, for a single or double with private bathroom are $100 to $145, and $145 to $185 for suites. Off season rates, November through April, for a single or double with private bathroom are $75 to $120, and $120 to $160 for suites. Minimum stay on weekends, holidays, and during August. Full prepayment is required seven days prior to your arrival.
CREDIT CARDS	Amex, MC, Visa
BREAKFAST	Full breakfast is served in the dining room.
AMENITIES	Bathrobes, clock radios, guest beverage area, bicycles, umbrellas, afternoon high tea is served in the parlor.
RESTRICTIONS	No smoking, no pets, children over 10 years old are welcome.
MEMBER	Professional Association of Innkeepers International, American Bed and Breakfast Association, Independent Innkeepers Association, Unique Northwest Country Inns, California Association of Bed and Breakfast Inns, Special Places
RATED	AAA 4 Diamonds, ABBA 3 Crowns, Mobil 3 Stars
KUDOS/COMMENTS	"Great hosts, outstanding guest rooms." ..."Like stepping into another era."... "Wonderful, couldn't say enough about it."

GRANDMOTHER'S HOUSE
BED & BREAKFAST

861 Howard Street, Ferndale, CA 95536   *707-786-9704*
Richard and Jacqueline Ramirez, Resident Owners

LOCATION	Four blocks north of downtown Ferndale. One block past the high school coming into town off Highway 101.
OPEN	All year
DESCRIPTION	1901 Queen Anne Eastlake Victorian with "light" Victorian decor.
NO. OF ROOMS	One room with private bathroom, two rooms share one bathroom.
RATES	Year round rates are $65 for singles, $70 for doubles. Entire home can be rented for $210. Call for cancellation policy, seven days advance notice required.
CREDIT CARDS	MC, Visa, Discover
BREAKFAST	Continental Plus served in the dining room. includes fresh juice and fruit, waffles, mufins, coffee, tea and hot chocolate.
AMENITIES	Robes, porches overlooking grazing cattle and buffalo, fireplace, self-service snacks available.
RESTRICTIONS	No smoking, no pets, children of any age are welcome. Outdoor residents include Chewy the dog, two cats, and a "Fluffy" rabbit.

SHAW HOUSE BED & BREAKFAST INN

703 Main Street, Ferndale, CA 95536   707-786-9958
Ken and Norma Bessingpas, Resident Owners   FAX 707-786-9958

LOCATION	Approximately four miles off Highway 101, in greater historic downtown Ferndale.
OPEN	All year
DESCRIPTION	An 1854 two-story Carpenter Gothic with French windows, six gables, french doors, and balconies, listed on the National Historic Register.
NO. OF ROOMS	Six rooms with private bathrooms. Try the Honeymoon Room for a treat.
RATES	Year round rates for a single or double with private bathroom are $70 to $135. Discounts are given to returning guests. Minimum stay during the Ferndale Fair in August. Cancellation policy requires seven days notice with $10 fee.
CREDIT CARDS	Amex, MC, Visa
BREAKFAST	Full breakfast is served in the dining room and changes everyday, a sample might include French toast, homemade syrup, fruit and beverages.
AMENITIES	Flowers, robes, slippers, cookies and coffee in the afternoon, bicycles, one-acre grounds with benches and gazebo.
RESTRICTIONS	No pets, children over five years of age are welcome. Resident cats include a stately Persian, Dudly, and a mix Kinzie.
REVIEWED	*Northern California Best Places*
MEMBER	American Bed and Breakfast Association, California Lodging Industry Association
RATED	ABBA 3 Crowns

FISH CAMP
(YOSEMITE NATIONAL PARK)

What a spot! At the south entrance to Yosemite National Park, and the Mariposa Grove of Giant Sequoias, the ancient ones. The Grizzly Giant is 2,700 years old! See them via open-air tram all summer. From here, make your way into the Park's splendors, and thank John Muir for it all. From Fresno it's 54 miles north on scenic Hwy. 41. Bass Lake is a nice stop on the way for water recreation.

APPLE TREE INN

1110 Highway 41, Fish Camp, CA 93623   209-683-5111
Vivien and Gerry Smith, Resident Owners

LOCATION	On Highway 41 south of Fish Camp, two miles south of Yosemite National Park.
OPEN	All year
DESCRIPTION	Six cottages on seven wooded acres.
NO. OF ROOMS	Six cottages with private bathrooms.
RATES	Year round rates for cottages with private bathrooms are $85 to $100. Minimum stay on holidays and weekends, two days notice for cancellation.
CREDIT CARDS	Amex, MC, Diners Club, Visa
BREAKFAST	Continental breakfast including freshly baked muffins, fruit and beverages is delivered to cottages.
AMENITIES	Gardens, views, private decks, TV, clock radios, fireplaces, two cottages have kitchens.
RESTRICTIONS	No pets. Local wildlife includes hummingbirds, deer, racoons, coyote, bears, fox and squirrels.
REVIEWED	*America's Wonderful Little Hotels and Inns, Weekend Get-a-Ways*
MEMBER	California Association of Bed and Breakfast Inns, Southern Yosemite Bed and Breakfast

KAREN'S BED & BREAKFAST YOSEMITE INN

1144 Railroad Avenue, Fish Camp, CA 93623   *209-683-4550*
Karen Bergh, Resident Owner   *800-346-1443*
FAX 209-683-4550

LOCATION	One quarter mile south of Chevron station on Highway 41. One mile south of Yosemite.
OPEN	All year
DESCRIPTION	A two-story 1989 contemporary country inn with country furnishings.
NO. OF ROOMS	Three rooms with private bathrooms.
RATES	Year round rates are $80 to $85 for a single and a double respectively. There is a two day minimum stay on holiday weekends. Cancellation requires seven days (21 days for holidays) notice and a $10 cancellation fee.
CREDIT CARDS	No
BREAKFAST	Full breakfast is served in the dining room and includes hot drinks, fruit juice, fresh fruit, waffles or pancakes or muffins, breakfast meats, eggs and potatoes.
AMENITIES	Afternoon refreshments, video and reading library, seasonal drinks, cookies, cakes, breads, fruit, cheese and nuts. Tour information for Yosemite.
RESTRICTIONS	No smoking (inside), no pets. Buster the cat weighs 20 pounds.
REVIEWED	*Americans Wonderful Little Hotels & Inns, Bed & Breakfast California, Bed & Breakfast in California, Bed & Breakfast Home Directory - West Coast, Bed & Breakfasts, Country Inns, The Definitive California Bed & Breakfast Guide*

FORESTVILLE

At the center of Sonoma's wine country. In the shadow of the Redwoods and just south of the Russian River, it's on Hwy. 116 north of San Francisco, between Hwy. 1 and 101.

THE FARMHOUSE INN & RESTAURANT

7871 River Road, Forestville, CA 95436 707-887-3300
Rebecca Smith, Resident Owner FAX 707-887-3311

LOCATION	From Highway 101 take River Road exit (Santa Rosa), head west on River Road. The Inn is 7.5 miles up on the left, across the street from Wohler Road.
OPEN	All year
DESCRIPTION	A restored 1878 two-story traditional farmhouse and cottages with white picket fences and gardens.
NO. OF ROOMS	Eight rooms with private bathrooms. Room #1 is especially nice.
RATES	Year round rates for a double room with private bathroom are $105 to $175, entire B&B rents for $1,135. Two night minimum stay on weekends, cancellation required seven days prior to arrival.
CREDIT CARDS	Amex, MC, Visa, Discover
BREAKFAST	Full breakfast, served in the dining room or outside on the deck, includes cereal, muffins, fruit, hot entree and beverages. Lunch and dinner are available at the restaurant located in the main house.
AMENITIES	Swimming pool and English gardens, phone, clock radios, fireplace, sauna, Jacuzzi tubs, wedding facilities for up to 250, business meetings, wheelchair accessible.
RESTRICTIONS	No smoking, no pets, Arthur, a feral cat, is still adjusting to domestic life.
REVIEWED	*Wine Country Access, Fifty Most Romantic Bed and Breakfasts in Northern California, The Definitive California Bed and Breakfast Touring Guide*
MEMBER	Country Inns of the Russian River

FORT BRAGG

Though small, this little seaport is big on logging, and has an active fishing fleet. It's also surrounded by Caspar Headlands State Beach and Recreation Area, Jughandle State Reserve, and lush MacKerricher State Park (save a day for this). Fun doings: homeward-bound Gray Whale Festival in March; tiny Noyo's fresh-off-the-boat fish and Salmon Barbecue Festival on July 4th; and major partying during Paul Bunyan Days over Labor Day weekend. This is lumber country—for a before-and-after look at the life of a tree, visit the Georgia Pacific Tree Nursery, followed by a tour of the Union Lumber Company Mill. Halfway between San Francisco and Eureka on scenic Hwy. 1.

AVALON HOUSE

561 Stewart Street, Fort Bragg, CA 95437   707-964-5555
Anne Sorrells, Resident Owner

COUNTRY INN BED & BREAKFAST

632 North Main Street, Fort Bragg, CA 95437   707-964-3737
Don & Helen Miller, Resident Owners   800-831-5327
Spanish spoken

LOCATION	In downtown Ft. Bragg.
OPEN	All year
DESCRIPTION	A 1892 two-story Victorian Town House with hanging flower baskets, contemporary and old fashioned furnishings, listed on the Fort Bragg Historic Register.
NO. OF ROOMS	Eight rooms with private bathrooms. Summertime is the best room according to Don.
RATES	Year round rates are $75 to $125 for a single or double with a private bathroom. There is a two day minimum stay on summer weekends and three night minimum stay on holiday weekends. Cancellation requires 72 hours notice.
CREDIT CARDS	MC, Visa
BREAKFAST	Continental Plus is served in the parlor and includes home baked nut and fruit breads, "surprise" muffins, orange juice, gouda cheese and beverages.
AMENITIES	Wine from 6 p.m. to retiring, fresh-cut flowers, brass and white enameled beds, hurricane lamps, maps, history books and off-street parking.
RESTRICTIONS	No smoking, no pets, children over 15 years of age are welcome.
REVIEWED	*Bed & Breakfast California, Country Inns, Lodges and Historic Hotels, Bed & Breakfast USA, Bed & Breakfast America, Bed & Breakfast North America*

GLASS BEACH B&B INN

726 North Main Street, Fort Bragg, CA 95437   707-964-6774
Nancy Cardenas, Resident Owner

GREY WHALE INN

615 North Main Street, Fort Bragg, CA 95437   707-964-0640
John & Colette Bailey, Resident Owners   800-382-7244
Spanish spoken   FAX 707-964-4408

LOCATION	In Fort Bragg, right on Main Street which is Highway 1.
OPEN	All year
DESCRIPTION	A four-story 1915 Colonial Revival inn with eclectic furnishings and ocean views
NO. OF ROOMS	Fourteen rooms with private bathrooms. Colette suggest the Sunrise room.
RATES	Year round rates are $60 to $160 for a single or a double with private bathroom. November through March rates are lower. There is a two night minimum stay on weekends and three nights on holidays. Cancellation requires seven days notice. Multiple night discounts available.
CREDIT CARDS	Amex, MC, Visa
BREAKFAST	Full breakfast is served in the dining room and includes a casserole, breads, "prize-winning" coffee cakes, fruit, cereal, yogurt and beverages.
AMENITIES	Telephones, recreation area with TV/VCR and pool table, tidepool explorations, complimentary teas and coffee in the parlor, fruit basket, meeting facilities for 20 to 30 people.
RESTRICTIONS	No smoking, children over 12 are welcome and there are limited accommodations for younger children. The resident cat is Sam.
REVIEWED	Fodor's California, Frommer's California, America's Wonderful Little Hotels & Inns, AAA Bed & Breakfast Guide—Northern California, American and Canadian B&Bs.
MEMBER	California Association of Bed & Breakfast Inns, Professional Association of Innkeepers International, Independent Innkeepers Association
RATED	AAA 2 Diamonds, ABBA 3 Crowns, Mobil 3 Stars

JUGHANDLE BEACH COUNTRY BED & BREAKFAST

32980 Gibney Lane, Fort Bragg, CA 95437   *707-964-1415*
Su & Jerry Schlecht, Resident Owners

LOCATION	Five miles north of the village of Mendocino, three miles south of Fort Bragg.
OPEN	All year
DESCRIPTION	A two-story 1883 Swedish farmhouse with country and antique furnishings.
NO. OF ROOMS	Four rooms with private bathrooms. Pick room 3.
RATES	Year round rates are $60 for a single with private bathroom and $75 to $95 for a double with private bathroom. The entire inn rents for $700 per weekend. There is no minimum stay and cancellation requires 48 hours notice.
CREDIT CARDS	MC, Visa
BREAKFAST	Full "gourmet breakfast"is served in the dining room.
AMENITIES	Coffee service in the rooms, old fashioned radios, woodstove and classical music in the parlor.
RESTRICTIONS	No smoking, no pets, children welcome. The official greeter is Maggie the cat.
REVIEWED	*America's Bed & Breakfast Inns*

The Lodge at Noyo River

500 Casa del Noyo Drive, Fort Bragg, CA 95437   707-964-8045
Paul Cadelago, Manager

PUDDING CREEK INN

700 North Main Street, Fort Bragg, CA 95437   707-964-9529
Garry & Carole Anloff, Resident Owners   800-227-9529
                                                  FAX 707-961-0282

LOCATION	At the north end of Fort Bragg on Highway 1 (aka Main Street).
OPEN	All year
DESCRIPTION	Two 1884 two-story Victorians connected by enclosed garden court and listed on the National Historic Register.
NO. OF ROOMS	Ten rooms with private bathrooms. Count's Room is the best in the house.
RATES	High season rates, June through September, for a single or double with private bathroom are $55 to $65, $10 less October through May. Two night minimum stay on weekends, five day cancellation notice required.
CREDIT CARDS	Amex, MC, Visa, Discover
BREAKFAST	Full breakfast served in the dining room includes an egg dish, fruit, yogurt, coffee cake, cereals and beverages. Special meals are available on request.
AMENITIES	Flowers, candy, newspaper, social hour, wine in your room, game room, enclosed garden court, laundry service, fax.
RESTRICTIONS	No smoking, no pets. Children of any age are welcome. Max the dog and Pudding the cat will welcome you.
REVIEWED	America's Wonderful Little Hotels and Inns, Bed and Breakfast California, Bed and Breakfast Country Inns, Recommended Country Inns—West Coast
MEMBER	National Bed and Breakfast Association, California Association of Bed and Breakfast Inns, Mendocino County Innkeepers Association
RATED	Mobil 3 Stars

RENDEZVOUS INN & RESTAURANT

647 North Main Street, Fort Bragg, CA 95437　　　　707-964-8142
Rose & Lionel Jacobs, Resident Owners　　　　　　800-491-8142
Spanish spoken

LOCATION	Two blocks north of downtown on the ocean side.
OPEN	All year
DESCRIPTION	A 1904 Edwardian inn with Shaker furnishings.
NO. OF ROOMS	Six rooms with private bathrooms.
RATES	Year round rates for a double room with private bathroom are $55 to $95. Minimum stay on holiday weekends, three day cancellation notice required.
CREDIT CARDS	MC, Visa, Discover
BREAKFAST	Continental Plus breakfast served in the dining room includes muffins, fresh fruit, omelettes, granola parfaits and beverages.
AMENITIES	No TV or phones to distrurb guests, queen beds
RESTRICTIONS	No smoking, no pets. You'll share your stay with kitties Sam and El Gato.
MEMBER	California Lodging Industry Association

SEA ESCAPE INN

18274 North Highway 1, Fort Bragg, CA 95437   707-964-6741
Tim & Holly Kuchar, Resident Owners   FAX 707-964-8685
Spanish spoken

LOCATION	One and a half miles south of Fort Bragg on the ocean side of the highway. Two driveways south of Medocino Coast Botanical Gardens, go west 1.4 mile to the ocean.
OPEN	All year
DESCRIPTION	A 1988 modern Redwood host home on five acres.
NO. OF ROOMS	One room with private bathroom.
RATES	Year round rates are $125 for a single or a double with a private bathroom. There is a minimum stay on major holiday weekends and cancellation requires seven days notice.
CREDIT CARDS	Amex, Discover, MC, Visa
BREAKFAST	Full breakfast is served in the dining room and includes home grown potatoes, onions & garlic with eggs from local chickens, fresh squeezed orange juice, homemade bread and abalone when available.
AMENITIES	Fireplace, flowers in room, refrigerator with bottle of cold wine, beer and mineral waters, chocolates, private beach for abalone diving and massage available at extra charge.
RESTRICTIONS	No smoking, no pets although there are exceptions. There are two horses Amboy and Demey;, two rabbits, Velvetine and Butterscotch and Amhurst the pheasants and some chickens.

TODD FARMHOUSE COUNTRY B&B

100 Highway 20, Fort Bragg, CA 95437   707-964-6575
Judy Haun & Bruce Johanson, Resident Owners

LOCATION	In the city limits of Fort Bragg, 15 miles from Mendocino.
OPEN	March 1 through December 1
DESCRIPTION	An 1898 two-story farmhouse and Dairy Cabin "furnished with some nice antiques" and views of the ocean.
NO. OF ROOMS	Two rooms and one cottage with private bathrooms.
RATES	High season April through October rates for a double room or suite with private bathroom are $75 to $100, cottage $85. Off season rates 10% less. Seven days cancellation notice required for full refund.
CREDIT CARDS	MC, Visa
BREAKFAST	Continental breakfast served in the dining room might include fresh apple pie, fruit, yogurt, granola, muffins and beverages.
RESTRICTIONS	No smoking, no pets. There are resident ducks and chickens.

FREESTONE

GREEN APPLE INN

520 Bohemian Highway, Freestone, CA 95472   707-874-2526
Rosemary Hoffman, Resident Owner

FREMONT

Named for John Fremont who loved the area, the city was created in 1956 by the incorporation of five San Francisco Bay communities and their agricultural lands. What's to do? Fremont Central Park and its Lake Elizabeth; Ardenwood Historic Farms; Mission San Jose; S.F. Bay National Wildlife Refuge and Coyote Hills Regional Park. Across South San Francisco Bay via Hwy. 101 and the Dumbarton Bridge, or north of San Jose on I-880.

LORD BRADLEY'S INN

43344 Mission Boulevard, Fremont, CA 94539   510-490-0520
Anne & Keith Medeiros, Resident Owners   FAX 510-657-7313
A little Spanishspoken

LOCATION	Take the Mission San Jose exit from Highway 680 and go 1/2 mile south on Mission Boulevard. The inn is in the Mission San Jose District adjacent to the Mission.
OPEN	All year
DESCRIPTION	An 1868 two-story Victorian inn with Victorian furnishings.
NO. OF ROOMS	There are eight rooms with private bathrooms. Ann suggests the Sir Keith's as her best room.
RATES	Year round rates are $65 to $75 for a single or double with a private bathroom. There is no minimum stay and cancellation requires five days notice.
CREDIT CARDS	Discover, MC, Visa
BREAKFAST	Continental Plus is served in the dining room.
AMENITIES	A doll collection is arranged throughout the inn. Gardens and patio available for meetings. The inn can handle weddings and receptions for up to 150 people.
RESTRICTIONS	No smoking inside the inn. Inquire about pets. The resident Scotties are called Heather and Shadow and the cat sometimes answers to Pashka.
MEMBER	California Lodging Industry Association

French Gulch

Time stands still in this historic mining town. On the high road to Trinity Lake, part of the awesome Whiskeytown Shasta-Trinity National Recreation Area. Nearby Whiskeytown Lake is among the best for boating, swimming, fishing and camping. Seventeen miles west of Redding via Hwy. 299 on Trinity Mountain Road.

French Gulch Hotel

14138 Main Street, French Gulch, CA 96033   916-359-2112
Marie & Gene Nixon, Resident Owners

LOCATION	From Highway 299 west go north three miles to French Gulch, cut-off in the center of town.
OPEN	From April 1 through December 12.
DESCRIPTION	A two-story, 1885 gold mining hotel with historic "but clean" interior furnishings on the National Register.
NO. OF ROOMS	One room with private bathroom, six rooms share two bathrooms. Marie suggests the bridal suite.
RATES	Year round rates are $65 to $75 for a single or double with a private bathroom, $50 to $60 for a single or a double with a shared bathroom. There is no minimum stay and cancellation requires seven days notice with a $10 cancellation fee.
CREDIT CARDS	MC, Visa
BREAKFAST	Full breakfast is served in the dining room and includes coffee, juice, assorted fruit plate and main entree. Dinner and special meals are available in restaurant.
AMENITIES	Robes, parlor with TV/VCR and meeting facilities, gazebo and waterfall.
RESTRICTIONS	No smoking, no pets and children over 12 are welcome.
MEMBER	California Hotel and Lodging Association
KUDOS/COMMENTS	"Nice rooms, well kept grounds, excellent food in their full restaurant."

GARDEN VALLEY

Tucked away in Gold Country with nary a word written about it (shame on all you travel writers!), but maybe that's the very reason to come here. No matter, it's part of the mythic Mother Lode, and very handy to Coloma's Marshall Gold Discovery State Historic Park. On Hwy. 193, east of Sacramento via Hwy. 50 and Hwy. 49.

MOUNTAINSIDE BED & BREAKFAST

5821 Spanish Flat Road, Garden Valley, CA 95633   916-626-0983
Paul & Mary Ellen Mello, Resident Owners   800-237-0832

LOCATION	Located 7.5 miles from Placerville, north on Spanish Flat Road off Highway 193. Look for our sign on Spanish Flat Road.
OPEN	All year
DESCRIPTION	A 1929, two-story country inn with 1920s decor on 80 acres.
NO. OF ROOMS	Four rooms with private bathrooms. Honeymoon room is recommended by Mary Ellen.
RATES	Year round rates for a double with private bathroom are $70 to $75. The attic sleeps up to eight with a private bathroom, rates are $75 for a couple, each additional person is $15. Cancellation requires seven days notice, plus $5 handling charge.
CREDIT CARDS	MC, Visa
BREAKFAST	Full breakfast is served in the dining room, breakfast room, or on the deck and includes fruit, juice, meat, egg dish, muffins or apple skillet cake, potato dish, baked tomatoes or Belgian Waffles.
AMENITIES	Robes, lots of decks, outdoor hot tub, piano and fireplace in parlor.
RESTRICTIONS	No smoking in the house, no pets. Outside resident pets include Tawny, a Yellow Labrador, and Fred the cat...good name for a cat, Fred. There is a heft and substance associated with that name that is not normally associated with a cats...TI
MEMBER	Historic Country Inns of El Dorado County

GEORGETOWN

This pretty New Englandish Victorian Gold Rush town is at the divide between the north and south forks of the American River. Stumpy Meadows Reservoir is a pretty 320-acre lake and a nice area for camping, or visit UC Berkeley's Blodgett Experimental Forest. Norrtheast of Sacramento via I-80 and Hwy. 193.

AMERICAN RIVER INN

Main and Orleans, Georgetown, CA 95634　　　　　916-333-4499
W. Collin, Resident Owner　　　　　　　　　　　800-245-6566
　　　　　　　　　　　　　　　　　　　　　　　FAX 916-933-9253

LOCATION	Turn East from Highway 193, inn is 2.5 blocks on north side of street.
OPEN	All year
DESCRIPTION	A restored three-story 1853 Victorian Miner's Boarding House, decorated with antiques.
NO. OF ROOMS	Seventeen rooms have private bathrooms, ten rooms have shared bathrooms. Check out #14.
RATES	Year round rates for single or double with private bathroom $95, $85 for single or double with shared bathroom, Honeymoon suites $115. Cancellation policy is ten days prior to arrival, 20 days on holiday weekends, with $10 processing fee.
CREDIT CARDS	Amex, MC, Diners Club, Visa, Discover
BREAKFAST	Full breakfast served in the dining room includes apple crepes, fresh fruit, muffins and beverages. Lunch and dinner catering is available for groups.
AMENITIES	Flowers, bikes, driving range and putting green, croquet, handicapped access in two rooms, afternoon wine and hors d'oeuvres.
RESTRICTIONS	No pets, children over nine years old are welcome.
REVIEWED	*Fifty Romantic Getaways in California*
MEMBER	California Association of Bed and Breakfast Inns

GEYSERVILLE

A tiny town at the foot of Geyser Peak, surrounded by grapes. The town's Fall Color Tour on the last Sunday in October is a good time to see grape leaves in a blaze of color. Anytime, Lake Sonoma Recreation Area is a great place to be for fishing, boating, or camping.

CAMPBELL RANCH INN

1475 Canyon Road, Geyserville, CA 95441   707-857-3476
Jerry & Mary Jane Campbell, Resident Owners   800-959-3878

LOCATION	Travel 1.6 miles west on Canyon Road exit off of Highway 101 at Geyserville.
OPEN	All year
DESCRIPTION	A two-story 1967 California Country inn on 35 acres with traditional furnishings.
NO. OF ROOMS	Five rooms with private bathrooms. Try the cottage.
RATES	Year round rates are $90 to $155 for a single with a private bathroom and $100 to $165 for a double with a private bathroom. With a Saturday, there is a two day minimum stay and a three day minimum stay on holiday weekends. Cancellation requires three days notice.
CREDIT CARDS	Amex, MC, Visa
BREAKFAST	Full breakfast is served in the dining room from a menu.
AMENITIES	Evening dessert with homemade pie or cake, tea or coffee, robes, flowers, all king beds, four rooms with balconies, swimming pool, pro tennis court, hot tub spa, bicycles.
RESTRICTIONS	No smoking, no pets, children over 12 are welcome. Maggie the Border Collie fetches tennis balls for guests.
REVIEWED	*Bed & Breakfast USA, AAA Bed & Breakfast Guide—Northern California*
MEMBER	California Association of Bed & Breakfast Inns, Wine Country Inns of Sonoma County
RATED	ABBA 3 Crowns
KUDOS/COMMENTS	". . .Comfortable ranch style home, great cooking, wonderful setting high on a hilltop."

HOPE-MERRILL HOUSE &
HOPE-BOSWORTH HOUSE

21253 and 21238 Geyserville Avenue, Geyserville, CA 95441 707-857-3356
Bob & Rosalie Hope, Resident Owners 800-825-4233
Spanish spoken FAX 707-857-4673

LOCATION	From Highway 101 take the Geyserville exit. Go north into town, the inns are on the west side of the road.
OPEN	All year
DESCRIPTION	Two separate Victorian buildings on California State Historic Register. Romantically restored and beautifully furnished with antiques throughout.
NO. OF ROOMS	12 rooms with private bathrooms. Rosalie recommends the Sterling Suite.
RATES	Year round rates are $95 to $125 for a single or a double and $140 for suites. There is a minimum two night stay on weekends and holidays. Cancellation requires seven days notice and a $10 fee.
CREDIT CARDS	Amex, MC, Visa
BREAKFAST	Full breakfast served in dining room. Lunch and dinner can be catered for group events.
AMENITIES	Heated swimming pool, private jacuzzi, gardens and gazebo. Handicapped room available, meeting facilities for small groups. Garden available for weddings.
RESTRICTIONS	No smoking, no pets
REVIEWED	*Bed and Breakfast California, Fifty Most Romantic Inns —Northern California, The Old House Lover's Guide to Inns and B&Bs, Historic Country Inns of California, Feather Beds and Flapjacks.*
MEMBER	California Association for Bed and Breakfast Innkeepers, Wine Country Inns of Sonoma County
RATED	Mobil 2 Stars
AWARDS	1989 American Home Award for Bed and Breakfast, National Trust for Historic Preservation
KUDOS/COMMENTS	"We often refer guests to Rosalie."

ISIS OASIS

20889 Geyserville Avenue, Geyserville, CA 95441 707-857-3524
Loreon Vigne, Resident Owner

GLEN ELLEN

This is Jack London country. The thing absolutely to do here is spend time at the Jack London State Historic Park. Also, Bouverie Audubon Preserve. In late summer, the Art Farm Festival of Classical Music is another must-do. North of San Francisco via Hwy. 101 and 121.

ABOVE THE CLOUDS INN

3250 Trinity Road, Glen Ellen, CA 95442   707-996-7371
Claude & Betty Ganaye, Resident Owners

GLENELLY INN

5131 Warm Springs Road, Glen Ellen, CA 95442   707-996-6720
Kristi Hallamore & Ingrid Hallamore, Resident Owners
Norwegian and Spanish spoken

LOCATION	From Arnold Drive in Glen Ellen, head west 1/3 mile on Warm Springs Road.
OPEN	All year
DESCRIPTION	A two-story 1916 French Colonial with antique and country furnishings.
NO. OF ROOMS	Eight rooms with private bathrooms. Kristi thinks Jack London is her best room.
RATES	Year round rates are $90 to $130 for a single or a double with private bathroom. There is a minimum stay on weekends (April through November) and cancellation requires seven days notice.
CREDIT CARDS	MC, Visa
BREAKFAST	Full breakfast is served in the dining room or in the guest room on request and includes orange juice, home baked breads or muffins, hot egg dishes or cobbler with bacon or sausage, fresh seasonal fruit, granola and yogurt.
AMENITIES	Flowers from the gardens, robes and extra big bath towels, hot tub in rose garden, hammock and swing under 200-year-old oak tree, homemade cookies, lemonade and sun tea always available.
RESTRICTIONS	No smoking and children are welcome with prior arrangement. The Chocolate Lab/Doberman dog is called Hershey and the two cats are called Greta and Nutmeg
REVIEWED	*America's Wonderful Little Hotels & Inns, Best Places to Kiss in Northern California, Bed & Breakfast in California, Karen Brown's California Country Inns & Itineraries, The Inn Guide, Northern California Best Places, Wine Country Access*
MEMBER	Professional Association of Innkeepers International, California Lodging Industry Association

JACK LONDON LODGE

13740 Arnold Drive, Glen Ellen, CA 95442   707-938-8510
Dale & Ann Bedard, Resident Owners

LOCATION	From San Francisco take Highway 121 to Arnold Drive and then straight for 10 to 15 minutes. From Sonoma or Santa Rosa take Highway 12 to the Glen Ellen sign at Arnold Drive. Turn west and go five minutes to center of town.
OPEN	All year
DESCRIPTION	1960 two-story California Country-style lodge on the tree-lined Sonoma Creek. Separate bar is a historic 1905 brick Chauvet-designed building.
NO. OF ROOMS	Twenty-two rooms with private bathrooms
RATES	May to November rates are $75 for single or double. Rates for the remainder of the year are $55 for single or double. There is no minimum stay and cancellation requires 48 hours notice.
CREDIT CARDS	MC, Visa
BREAKFAST	Continental breakfast served on weekends and holidays all year and on weekdays from June 15th to September 15th. Lunch and dinner available at the Londons Grill Restaurant.
AMENITIES	Phone and TV in rooms. Pool with view of the creek. Jack London Saloon in historic building.
RESTRICTIONS	No pets.
REVIEWED	*The Berkeley Guides, Budget Travelers Guide*

JVB VINEYARDS

14335 Sonoma Highway, Glen Ellen, CA 95442   707-996-4533
Beverly & Jack Babb, Resident Owners

TANGLEWOOD HOUSE

250 Bonnie Way, Glen Ellen, CA 95442   *707-996-5021*
John & Mary Field, Resident Owners

LOCATION	From the village of Glen Ellen, take Arnold Drive 1/2 mile to Dunbar Road, turn left and drive 1/2 mile to Bonnie Way. The host home is at the intersection of Dunbar and Bonnie Way.
OPEN	All year
DESCRIPTION	A 1963 country ranch host home with country pine and antique furnishings.
NO. OF ROOMS	One bedroom suite, sitting room, fireplace with private bathroom and private entrance.
RATES	Year round rates for a single or a double with a private bathroom are $115. There is a two day minimum stay on spring, summer and fall weekends and cancellation requires 48 hours notice.
CREDIT CARDS	No
BREAKFAST	Full breakfast served in the guest room includes hot dishes such as eggs or pancakes plus fresh fruit, juice, muffins and coffee.
AMENITIES	A bottle of wine, cheese and crackers, cable TV, and an acre of secluded gardens with a pool and gazebo.
RESTRICTIONS	No smoking, no pets and children over 12 are welcome. The resident Collies are Cleo and Austin.
MEMBER	Bed & Breakfast Association of Sonoma Valley.

GLENHAVEN

Another quiet little gem on the southeast shore of Clear Lake. Look for wineries nearby. On Hwy 20 southeast of Fort Bragg and Hwy. 101.

KRISTALBERG BED & BREAKFAST

715 Pearl Court, Glenhaven, CA 95443   707-274-8009
Merv Myers, Resident Owner
German, Spanish and French spoken

LOCATION	Four miles east of Lucerne, .5 miles off of Highway 20, turn left on Bruner Drive, go to the end, left on Pearl Court.
OPEN	All year
DESCRIPTION	A three-story 1987 Cape Cod with European and Victorian antique furnishing.
NO. OF ROOMS	Two rooms with private bathrooms and one room shares one bathroom. Merv likes the Master Suite.
RATES	High season, May through October, rates are $90 for a single or a double with a private bathroom, $60 for a single or a double with a shared bathroom and $150 for the suite. Low season, November through April, rates are $80 for a single or a double with a private bathroom, $55 for a single or a double with a shared bathroom and $125 for the suite. There is no minimum stay and cancellation requires seven days notice.
CREDIT CARDS	Amex, Discover, MC, Visa
BREAKFAST	Continental Plus is seved in the dining room and includes fruit with yogurt and granola, quiche, blackberry shortcake, oatmeal & raisins with fruit, egg custard or cornbread-fruit compote. Dinner is also available.
AMENITIES	TV, flowers, live organ music, whirlpool tub in master suite, after-dinner sherry, afternoon refreshment, hot tub, balconies on lake side of house.
RESTRICTIONS	Smoking outside, no pets, single child okay. The resident Australian shepherd is called Dingo and is friendly.
MEMBER	California Association of Bed & Breakfast Inns

GRASS VALLEY

The town's place in history centers around the billion dollars in gold mined from hardrock. Check it all out at the 784-acre Empire Mine State Historic Park. Times to be here: in June for the Cornish Miners' Picnic, Bluegrass Festival, and Music in the Mountains Summer Festival (a two-week shared event with Nevada City). At the gateway to Tahoe National Forest and the new Yuba-Donner Scenic Byway, and very handy to Englebright Lake State Recreation Area. From Sacramento, 60 miles northeast via I-80 and Hwy. 49.

ANNIE HORAN'S B&B

415 West Main Street, Grass Valley, CA 95945   916-272-2418
Tom & Pat Kiddy, Resident Owners

GOLDEN ORE B&B INN

448 South Auburn Street, Grass Valley, CA 95945   916-272-6872
Kacie Collins, Manager

THE HOLBROOKE

212 West Main, Grass Valley, CA 95945   916-273-1353
Linda Rasor, Manager

MURPHY'S INN

318 Neal Street, Grass Valley, CA 95945	916-273-6873
Tom & Sue Myers, Resident Owners	FAX 916-273-6873

LOCATION	From Highway 49 take Colfax 174 exit, left on South Auburn, left on Neal Street.
OPEN	All year
DESCRIPTION	A two-story 1866 wood frame inn with an interior in the style of the period.
NO. OF ROOMS	Eight rooms with private bathrooms. Sue says that Theodosia's suite is the best room.
RATES	Year round rates are $75 to $135 for a double with a private bathroom. There is a minimum stay if staying over a Saturday night and cancellation requires seven days notice.
CREDIT CARDS	Amex, MC, Visa
BREAKFAST	Full breakfast served in the dining room includes an entree, fruit, muffin and beverages.
AMENITIES	In-room phone service on request, TV in all rooms, carriage rides on Friday, Saturday and Sunday (fee).
RESTRICTIONS	No smoking, no pets.
MEMBER	California Association of Bed & Breakfast Inns

SWAN-LEVINE HOUSE

328 South Church Street, Grass Valley, CA 95945	916-272-1873
Howard & Margaret Levine, Resident Owners	

LOCATION	Two blocks from downtown Grass Valley.
OPEN	All year
DESCRIPTION	Three-story 1880 Queen Anne Victorian with eclectic Victorian furnishings. `
NO. OF ROOMS	Four rooms with private bathrooms. Ask for the suite.
RATES	Year round rates for a single or double room with private bathroom are $70 to $85. Cancellation requires 48 hours notice.
CREDIT CARDS	Amex, MC, Visa
BREAKFAST	Full breakfast served in the dining room might include eggs Mexican style, pancakes, sausage, crepes, fresh baked breads and beverages.
AMENITIES	Badminton court, exercise pool, instruction or demonstration in the art of printmaking.
RESTRICTIONS	No smoking, pets and children are welcome. Resident pets that "find our house" include four cats and a naturally friendly Black Lab/Golden Retriever mix, Cinnamon.
MEMBER	California Association of Bed and Breakfast Inns, Historic Inns of Grass Valley and Nevada City

GROVELAND

This pleasant little mountain resort community is also a jumping off place for whitewater rafting. On Hwy. 120 at the west entrance into Yosemite.

BERKSHIRE INN

19950 Highway 120, Groveland, CA 95321   209-962-6744
Bob & Dody Yates, Resident Owners

THE GROVELAND HOTEL, AN HISTORIC COUNTRY INN

18767 Main Street, Groveland, CA 95321   209-962-4000
Peggy A. & Grover Mosley, Resident Owners   800-273-3314
Some Spanish spoken   FAX 209-962-6674

LOCATION	Two hours from San Francisco. Take Highway 80 East to Highway 680 East. Head east on Highway 580 to Highway 120. Highway 120 East heads right through Groveland. The hotel is on Highway 120 (Main Street) on the east end of town.
OPEN	All year
DESCRIPTION	A two-story, 1849 Monterey Colonial hotel and a 1914 Queen Anne with Victorian antiques.
NO. OF ROOMS	Seventeen rooms with private bathrooms.
RATES	Year round rates for a double room with private bathroom are $85 to $105, and $165 for suites. No minimum stay required, 24 hours cancellation notice with $10 fee.
CREDIT CARDS	Amex, MC, Diners Club, Visa, Discover
BREAKFAST	Continental Plus breakfast served at a spot of your choice in the hotel includes fresh muffins, breads, cereal and beverages. Lunch and dinner are available upon request for groups.
AMENITIES	Robes, phones, down comforters, evening wine, TV in the parlor, verandas, courtyard dining in the summer. Suites have fireplaces, spa tubs and "teddy bear adoption services." Conference room is available.
RESTRICTIONS	No smoking. A "Halloween Kitty", Elvira, cruises the grounds.
REVIEWED	*AAA Bed & Breakfast Guide—Northern and Central California*
MEMBER	Professional Association of Innkeepers International, American Bed and Breakfast Association, California Association of Bed and Breakfast Inns, Independent Innkeepers Association
RATED	ABBA 1 Crown

HOTEL CHARLOTTE

PO Box 787, Groveland, CA 95321   209-962-6455
Ruth Kraenzel. Resident Owner

GUALALA

An old lumber town (Wah-LA-la) on the Gualala River and at the south end of the rugged Mendocino Coast. This is one of the best whalewatching spots on the north coast. Del Mar Landing, an ecological reserve of virgin coastline, seals and tidepools can be reached via Gualala Point County Park.

NORTH COAST COUNTRY INN

34591 South Highway 1, Gualala, CA 95445   707-884-4537
Loren & Nancy Flanagan, Resident Owners   800-959-4537
Spanish spoken

LOCATION	Four miles north of Gualala at the intersection of Highway 1 and Fish Rock Road, which is identified by a highway sign and mile marker 5.12.
OPEN	All year
DESCRIPTION	Multi-story 1951/1984 rustic board-and-batten inn with country furnishings.
NO. OF ROOMS	Four rooms with private bathrooms.
RATES	Year round rate for a single or double room with private bathroom is $135. Two night minimum on weekends, three nights on holidays, five day cancellation notice required.
CREDIT CARDS	Amex, MC, Visa
BREAKFAST	Full breakfast served in guestroom includes seasonal fruit, hot entree, oven-fresh baked goods and fresh ground coffee.
AMENITIES	Hillside hot tub under the pines, upper garden gazebo, coffee, juice and tea in guest rooms, games, guestroom libraries, fireplaces and chocolates, private decks, off-road parking.
RESTRICTIONS	No smoking, no pets, children over 12 years old are welcome. Two cats, Sam and Sally, will share your visit.
MEMBER	California Association of Bed and Breakfast Inns
RATED	Mobil 2 Stars

THE OLD MILANO HOTEL

38300 Highway One, Gualala, CA 95445   707-884-3256
Leslie Linscheid, Resident Owner
Spanish spoken

LOCATION	One mile north of Gualala on the west side of Highway 1.
OPEN	All year
DESCRIPTION	1905 two-story Victorian with authentic Victorian period decor on three acres of ocean-front property. Listed on National Registor of Historic Places.
NO. OF ROOMS	Three rooms with private bathrooms, six rooms share two bathrooms. Ocean View room Number 4 is highly recommended.
RATES	High season rates, April through October, for a double with private bathroom are $135 to $165, and a double with shared bathroom is $80 to $100, suites $165, guesthouse $135, entire B&B can be rented for $1,065. Off season rates, November through March, except weekends and holidays, are 25% less. Minimum stay on Saturdays, three day cancellation policy.
CREDIT CARDS	MC, Visa
BREAKFAST	Complete country breakfast served in dining room or guestroom.
AMENITIES	Outdoor hot tub perched on the cliffside overlooking the ocean. Award winning restaurant.
RESTRICTIONS	No smoking, no pets, children over 14 years welcome.
REVIEWED	*The Official Guide to America's Historic Inns, Best Choices on the California Coast, Country Inns of the West Coast, American and Canadian Bed and Breakfasts*
KUDOS/COMMENTS	"Comfortable old style hotel by the ocean. Very good food, outstanding breakfast." ..."Spectacular setting, quaint rooms."

SAINT ORRES

36601 South Highway 1, Gualala, CA 95445   *707-884-3303*
Eric Black, Ted Black, and   *FAX 707-884-1543*
Rosemary Campiformio, Resident Owners

LOCATION	On the south coast of Mendocino County, three miles north of Gualala.
OPEN	All year
DESCRIPTION	A 1970 two-story hotel with two copper "onion domes" and cottages on 42 acres.
NO. OF ROOMS	Eleven rooms with private bathrooms, eight rooms share three bathrooms. Sequoia Room is highly recommended.
RATES	Year round rates for a single or double room or cottage with private bathroom are $85 to $180, and $50 to $75 for a single or double room with shared bathroom. Suites rent for $270. Minimum stay required on weekends and holidays, 72 hours notice for cancellation.
CREDIT CARDS	MC, Visa
BREAKFAST	Full breakfast served in the hotel dining room or delivered to cottage includes a rotating main dish like fritatta, rice pudding, or waffles, fruit, breakfast breads, granola and beverages. Dining room is open to the public for dinner.
AMENITIES	Various hotel rooms include ocean views, fireplaces and decks, cottages share spa, hot tub, and sundeck.
RESTRICTIONS	No smoking in public areas, no pets.
REVIEWED	*Best Places to Kiss in Northern California, Bed and Breakfast California, Country Inns of the Far West*

WHALE WATCH INN

35100 Highway 1, Gualala, CA 95445   707-884-3667
Jim & Kazuko Popplewell, Resident Owners   800-942-5342
Spanish spoken

LOCATION	Approximately three hours north of San Francisco. On Highway 1, four miles north of Gualala on the ocean side of the highway.
OPEN	All year
DESCRIPTION	A 1985 contemporary country inn with sweeping ocean views.
NO. OF ROOMS	Eighteen rooms with private bathrooms. Most popular room is the Bath Suite.
RATES	Year round rates for a single or double room with a private bathroom are $170 to $255. Two night stay required on weekends, three nights on holidays. No cancellation penalty with five days notice.
CREDIT CARDS	Amex, MC, Visa
BREAKFAST	Full breakfast served in guestroom includes fresh fruit and juices, homemade bread, hot entree, and beverages. Snack baskets are available including cheese, crackers, fruit, cookies and wine.
AMENITIES	All rooms have private decks, fireplaces, queen beds, down comforters. Saturday evening social hour includes appetizers, wine and assorted beverages, eight rooms have two person whirlpool tubs, four rooms have regular whirlpool tubs.
RESTRICTIONS	No smoking, no pets.
REVIEWED	*Weekends for Two in Northern California, Best Places to Kiss in Northern California, Best of San Francisco*
KUDOS/COMMENTS	"Extraordinary views from every room."

GUERNEVILLE

Pronounce it GURN-ville, never mind that the founder's name is pronounced Gurn-ee. This is the "big city" of the Russian River area, the place for tubing, canoeing and rafting the Russian. The Russian River Jazz Festival in September is a very major event. Be around for the Crab Feed in February, but you may want to skip the Slug Fest in March that honors the redwood forest-dwelling banana slug. At the south entrance to Armstrong Redwoods State Reserve, via Hwy. 1 and 116.

APPLEWOOD

13555 Highway 116, Guerneville, CA 95446　　　　　　707-869-9093
James Caron & Darryl Notter, Resident Owners

LOCATION	Applewood is 3/4 miles south of downtown Guerneville, at intersection of River Road and Highway 116 in Pocket Canyon.
OPEN	All year
DESCRIPTION	1922 three-story California Mission Revival on six wooded acres and the County Historic Register
NO. OF ROOMS	Sixteen rooms with private bathrooms. Try the Slavianka Suite.
RATES	Year round rates for a double are $115 to $225. Minimum stay on weekends and holidays. There is a 10 day cancellation policy with a $15 processing fee.
CREDIT CARDS	Amex, MC, Visa, Discover
BREAKFAST	Full breakfast served in the dining room. Dinner available.
AMENITIES	Swimming pool, jacuzzi, flowers, phones, TV, some rooms have fireplaces and/or jacuzzis, private patios or balconies. Handicapped access, meeting rooms available.
RESTRICTIONS	No smoking, no pets, the inn is not suitable for children. "Will share our dogs", Norton and Balki...There have been a couple of dogs we've encountered that we would have been willing to share...like the Boxer that ate the couch...TI
REVIEWED	*Northern California Best Places, The Napa Sonoma Book, California Country Inns and Itineraries, Country Inns of the Far West-California.*
RATED	Mobil 3 Stars
KUDOS/COMMENTS	"Posh - very nice - good restaurant."... "A charming and elegant Revival mansion. Tastefully decorated, with stupendous dinners served five nights a week (Tuesday through Saturday)."

CREEKSIDE INN & RESORT

16180 Neeley Road, Guerneville, CA 95446	*707-869-3623*
Lynn Crescione, Resident Owner	*800-776-6586*
Spanish spoken	*FAX 707-869-1417*

LOCATION
North of Santa Rosa, take River Road exit off Highway 101. Drive west 15 miles to the four way intersection in Guerneville. Turn left onto Highway 116, continue across the bridge to Neeley Road. Turn right .2 miles, inn is on the right.

OPEN
All year

DESCRIPTION
A Tudor inn built in the late 1930s, surrounded by ten cottages.

NO. OF ROOMS
Two rooms with private bathrooms, four rooms share two bathrooms, ten cottages with kitchens. Lynn recommends the Victorian Room.

RATES
Year round rates for a single or double with private bathroom are $95 to $110, and $40 to $65 for a single or double with shared bathroom. Suites are $95 to $110, cottages with kitchens are $58 to $125. Entire B&B rents for $370 to $460. Minimum stay required June through September, cancellation policy requires 14 days notice for weekends, three days notice for weekdays.

CREDIT CARDS
MC, Visa, Discover

BREAKFAST
Continental Plus breakfast is served in the dining room and includes beverages, seasonal fruit and an egg or cheese dish.

AMENITIES
Pool, rose gardens, flowers, pool table, table tennis, badminton, video games, large lounge with TV and VCR, meeting room for 20, wheel chair access to the inn, one handicapped accessible cottage.

RESTRICTIONS
No smoking, no pets.

REVIEWED
Northern California Handbook, Best Places to Stay in Northern California, Weekend Adventures for City Weary People

FERN GROVE INN

16650 River Road, Guerneville, CA 95446	*707-869-9083*
Bob Klein, Manager	

RIDENHOUR RANCH HOUSE INN

12850 River Road, Guerneville, CA 95446   707-887-1033
Diane & Fritz Rechberger, Resident Owners   FAX 707-869-2967
German spoken

LOCATION	Seventy five minutes from San Francisco, 12 miles from Highway 101 west. East of Guerneville four miles, 500 yards from Korbel Champagne Cellar.
OPEN	All year
DESCRIPTION	This 1906 farmhouse on 2.25 acres is decorated with an eclectic mix of English and American antiques.
NO. OF ROOMS	Eight rooms with private bathrooms.
RATES	Year round rates $95 to $130. Two night minimum stay on weekends, seven day cancellation policy.
CREDIT CARDS	Amex, MC, Visa
BREAKFAST	Full breakfast served in the dining room or country kitchen includes fruit, breads, cakes and an egg dish.
AMENITIES	Flowers, robes, hot tub, cookies and fruit in the afternoon, sherry and port always available. Handicapped access in one room.
RESTRICTIONS	No smoking, no pets. A charming menagerie of dogs and cats includes Hildegard, a Corgi mix, who loves to challenge guests to a soccer match.
REVIEWED	*Northern California Best Places, Bed and Breakfast and Country Inns, Access to Wine Country*
MEMBER	Wine Country Inns of Sonoma County

SANTA NELLA HOUSE

12130 Highway 116, Guerneville, CA 95446   707-869-9488
Joyce & Ed Ferrington, Resident Owners

LOCATION	From Highway 101 north, above Petaluma take the off ramp marked 116 "Sebastopol." Travel west through Sebastopol on to the next village, Forestville. Go 4.5 miles west of Forestville, the inn is on the left side.
OPEN	Seasonal from March 1 through December 15.
DESCRIPTION	A circa 1865 Victorian-Italianiate two-story farmhouse with veranda and Victorian interior furnishings.
NO. OF ROOMS	Four rooms with private bathrooms. The best room is the Gold room.
RATES	Year round rates are $90 to $95 for a single or a double with private bathrooms. There is a minimum stay on weekends and holidays and cancellation requires seven days notice.
CREDIT CARDS	Amex, MC, Visa
BREAKFAST	Full breakfast served in the dining room includes eggs benedict or waffles or omelette, "almost sinfully exotic" fruit plates and beverages.
AMENITIES	Hot tub under the Redwoods, meeting room and "funky" pool table on the veranda.
RESTRICTIONS	No smoking, no pets
REVIEWED	*Frommer's 100 best Bed & Breakfasts—North America.*

HALF MOON BAY

This small, once Spanish/Portuguese farming community is now a trendy Bay Area suburb that's a charmer. It's a good launching spot for coastal sightseeing and whalewatching cruises, and plenty of sandy beaches for exploring. Absolutely check out Fitzgerald Marine Reserve, Northern California's largest natural tidepools. Main events include the Portuguese Chamarita celebration in spring and Harbor Day in September. But the biggie is the Art and Pumpkin Festival in October. On the San Mateo Coastline of the San Francisco Peninsula via Hwy. 1.

CYPRESS INN

407 Mirada Road, Half Moon Bay, CA 94019   *415-726-6002*
Suzie Lankes and Dan Floyd, Resident Owners   *800-832-3224*
French, German spoken   *FAX 408-458-0989*

LOCATION	On the beach from Highway 1 between Princeton Harbor and Half Moon Bay, take Medio to the corner of Mirada.
OPEN	Year round
DESCRIPTION	1990 contemporary three-story inn with contemporary and folk art decor.
NO. OF ROOMS	Eight rooms with private bathrooms. Try the Penthouse Suite for a treat.
RATES	Year round rates for a single or double with a private bathroom are $160 to $275. Minimum stay required over Saturday night, three day cancellation notice.
CREDIT CARDS	Amex, MC, Visa
BREAKFAST	Full breakfast is served in the dining room or in your guestroom.
AMENITIES	TV, VCR, fireplace, soaking tubs, wine, hors d'oeuvres, desserts.
RESTRICTIONS	No smoking.
REVIEWED	*Fifty Most Romantic Inns, Best Places to Kiss in Northern California*
MEMBER	Half Moon Bay Bed and Breakfast Association
RATED	AAA 3 Diamonds

MILL ROSE INN

615 Mill Street, Half Moon Bay, CA 94019   *415-716-9794*
Terry & Eve Baldwin, Resident Owners

KUDOS/COMMENTS   "Beautiful gardens, comfortable rooms."

OLD THYME INN

779 Main Street, Half Moon Bay, CA 94019   *415-726-1616*
George & Marcia Dempsey, Resident Owners
Spanish and French Spoken

LOCATION	In the Old Town part of Half Moon Bay, seven blocks south of the intersection of Main Street and Highway 92.
OPEN	All year
DESCRIPTION	A two-story 1899 Queen Anne Victorian with Victorian and turn-of-the-century furnishings and a 50 variety herb garden.
NO. OF ROOMS	Seven rooms with private bathroooms. Try the Garden Suite upstairs that has a private entrance.
RATES	Year round rates for a single or double range from $70 to $210. There is a two day minimum stay on some summer weekends and cancellation requires one week's notice.
CREDIT CARDS	MC, Visa
BREAKFAST	Full breakfast is served in the dining room or guestrooms and includes specially blended coffees, a large selection of teas, fruit juices, daily fresh baked bread, egg dishes, fresh fruit dishes and muffins.
AMENITIES	Spa tubs, fireplaces, fresh flowers, wine and sherry in the evenings, robes, down pillows, free "cutting kit" for the herb garden, meeting facilities and some TV and telephones.
RESTRICTIONS	No smoking, no pets, children over 10 years of age are welcome. The "very rare" purebred Scottish Fold cats are Myles and Coco.
REVIEWED	*America's Wonderful Little Hotels & Inns, Recommended Country Inns—West Coast, Away for the Weekend in Northern California, Best Places to Kiss in Northern California*
MEMBER	Professional Association of Innkeepers International
RATED	Mobil 3 Stars
KUDOS/COMMENTS	"Good place to stay, friendly hosts."

SAN BENITO HOUSE

356 Main Street, Half Moon Bay, CA 94019   *415-726-3425*
Carol Mickelson, Resident Owner

THE ZABALLA HOUSE B&B

324 Main Street, Half Moon Bay, CA 94019
Kerry Pendergast, Resident Owner

415-726-9123

LOCATION	In beautiful downtown Half Moon Bay, one block south of Highway 92 and four blocks east of Highway 1.
OPEN	All year
DESCRIPTION	A two-story 1859 Victorian surrounded by gardens with Victorian eclectic interior furnishings.
NO. OF ROOMS	Nine rooms with private bathrooms. The Innkeeper suggests #7.
RATES	Year round rates are $85 to $160 for a single with a private bathroom, $90 to $165 for a double with a private bathroom, mid-week rates for a single are $60 to $120 and $65 to $125 for a double. There is no minimum stay and cancellation requires 72 hours notice.
CREDIT CARDS	Amex, Discover, MC, Visa
BREAKFAST	Full breakfast is served buffet-style in the dining room and includes homemade granola, muffins, coffee cake, fruit salad, hot egg/cheese dish.
AMENITIES	Fresh flowers in all rooms, wine and cheese served in the parlor in the evenings, some rooms have double-sized whirlpool tubs and fireplaces. Resident ghost in Room 6.
RESTRICTIONS	No smoking, children over six are welcome, pets are negotiable but usually okay. The resident rooster wakes up room #7 at 6 a.m.
REVIEWED	*Bed, Breakfast and Bike - Northern California, Northern California Best Places, The Definitive California Bed & Breakfast Guide, Karen Brown's California Country Inns and Itineraries, Northern California Handbook, Best Places to Kiss in Northern California, Country Inns and Backroads*
MEMBER	Professional Association of Innkeepers International, California Lodging Industry Association
RATED	Mobil 2 Stars

HEALDSBURG

Once a trading post founded by gold miner Harmon Heald. The Alexander, Dry Creek and Russian River valleys converge here to make this a prime winegrowing region with more than 50 wineries. So . . . would believe a Zucchinifest in August? The downtown Plaza is the spot for concerts, celebrations, picnics, and rest between shopping. About 70 miles north of San Francisco via Hwy. One. Be here for the main event: Russian River Wine Festival in mid-May.

BELLE DE JOUR INN

16276 Healdsburg Avenue, Healdsburg, CA 95448　　　707-431-9777
Tom & Brenda Hearn, Resident Owners　　　FAX 707-431-7412

LOCATION	From Highway 101 take Dry Creek Road exit, turn right and go to the second traffic light, turn left on Healdsburg Avenue and continue one mile, Simi Winery visitor center is on the left, turn right up the tree-lined drive.
OPEN	All year
DESCRIPTION	An 1870s Italiante farmhouse and cottages with California country furnishings, on six acres.
NO. OF ROOMS	Four rooms with private bathrooms. Brenda recommends the Terrace Room.
RATES	Year round rates are $110 to $185 for a single or a double with a private bathroom. There is a two day minimum stay when a Saturday is included and three days on major holidays. Cancellation requires seven days with a $15 fee.
CREDIT CARDS	MC, Visa
BREAKFAST	Full breakfast is served in the farmhouse dining room or on the garden deck and includes house blend coffee, teas, fresh juice, fresh fruit, two types of baked goods, quiche, fritata, omelettes and specialty dishes.
AMENITIES	Flowers, robes, hair dryers, telephones in room, refrigerators, bottled water, candy, fresh fruit, ceiling fans, fireplaces, Jacuzzi tubs for two, steambath, hammocks and gardens.
RESTRICTIONS	No smoking, no pets, children are not encouraged. The resident cats are Beast, Zubie and Ivan... Great names!...TI
REVIEWED	*Special Places for Discerning Travelers, B&B California, Wine Country Access, California Country Inns & Itineraries, California B&B Guide, Away for the Weekend, Best Places to Kiss in Northern California*
MEMBER	California Association of Bed & Breakfast Inns
KUDOS/COMMENTS	"Four very nice cottage type accomodations." ... "immaculate, beautiful surroundings, friendly innkeepers and excellent homemade food."

CALDERWOOD INN

25 West Grant Street, Healdsburg, CA 95448   707-431-1110
Bob & Chris Maxwell, Resident Owners

CAMELLIA INN

211 North Street, Healdsburg, CA 95448   707-433-8182
Del, Ray & Lucy Lewand, Resident Owners   800-727-8182
FAX 707-433-8130

LOCATION	Take Highway 101 north to the Central Healdsburg exit, at 4th traffic light turn right on North Street, the inn is 2.5 blocks on the left.
OPEN	All year
DESCRIPTION	A two-story 1869 Italianate Victorian with antique furnishings.
NO. OF ROOMS	Nine rooms with private bathrooms. The most popular room is the Tower West.
RATES	Year round rates are $60 to $125 for a single or a double with a private bathroom, the suite is $105 and the entire inn rents for $1,000. There is a minimum stay when Saturday is involved and cancellation requires seven days notice.
CREDIT CARDS	Amex, MC, Visa
BREAKFAST	Full breakfast is served in the dining room and includes fresh fruit, yogurt, juice, cereal, fresh sourdough, main dish such as quiche and beverages.
AMENITIES	Fresh flowers, hosted afternoon beverage and snacks by the swimming pool in the summer, evening beverages in the winter, tubs for two and fireplaces in several rooms and special events such as a Robert Burns Dinner.
RESTRICTIONS	No smoking indoors, no pets.
REVIEWED	*America's Wonderful Little Inns & Hotels, Best Places to Kiss in Northern California, Recommended Country Inns in Northern California, 50 Romantic Getaways, Weekends for Two in Northern California*
MEMBER	Professional Association of Innkeepers International, California Association of Bed & Breakfast Inns, Wine Country Inns of Sonoma
KUDOS/COMMENTS	"Beautiful rooms with fireplaces, whirlpool tubs and lovely gardens"

FRAMPTON HOUSE

489 Powell Avenue, Healdsburg, CA 95448   707-433-5084
Paula Bogle, Resident Owner

THE GEORGE ALEXANDER HOUSE

423 Matheson Street, Healdsburg, CA 95448   707-433-1358
Phyllis & Christian Baldenhofer, Resident Owners   800-310-1358
FAX 707-433-1367

LOCATION	Take the Central Healdsburg exit and drive 1/2 miles to the third traffic light, that is Matheson Street. Turn right.
OPEN	All year, closed Thanksgiving to Christmas
DESCRIPTION	A 1905 two-story Late Queen Anne with Victorian furnishings.
NO. OF ROOMS	Four rooms with private bathrooms. The Back Porch may be the best room.
RATES	Year round rates are $80 to $150. Three rooms require a minimum stay and cancellation requires seven days notice.
CREDIT CARDS	MC, Visa
BREAKFAST	Full breakfast is served in the dining room and includes beverages, fresh fruit, one or more homebaked breads, a main dish plus side dishes such as potatoes with baked eggs.
AMENITIES	Robes, mineral water, juice in the refrigerator, bathroom basket and two guest parlors.
RESTRICTIONS	No smoking, no pets, resident cats are Moose and Magic.
REVIEWED	*Bed & Breakfast California, America's Wonderful Little Hotels & Inns*
MEMBER	California Association of Bed & Breakfast Inns
KUDOS/COMMENTS	"Beautiful restored Victorian with exceptional baths. Creative breakfasts to the nth degree."

GRAPE LEAF INN

539 Johnson Street, Healdsburg, CA 95448   707-433-8140
Terry and Karen Sweet, Resident Owners

LOCATION	From Highway 101 take the Healdsburg exit. Grape Leaf is on the corner of Johnson and Grant Streets.
OPEN	All year, except Christmas Eve and Christmas Day.
DESCRIPTION	A beautifully restored turn-of-the-century Queen Anne Victorian home. Furnished in classic, comfortable period furnishings.
NO. OF ROOMS	Seven rooms have private bathrooms.
RATES	Year round rates run $90 to $150, with a $30 discount for singles. Minimum stay two nights on most weekends. Seven day cancellation policy.
CREDIT CARDS	MC, Visa, Discover
BREAKFAST	Full breakfast served in the dining room includes "scrumptious" egg dishes, breakfast meats, roasted red potatoes, fresh breads, muffins and coffee.
AMENITIES	Wrap around porch, complimentary selection of Sonoma County wines served each evening with an assortment of cheeses and French bread.
RESTRICTIONS	No smoking, no pets. Children over 11 years welcome. A tribe of lovable Labradors includes Dano, Smokey, and Jasmine (aka "Jazzy Girl").
REVIEWED	*Bed and Breakfast in California, Best Places to Kiss in San Francisco and the Bay Area, America's Wonderful Little Hotels and Inns, Where to Stay in Northern California, Recommended Country Inns — West Coast*
MEMBER	California Association of Bed and Breakfast Inns, California Lodging Industry Association
KUDOS/COMMENTS	Another innkeeper wrote, "Our guests recommend it to our guests."

HAYDON STREET INN

321 Haydon Street, Healdsburg, CA 95448   *707-433-5228*
Richard and Joanne Claus, Resident Owners
Some Spanish spoken

LOCATION	Take north Highway 101 to the Central Healdsburg exit. Take Healdsburg Avenue to Matheson, turn right. Three blocks to Fetch, turn right. Two blocks to Hayden, turn left.
OPEN	All year, except December 15 through January 1.
DESCRIPTION	A two-story 1912 Victorian, Craftsman and cottage furnished with antiques.
NO. OF ROOMS	Eight rooms including the cottage, most with private bathrooms.
RATES	Year round rates for a double with private bathroom are $105 to $150, and $75 to $105 for a single or double with shared bathroom.
CREDIT CARDS	Amex, Diners Club, Discover
BREAKFAST	Full country breakfast served in the dining room.
AMENITIES	Wine and cheese in the parlor, large front porch with wicker furniture, ceiling fans, double whirlpool tubs for two under skylights.
RESTRICTIONS	No smoking, no pets. Resident cat, Calicat
MEMBER	California Association of Bed and Breakfast Inns
KUDOS/COMMENTS	"Now that Joanne Claus, the original owner, is back, things are up to snuff!"

HEALDSBURG INN ON THE PLAZA

110 Matheson, Healdsburg, CA 95448   707-433-6991
Genny Jenkins, Resident Owner   800-431-8663

LOCATION
: From Highway 101, take Central Healdsburg exit, go north to third stop light, turn right, third building on the right.

OPEN
: All year

DESCRIPTION
: A 1900 two-story Victorian Commercial hotel with Victorian furnishings. The hotel is on the California Historic Register.

NO. OF ROOMS
: Ten rooms with private bathroom. Pick Stardance.

RATES
: High season, August through November, rates are $135 to $175 for a single or a double with a private bathroom. Low season, Decmber through July, rates are $115 to $175 for a single or a double with a private bathroom. There is no minimum stay and cancellation requires three days notice and a $15 fee.

CREDIT CARDS
: MC, Visa

BREAKFAST
: Full breakfast is serve in the solarium and includes granola or baked hot oatmeal, juice, egg & cheese entree, potatoes, meat, salads and fresh fruits. Special meals are available.

AMENITIES
: Fireplaces in rooms, old fashioned tubs for two with rubber duckie, TV/VCR, large video library, 24 hour cookies, wine, art gallery, central air conditioning and telephones.

RESTRICTIONS
: No smoking, no pets, children over seven are welcome.

REVIEWED
: *America's Wonderful Little Hotels & Inns, Definitive California B&B Touring Guide, Best Places to Kiss in Northern California, Feather Beds and Flapjacks—A Preservationists Guide to Historic B&Bs, Inns and Small Hotels.*

MEMBER
: Professional Association of Innkeepers International, California Association of Bed & Breakfast Inns

MADRONA MANOR

1001 Westside Road, Healdsburg, CA 95448   707-433-4231
John & Carol Muir, Resident Owners   800-258-4003
Spanish spoken   FAX 707-433-4003

LOCATION	From Highway 101, take the Central Healdsburg exit, travel north on Healdsburg Avenue. Where three streets come together, Healdsburg Avenue, Vine and Mill, turn left sharply onto Mill. Less than one mile from town you'll see the arches.
OPEN	All year
DESCRIPTION	Three-story 1881 Gothic Victorian with eclectic furnishings and located on eight landscaped and wooded acres.
NO. OF ROOMS	Twenty one rooms with private bathrooms.
RATES	Year round rates are $135 for a single with private bathroom, $135 to $185 for a double with private bathroom. Suites are $185 to $225. Minimum stay required in the Mansion, April through November. Five day cancellation policy, plus $10 cancellation fee.
CREDIT CARDS	Amex, MC, Diners Club, Discover
BREAKFAST	Full breakfast served in the dining room. includes fresh juices, hot cereal, homemade granola, eggs, sheeses, meats, pastries, coffee and tea. Dinner available seven nights a week, also serve Sunday Brunch.
AMENITIES	Fresh garden flowers, robes, swimming pool, fresh baked chocolate chip cookies, champagne for anniversary guests. Handicapped access, meeting facilities, air conditioning and phones.
RESTRICTIONS	None. Resident eclectic cat is named Tiger.
REVIEWED	*Karen Brown's California County Inns and Itineraries, Best Places to Kiss in Northern California, Elegant Small Hotels*
MEMBER	Professional Association of Innkeepers International, Independent Innkeepers Association

THE RAFORD HOUSE

10630 Wohler Road, Healdsburg, CA 95448   707-887-9573
Carole and Jack Vore, Resident Owners   FAX 707-887-9597

LOCATION	Three miles north of Santa Rosa, take River Road exit from Highway 101. Drive west 7.5 miles to Wohler Road.
OPEN	All year, except Christmas weekend.
DESCRIPTION	An 1880s two-story Victorian summer house on four acres, surrounded by rose gardens and towering palm trees. On the Sonoma County Historic Register.
NO. OF ROOMS	Five rooms with private bathrooms, two rooms share a bathroom. The Bridal Suite is a gem.
RATES	Year round rates for a single or double with private bathroom are $95 to $130, and $85 for a single or double with a shared bathroom. Minimum two night stay on weekends, April through October. One week cancellation notice required for a full refund.
CREDIT CARDS	Amex, MC, Visa, Discover
BREAKFAST	Full breakfast, includes hot entree, fresh fruit, croissants, muffins and beverages is served in the dining room.
AMENITIES	Two rooms have fireplaces, evening refreshments and local wines are served in the common area.
RESTRICTIONS	No smoking, no pets, children not encouraged. Peaches, a Sheltie mixed breed, serves as the "official greeter and guide, from the parking area to the front door."
REVIEWED	*Country Inns of California, Bed and Breakfast California, The Official Guide to American Historic Bed and Breakfast Inns and Guesthouses*
MEMBER	Professional Association of Innkeepers International, California Association of Bed and Breakfast Inns

VILLA MESSINA

316 Burgundy Road, Healdsburg, CA 95448   *707-433-6655*
Jerry Messina, Resident Owner   *FAX 707-433-4515*

LOCATION — Take Highway 101 to the Dry Creek Road exit. Go east to the second stoplight and turn left on Healdsburg Avenue. Go one block after the first stoplight and turn left on Chiquita Road. Proceed under freeway and take the first right on Burgandy Road. At divide turn left, Villa Messina is the second driveway on the right.

OPEN — All year

DESCRIPTION — 1987 two-story villa with antique and contemporary furnishings.

NO. OF ROOMS — Five rooms with private bathrooms. The Master Bedroom Suite is the best in the house.

RATES — Year round rates for a double room with private bathroom are $130 to $250. There is a two night minimum stay on weekends and seven days notice required for cancellation.

CREDIT CARDS — Amex, MC, Diners Club, Discover

BREAKFAST — Full breakfast including fruit.

AMENITIES — Flowers, robes, telephones, TV in rooms, meeting facilities.

RESTRICTIONS — No smoking, no pets. Resident critters are two Rottweilers, Frieda and Max, Jucinda the Potbelly Pig and llamas Cancun and Zorba.

MEMBER — California Association of Bed and Breakfast Inns

KUDOS/COMMENTS — ". . .spectacular house and views, fun, gregarious innkeepers."

HOMEWOOD

On Lake Tahoe's west shore and away from the crowds of Olympic Valley (Squaw Valley),

CHANEY HOUSE

4725 West Lake Boulevard, Homewood, CA 96141   916-525-7333
Gary and Lori Chaney, Resident Owners

LOCATION	Located 5 miles south of Tahoe City on Highway 89 (West Lake Boulevard). Look for the Chaney sign with the physical address 4725 on the right.
OPEN	All year
DESCRIPTION	A 1928 two-story native stone home with native pine accents on the shore of Lake Tahoe. Eighteen inch thick stone walls, gothic arches and massive stone fireplace.
NO. OF ROOMS	Four rooms with private bathrooms.
RATES	Year round rates for all rooms are $100 to $115. Two day minimum stay required, cancellation requires 14 days notice, 30 days notice for holidays.
CREDIT CARDS	No
BREAKFAST	Full breakfast served in the dining room, or the patio in summer, includes beverages, bundt cakes and egg dishes.
AMENITIES	Three patios, private pier, TV/VCR/CD, close to all Tahoe outdoor activities.
RESTRICTIONS	Smoking outside only, no pets, children over 12 years old are welcome. There is a resident Golden Retriever.
REVIEWED	*Bed and Breakfast California, Bed and Breakfasts in California, Fodor's West Coast B&Bs Country Inns and Weekend Pleasures*
MEMBER	American Bed and Breakfast Association, California Association of Bed and Breakfast Inns
RATED	ABBA 2 Crowns

ROCKWOOD LODGE

5295 West Lake Boulevard, Homewood, CA 96141   916-525-5273
Louis Reinkens, Resident Owners

HOPE VALLEY

SORENSEN'S RESORT

14255 Highway 88, Hope Valley, CA 96120   *916-694-2203*
Patty & John Brissenden, Resident Owners

HOPLAND

If you're heading through inland Mendocino County, stop here for a respite. This may be wine country, but teeny Hopland—named for the hops once grown in the area—offers a good brew. Or head over to the Hopland Indian Rancheria for high-stakes bingo. On Hwy. 101, 13 miles south of Ukiah.

THATCHER INN

13401 South Highway 101, Hopland, CA 95449   *707-744-1890*
Carmen Gleason, Manager   *800-266-1891*
                                                          FAX 707-744-1219

LOCATION	On Highway 101 on the right side of highway. (No freeway off-ramps.)
OPEN	All year. Closed Jan 1st through 15th for deep cleaning.
DESCRIPTION	An 1890 Victorian Country Inn with period furnishing.
NO. OF ROOMS	Twenty rooms with private bathrooms. For a special stay request the Lotti Room.
RATES	Year round rates are singles $81 to $135; doubles $90 to $105; suites $120 to $150. Reservation/cancellation policy: five days prior to arrival.
CREDIT CARDS	Amex, MC, Visa
BREAKFAST	Full country style breakfast ordered from menu served in the dining room. Lunch and dinner also available.
AMENITIES	Rooms have robes for guests, telephone, clock-radios, and period furnishings. English style library and the Lobby Bar has one of the largest selections of single malt scotch whiskey collections in the west. A swimming pool is available in the patio garden area. Private parties for up to 75 people may be arranged and a meeting area is available for up to 35 people.
RESTRICTIONS	No smoking, no pets.
MEMBER	California Association of Bed & Breakfast Inns, American Bed & Breakfast Association
RATED	AAA 2 Diamonds, ABBA 4 Crowns

INVERNESS

This is a beauty, with a location that's to die for: on the Point Reyes Peninsula and Tomales Bay, at the entrance to the most stunning part of Point Reyes National Seashore. Explore the half-moon beach and secret coves of the Bay, and visit the oyster farms, for which the town is noted. From San Francisco, head north on Hwy. 1 and Point Reyes Road.

THE ARK

180 Highland Avenue, Inverness, CA 94937   *415-663-9338*
Jim Van der Ryn, Resident Owner   *800-808-9338*
Spanish spoken

LOCATION	From Highway 101 take San Anselmo-Sir Francis Drake Boulevard exit. Go west 25 miles to Olema. Turn north on Highway 1 for 1 block, turn left on Bear Valley Road. Go 2.3 miles to end of road, turn left at stop sign onto Sir Francis Drake Boulevard. Go 3 miles to Inverness, turn left on Inverness Way, go 3 blocks, turn left on Highland Avenue, go 1 mile to the inn.
OPEN	All year
DESCRIPTION	1971 rustic cottage furnished with an eclectic collection of original art and weavings.
NO. OF ROOMS	Two bedroom cottage with private bathroom.
RATES	Year round rate for two people is $135, and $15 per person up to four people. Discount of 20% off peak season midweek. Ten day cancellation notice required with $10 fee.
CREDIT CARDS	No
BREAKFAST	Continental Plus breakfast supplies stocked in the cottage kitchen include fresh seasonal fruit, granola, yogurt, local organic milk, "home raised" eggs, pastries, home baked bread, homemade jam and beverages.
AMENITIES	Flowers, phone, TV, woodstove, fireplace, kitchen, picnic and BBQ area, stereo, small book collection, games.
RESTRICTIONS	No smoking indoors.
REVIEWED	*Bed & Breakfast California*
MEMBER	California Association of Bed and Breakfast Inns

BAYSHORE COTTAGE

12732 Sir Francis Drake Boulevard, Inverness, CA 94937   *415-669-1148*
Mare M. Hansen, Resident Owner
French spoken

LOCATION	South of Inverness .75 mile, directly on Tomales Bay. It is 3.1 miles west and north from the intersection of Sir Francis Drake Boulevard and Highway 1 at Point Reyes Station. On Sir Francis Drake Boulevard at Willow Point.
OPEN	All year
DESCRIPTION	A 1988 Cape Cod cottage with painted knotty pine walls and hardwood floors, in a garden setting on Tomales Bay.
NO. OF ROOMS	One cottage with private bathroom.
RATES	Year round rate for the cottage is $125. Two night minimum stay on weekends, ten day cancellation notice required with $15 fee.
CREDIT CARDS	No
BREAKFAST	Cottage kitchen is provisioned with full breakfast options including variety of juices, fresh fruit basket, hot and cold cereal, pancake mix, yogurts, eggs, bagels, English muffins and beverages.
AMENITIES	Queen size Eurobed, down quilts and pillows, flowers, candles, outdoor hot tub, pier and gazebo, sherry, adjacent library with TV/VCR, books, binoculars.
RESTRICTIONS	No smoking, no pets. Three resident Yellow Labs are: Louis, Nina and Tito and the cat is Petit Chat.
REVIEWED	*AAA Bed & Breakfast Guide—Northern and Central California*

BLACKTHORNE INN

266 Vallejo Avenue, Inverness, CA 94956   *415-663-8621*
Susan Wigett, Resident Owner

DANCING COYOTE BEACH

12974 Sir Francis Drake Boulevard, Inverness, CA 94937   415-669-7200
John Phillips, Resident Owner

LOCATION	One tenth of mile from greater downtown Inverness. From Highway 1 north turn left on Bear Valley Road and follow the signs into town.
OPEN	All year
DESCRIPTION	Four 1971 glass and wood cottages with California cottage furnishings.
NO. OF ROOMS	Four cottages with private bathroom.
RATES	Year round rates are $95 to $125 per night for a single or a double with a private bathroom. There is a two night minimum stay on the weekend and there is a cancellation policy.
CREDIT CARDS	No
BREAKFAST	Continental breakfast is stocked in the cottage and includes beverages, breakfast breads, yogurt and cereal.
AMENITIES	Each cottage has a fireplace, skylight, private kitchen and deck.
RESTRICTIONS	Smoking on deck only.
REVIEWED	*Best Places to Kiss in Northern California*

FAIRWINDS FARM COTTAGE

82 Drake's Summit, Inverness, CA 94937   *415-663-9454*
Joyce H. Goldfield, Resident Owner
Sign language

LOCATION	From Point Reyes Station turn right over green bridge, take next immediate right (sign reads "Inverness"), go 1 mile and road curves to right—start looking on your left for 2 white houses and a school bus stop ("Balboa"). Turn left up Balboa and go 2 miles to dead end. Our driveway is directly to your right.
OPEN	All year
DESCRIPTION	1964 carriage house cottage is furnished with oak antiques.
NO. OF ROOMS	One large cottage with private bathroom.
RATES	Year round rate for entire cottage is $125 for two people, and $25 each additional person. Stay for seven nights and pay for six. Two night minimum on weekends, 14 day cancellation notice required.
CREDIT CARDS	No
BREAKFAST	Full breakfast provisions in the cottage kitchen include muffins, breads, scones, bacon, eggs, cheese, onions, garlic, herbs, waffles and beverages.
AMENITIES	Evening snacks provided, flowers, robes, hot tub with ocean view, TV, stereo, VCR with 400+ movies, garden with giant pine trees, two person swing, ponds with fish and waterfalls, separate child's playhouse filled with toys, large library, musical instruments, surrounded by 75,000 acres of wilderness.
RESTRICTIONS	No smoking, no pets, children of all ages welcome. Animals abound at the cottage and include donkeys, horses, dogs, cats and an angora goat . . . "all very sweet."
MEMBER	Coastal Lodging Association

HOTEL INVERNESS

PO Box 780, Inverness, CA 94937   *415-669-7393*
Susan & Tom Simms, Resident Owners

LAUREL RIDGE COTTAGE INN

217 Laurel Street, Inverness, CA 94937   415-663-1286
Rita K. & Bill Landis, Resident Owners   800-853-2074
                                                          FAX 415-663-9418

LOCATION	Laurel Street is a private road 2 miles from Point Reyes Station, west on Sir Francis Drake Boulevard. Our cottage is .5 mile to the west of Drake Boulevard on the Inverness Ridge.
OPEN	All year
DESCRIPTION	1992 contemporary rustic cottage with antique furnishings.
NO. OF ROOMS	One bedroom with private bathroom living room and kitchenette.
RATES	Cottage rents for $135 per day and includes kitchenette, living area, bedroom and bathroom.
CREDIT CARDS	No
BREAKFAST	Continental Plus breakfast brought to the cottage includes rolls, eggs, cereals and beverages.
AMENITIES	Fresh fruit, daily maid service, flowers, robes, cable TV, lounge chairs on two decks overlooking a canyon, wood stove.
RESTRICTIONS	No smoking, no pets.
MEMBER	California Association of Bed and Breakfast Inns

MANKA'S INVERNESS LODGE

PO Box 1110, Inverness, CA 94937   415-669-1034
Margaret Grade, Resident Owner

MARSH COTTAGE BED & BREAKFAST

PO Box 1121, Point Reyes Station, CA 94956   415-669-7168
Wendy Schwartz, Resident Owner

Patterson House

12847 Sir Francis Drake Boulevard, Inverness, CA 94937   *415-669-1383*
Rosalie Patterson, Resident Owner   *FAX 415-669-1383*
Spanish, French, German spoken

LOCATION	Across from Inverness Yacht Club and Tomales Bay, turn left up driveway.
OPEN	All year
DESCRIPTION	Built in 1916 this Craftsman host home with "comfortable' eclectic furnishings, features porches and decks overlooking Tomales Bay.
NO. OF ROOMS	Five rooms with private bathrooms. Room #1 features with best view.
RATES	Year round rates for a single or double room with private bathroom $125 to $145 weekends, $85 to $100 midweek. Two night minimum on holiday weekends, seven day cancellation notice required.
CREDIT CARDS	MC, Visa
BREAKFAST	Full breakfast on weekends, Continental Plus on weekdays, is served in the dining room and might include fresh seasonal fruit, waffles, pancakes, eggs, quiche, bacon, ham, croissants, other pastries and beverages. Menu changes daily.
AMENITIES	Fresh flowers, hot tub jacuzzi on deck, 6' clawfoot bathtubs, two rooms with private porches, king and queen beds, phone and fax available, common room with stone fireplace.
RESTRICTIONS	No smoking inside, no pets, children over 10 years old are welcome on weekdays.

ROSEMARY COTTAGE

75 Balboa Avenue, Inverness, CA 94937   *415-663-9338*
Suzanne Storch, Resident Owner   *800-808-9338*
Spanish spoken

LOCATION	From Highway 101 take the San Anselmo-Sir Francis Drake Boulevard exit. Drive west 25 miles to Olema. Turn right (north) onto Route 1 for .10 mile. Turn left onto Bear Valley Road, drive 2.3 miles to stop sign. Turn left 1 block, turn left onto Balboa Avenue. Go .5 mile, driveway is on the left.
OPEN	All year
DESCRIPTION	1987 French Country cottage with some antiques and oriental rugs.
NO. OF ROOMS	Two room cottage with private bathroom.
RATES	Year round rate for two people is $135, and $15 per extra person. Twenty percent discount available off-season. Ten day cancellation notice with $10 fee.
CREDIT CARDS	No
BREAKFAST	Continental Plus breakfast provisions are stocked in the cottage including fresh fruit, granola, "home raised" eggs, yogurt, pastries, homebaked bread, homemade jam and beverages.
AMENITIES	Flowers, herb garden, woodstove, telephone, TV, AM/FM radio and tape player, games, small book collection, binoculars, BBQ and picnic area, large deck, well equipped kitchen.
RESTRICTIONS	No smoking inside. Fluffy is the resident cat.

SANDY COVE INN

12990 Sir Francis Drake Boulevard, Inverness, CA 94937   *415-669-2683*
Kathy and Gerry Coles, Resident Owners   *800-759-2683*
Spanish, German, Italian spoken   *FAX 415-669-7511*

LOCATION	One mile past the town of Inverness on Tomales Bay.
OPEN	All year
DESCRIPTION	1986 two-story beachfront Cape Cod inn with Adirondack decor.
NO. OF ROOMS	Three rooms with private bathrooms.
RATES	Year round rates for a double room with private bathroom are $115 to $145, depending on time of week. Two-night minimum stay on weekends, 14-day cancellation notice plus $15 fee.
CREDIT CARDS	Amex, MC, Visa, Discover
BREAKFAST	Full breakfast served in guestroom or in the solarium might include organic apple pancakes, strawberry frappe, and fresh baked goods. Menu varies with the season, dietary restrictions are respected. Picnic baskets available if ordered in advance.
AMENITIES	Robes, phone in room, beverages, fresh fruit and cheese, tapes, radio, library and fireplace in room, private deck, beach towels and chairs, backpacks, sitting area in each room, refrigerators, wine and cheese on apprival.
RESTRICTIONS	No smoking anywhere, no pets, children are not encouraged. "Kind and loving" farm animals on the premises.

TEN INVERNESS WAY

10 Inverness Way, Inverness, CA 94937   *415-669-1648*
Mary E. Davies, Resident Owner

LOCATION	From Olema, turn right on Highway 1, turn left on Bear Valley Road. Drive three miles to stop sign. Turn left, drive four miles to Inverness. Turn left on 2nd Inverness Way, look for the sign on the right.
OPEN	All year
DESCRIPTION	1904 two-story California Redwood shingle with "comfortable" antiques.
NO. OF ROOMS	Five rooms with private bathrooms. Check out the Garden Suite.
RATES	Year round rates for a single or a double with a private bathroom are $110 to $160. Two night minimum stay on weekends, seven day cancellation policy.
CREDIT CARDS	MC, Visa
BREAKFAST	Full breakfast served in the dining room.
AMENITIES	Fresh flowers, robes, homemade cookies, hot tub in garden.
RESTRICTIONS	No smoking, no pets, children of all ages are welcome.
REVIEWED	*Karen Brown's California's Country Inns and Itineraries, Recommended Country Inns—West Coast*
MEMBER	Professional Association of Innkeepers International
KUDOS/COMMENTS	"Comfortable, homey, relaxing atmosphere — simple comforts."

IONE

This tiny Gold Country town is home to the new Mule Creek State Prison. The gloomy Preston School of Industry, now an historic monument (and appropriately condemned) was the state's first reform school. Handy to Jackson, and vicinity of Camanche and Pardee Reservoirs and Lake Amador. Southeast of Sacramento, via Hwy. 16 and 124.

THE HEIRLOOM

214 Shakeley Lane, Ione, CA 95640   619-274-4468
Melisande Hubbs & Patricia Cross, Resident Owners
Portuguese spoken

LOCATION	At the intersection of Highway 124 and Highway 104 go west on Shakeley Lane (Highway 124 becomes Shakeley Lane). House is in the first block on the left, down a lane about 500 feet.
OPEN	All year except Thanksgiving, Christmas Eve and Christmas Day.
DESCRIPTION	An 1863, two-story, Southern Antebellum Greek Revival inn, with columns and balconies. Dedicated as an Historic Landmark by California Native Sons of the Golden West.
NO. OF ROOMS	Four rooms with private bathrooms, two rooms with shared bathroom. Melisande recommends the Winter Room.
RATES	Year round rates for a single or double with private bathroom are $65 to $92, and $55 to $85 for a single or double with shared bathroom. Two-room cottage rents for $170, entire inn rents for $500. No minimum stay, 72 hour cancellation policy.
CREDIT CARDS	Amex, MC, Visa
BREAKFAST	Full breakfast served in the dining room, on the balcony, or in the garden includes fresh squeezed orange juice, fresh seasonal fruit, breads, hot entree like souffles, crepes or Eggs Benedict and beverages. Dietary restrictions accommodated on request.
AMENITIES	Afternoon refreshments, gardens with glider and hammocks, croquet, fireplaces and woodstoves, flowers, fruit and candy in rooms, grand piano, bath sheets.
RESTRICTIONS	No smoking, no pets.
REVIEWED	*Recommended Country Inns—West Coast, Best Places to Stay in Northern California, National Trust Guide to Historic Bed and Breakfasts, Bed and Breakfast USA, Best Places to Kiss in Northern California*
MEMBER	California Association of Bed and Breakfast Inns, Bed and Breakfast Innkeepers of Amador County
KUDOS/COMMENTS	"Gracious hospitality, conscientious innkeepers, excellent breakfast."... "Innkeepers Pat & Milisande are the heart of their lovely home - great cooks, delightful hostesses."... "Probably the most comfortable place we have ever stayed."

ISLETON

On Andrus Island in the Sacramento Delta, the town is shadowed by remnants of its Chinatown past. About 30 miles northwest of Stockton via I-5 and Hwy. 12.

DELTA DAZE INN

20 Main Street, Isleton, CA 95641   916-777-4667
Frank & Shirley Russell, Resident Owners

LOCATION	Turn right at the "Y", Main Street, and go 1-1/2 blocks to the inn on the right-hand side.
OPEN	All year
DESCRIPTION	A two-story 1926 "Prohibition - Asian" redone "bawdy house" with "delta style" furnishings.
NO. OF ROOMS	Twelve rooms with private bathrooms. Try the levee suite.
RATES	High season, May through October, rates are $90 for a single or a double with private bathroom and $125 for a suite. Low season, November through April, rates are $49.50 for a single or a double with a private bathroom and $69.50 for a suite. There is a minimum stay for holidays and special events and cancellation requires seven days notice.
CREDIT CARDS	Amex, MC, Visa
BREAKFAST	Full breakfast served in the dining room includes fruit, juice, bran muffins, biscuits & gravy, sausage & eggs and sourdough casserole, waffles and pancakes.
AMENITIES	Levee tea at three, soda fountain, goodies, complimentary use of bicycles, meeting facilities and handicapped access.
RESTRICTIONS	No smoking except in three rooms, no pets.
REVIEWED	*American & Canadian B&Bs*
MEMBER	American Bed & Breakfast Association, California Association of Bed & Breakfast Inns
RATED	AAA 2 Diamonds

JACKSON

Still brisk and lively, this is the place to be for a little fun a la "Rush" (John Wayne used to hang out here a lot). Best places to visit include the County Museum, and the St. Sava Serbian Orthodox Church and its sanctuary. In April, the Mother Lode Dixieland and Jazz Benefit are worth a listen. From Sacramento, 44 miles southeast via Hwy. 16 and 49.

ANN MARIE'S COUNTRY INN

410 Stasal Avenue, Jackson, CA 95642   *209-223-1452*
Alberta Thomas, Resident Owner

LOCATION	Just off Highway 88 in downtown Jackson. Left on North Main Street to first stop light, right on North Street, left on Stasel.
OPEN	All year
DESCRIPTION	An 1892 Victorian and cottage with antique "but not Victorian" furnishings.
NO. OF ROOMS	Two rooms with private bathrooms
RATES	Year round rates for a single, double or the cottage are $85 to $100.
CREDIT CARDS	MC, Visa, Discover
BREAKFAST	Full breakfast is served in the dining room or guest room and includes hot fruit dish, breads, muffins, pastry, egg dish, home fried potatoes, fresh fruit and beverages.
AMENITIES	Woodburning stove in parlor and potbelly stove in the cottage.
RESTRICTIONS	No smoking, no pets. The dog is Tizzy and the cats often respond to the names Jackie, O.J. and J.J.
REVIEWED	*The Best of Gold Country, Bed & Breakfast California*

COURT STREET INN

215 Court Street, Jackson, CA 95642   209-223-0416
Janet & Lee Hammond, Resident Owners   800-200-0416

LOCATION	Two blocks west on Court Street from the center of Main Street.
OPEN	All year
DESCRIPTION	A two-story 1872 Victorian farmhouse with guesthouse and 1900-1930s American antique furnishings. On the State and National Historic Registers
NO. OF ROOMS	Seven rooms with private bathrooms and one room shares one bathroom. The Hammonds recommend the Indian House.
RATES	Year round rates are $85 to $125 for a single or double with a private bathroom. The suite is $125 and the guesthouse is $100 to $130 for a double. Rates are lower Sunday through Thursday. There is no minimum stay.
CREDIT CARDS	Amex, MC, Visa
BREAKFAST	Full breakfast is served in the dining room or guestroom and includes a main entree, potato dish, meat, fresh fruit and beverages. Picnic baskets are available.
AMENITIES	Fresh flowers, terry robes, outdoor hot tub, TV available for each room, iron and ironing board, hors d'oeuvres, fireplaces, private decks and pond with waterfall.
RESTRICTIONS	No smoking, no pets.
REVIEWED	*Bed & Breakfast California, Northern California Best Places, The Best Places to Kiss in Northern California*
MEMBER	Professional Association of Innkeepers International, California Association of Bed & Breakfast Inns, Amador County Bed & Breakfast Association

GATE HOUSE INN

1330 Jackson Gate Road, Jackson, CA 95642	*209-223-3500*
Keith & Gail Sweet, Resident Owners	*800-841-1072*
	FAX 209-223-1299

LOCATION

The inn is located 1.3 miles north of the center of Jackson. Take Main Street, that becomes Jackson Gate, and the inn is on the right side of thr road just past Terejas Restarant.

OPEN

All year

DESCRIPTION

A two-story 1902 Victorian and cottage with Victorian furnishings throughout. Listed on the State Historic Register.

NO. OF ROOMS

Five rooms with private bathrooms. Pick the summer house as the best room.

RATES

Year round rates are $85 to $120 for a single or double with private bathroom; $95 for a suite; $120 for the guesthouse and the entire inn rents for $470. There is a minimum stay on weekends when a Saturday is involved and cancellation requires seven days notice with a $10 charge.

CREDIT CARDS

Amex, Discover, MC, Visa

BREAKFAST

Full breakfast is served in the dining room or guest room and includes hot drinks, juices, breads, fruit, meat and main dish.

AMENITIES

Fresh flowers in rooms daily, fresh fruit, homemade cookies, candy available in all public rooms, afternoon tea and hors d'oeuvres, chocolate turn downs, pool and patio with BBQ facilities, ping pong and exercise room.

RESTRICTIONS

No smoking, children over 12 are welcome.

MEMBER

Professional Association of Innkeepers International, Amador County Bed & Breakfast Association, California Association of Bed & Breakfast Inns

RATED

AAA 3 Diamonds

THE WEDGEWOOD INN

11941 Narcissus Road, Jackson, CA 95642	*209-296-4300*
Vic & Jeannine Beltz, Resident Owners	

JAMESTOWN

Railfans will love this place—the 26-acre Rail Town 1897 State Historic Park includes a roundhouse, station, trains and yard facility, and you can watch maintenance and restoration of equipment. Hollywood likes pretty "Jimtown" too: check out the "Back to the Future III" movie set. There's a Gunfighters Rendezvous in April. East of Stockton via Hwy. 120 and 49.

HISTORIC NATIONAL HOTEL

77 Main Street, Jamestown, CA 95327　　　　　209-984-3446
Stephen Willey, Resident Owner　　　　800-446-1333, ext 286
German, Spanish spoken　　　　　　FAX 209-984-5620

LOCATION	Main Street, center of town.
OPEN	All year
DESCRIPTION	Restored two-story 1859 California Gold Rush hotel and restaurant furnished with original antiques and on the California State Historic Register.
NO. OF ROOMS	Five rooms with private bathrooms, six rooms have antique basins and share two bathrooms. Room Nine is the best in the house.
RATES	Year round rate, for a single or a double with private bathroom is $80, a single or a double with shared bathroom $65. Entire hotel can be rented for $790. No minimum, stay and 72 hour cancellation required.
CREDIT CARDS	Amex, MC, Diners Club, Visa, Discover, Carte Blanche
BREAKFAST	Continental Plus is served and includes fresh fruit, cereals, homemade breads, hard-boiled eggs, coffee, tea and morning paper. Other meals are available in the restaurant.
AMENITIES	Fresh flowers, brass beds and patchwork quilts, robes, TV on request, meeting facilities and friendly resident ghost.
RESTRICTIONS	Smoking in designated areas only, children over eight years welcome, pets of any age welcome with prior approval.
REVIEWED	*Recommended Country Inns—West Coast, Northern California Best Places, The Best Bed and Breakfast Country Inns, Country Inns of the Far West, Weekend Adventures for City Weary People*
MEMBER	National Bed and Breakfast Association, California Association of Bed and Breakfast Inns, Gold Country Inns of Tuolumne County

JAMESTOWN HOTEL

PO Box 539, Jamestown, CA 95327   209-984-3902
Chris Dolan, Manager

THE PALM HOTEL BED & BREAKFAST

10382 Willow Street, Jamestown, CA 95327   209-984-3429
Rick & Sandy Allen, Resident Owners

LOCATION	One block off of Main Street.
OPEN	All year
DESCRIPTION	A 1900s two-story Victorian mansion with eclectic and Victorian furnishings.
NO. OF ROOMS	Five rooms with private bathrooms and four rooms share 1 1/2 bathrooms. The new owners like the grand suite.
RATES	Year round rates are $80 to $100 for a single or a double with a private bathroom, $60 to $80 for a single or double with a shared bathroom and $95 to $130 for a suite. There is no minimum stay and cancellation requires five days notice.
CREDIT CARDS	Amex, MC, Visa
BREAKFAST	Full breakfast served in the dining room, lobby or porch includes eggs, potatoes, breads, fruits, beverages and the specialty: baked apple crisp.
AMENITIES	Flowers, robes, TV, local candy on every pillow, handicapped access and parlor soda fountain.
RESTRICTIONS	No smoking, no pets
REVIEWED	Historic Inns of California's Gold Country Cookbook and Guide.

ROYAL HOTEL

18239 Main Street, Jamestown, CA 95327   209-984-5271
Nancy and Bob Bosich, Resident Owners   FAX 209-984-1675

LOCATION	Downtown, across from the community park and gazebo.
OPEN	All year
DESCRIPTION	1922 two-story Victorian hotel and cottages Victorian country inn surrounded by landscaped grounds.
NO. OF ROOMS	Ten rooms with private bathrooms, nine rooms with shared bathrooms. Pick the Honeymoon Cottage.
RATES	Year round rates are from $35 to $85, average around $55. No minimum stay, 72 hours cancellation notice.
CREDIT CARDS	Amex, MC, Visa
BREAKFAST	Continental Plus is served in the parlor and includes seasonal fruit, granola, yogurt, muffins and bread coffee and tea.
AMENITIES	Old fashioned balconies, barbecues, air conditioning, fireplace, bookshop, community kitchen, laundry facilities and RV parking.
RESTRICTIONS	No smoking, no pets, children OK...a matter of opinion...TI

JENNER

In Sonoma County on the north end of spectacular Sonoma Coast State Beaches. Marvelous tidepools, and perfect for everything except swimming. From here, the Russian River flows past into the Pacific. On Highway 1 north of Bodega Bay, 12 miles south of Fort Ross State Historic Park.

MURPHY'S JENNER INN

10400 Coast Highway One, Jenner, CA 95451   707-865-2377
Richard and Sheldon Murphy, Resident Owners   800-732-2377
     FAX 707-865-0829

LOCATION	From Highway 101, take Central Petaluma exit west to Coast Highway 1, then north to Jenner. Don't blink and you'll see us.
OPEN	All year
DESCRIPTION	Built in 1895 and 1948, this seaside resort includes a redwood lodge building and seven traditional coastal cottages. Furnishings may be country Victorian or rustic and woodsy.
NO. OF ROOMS	Thirteen rooms or cottages with private bathrooms. The Rosewater Cottage is the best in the bunch.
RATES	High season rates, April through October, for double rooms, suites or cottages with private bathrooms are $65 to $165, 15% discount off season, midweek. Two night minimum stay on weekends, three nights on holidays. Refund less $10 processing fee with seven days notice.
CREDIT CARDS	Amex, MC, Visa
BREAKFAST	Continental Plus breakfast served in the lodge parlor includes fresh fruit, warm pastries and muffins, granola and beverages. There is a full restaurant in the lodge building independent of the inn.
AMENITIES	Most rooms have private decks or porches with water views. Fireplaces, kitchens, and hot tubs available. Teas, apertifs, games, books and magazines, small boat launch with river estuary, conference and retreats accomodated, full wedding and reception services.
RESTRICTIONS	Smoking allowed on decks, no pets. The surrounding area includes a wildlife sanctuary.
MEMBER	California Association of Bed and Breakfast Inns

KLAMATH

REQUA INN

451 Requa Road, Klamath, CA 95548   707-482-8205
Sue Reese, Leo & Melissa Chavez, Resident Owner

LAKE TAHOE

This is the largest alpine lake on the North American continent, with water so pure (99.7 percent) it's almost distilled, and so clear objects can be seen 75 feet down. Among its surrounding natural wonders are world class skiing, Sugar Pine Point State Park, Pope-Baldwin Recreation Area, glorious Emerald Bay, the Desolation Wilderness, and the many little civilizations that populate the lake's shores. East of Sacramento on I-80 or Hwy. 50.

ALPENHAUS COUNTRY INN

6941West Lake Boulevard, Tahoma, CA 96142   916-525-5000
Allen & Patricia Multon, Resident Owners
Spanish, French and Italian spoken   FAX 916-525-5266

LOCATION	Exit Highway 80 at Truckee at the Lake Tahoe exit, proceed 15 miles to Tahoe City, turn right at first light on Highway 89, proceed 7.5 miles towards Emerald Bay, the inn is in the heart of Tahoma.
OPEN	All year
DESCRIPTION	A three-story late 1930s old Tahoe style log frame with country furnishings and restaurant
NO. OF ROOMS	Eleven rooms with private bathrooms and two rooms share two bathrooms. Pick Amy's honeymoon cottage.
RATES	Year round rates range from $80 to $90 for a double with private bathroom, $70 to $80 for a double with a shared bathroom, suites range from $115 to $125, the guesthouse ranges from $95 to $150. There is a minimum stay and slightly higher rates for holiday periods and cancellation requires two weeks notice.
CREDIT CARDS	Amex, MC, Visa
BREAKFAST	Full breakfast (except for cottage guests) is served in the dining room and includes a choice of french toast, bacon & eggs, omelette of the day, pancakes and beverages. Lunch and dinner are available and special allergy-free meals and set price dinners for groups are available by prior agreement.
AMENITIES	Telephones, heated swimming pool, spa, bike rental.
RESTRICTIONS	No smoking, no pets, children of all ages are welcome.
REVIEWED	*AAA Bed & Breakfast Guide—Northern California*
MEMBER	California Association of Bed & Breakfast Inns
RATED	AAA 2 Diamonds

THE CHRISTIANIA INN

3819 Saddle Road, South Lake Tahoe, CA 96151   916-544-7337
Jerry and Maggie Mershon, Resident Owners   FAX 916-544-5342
Spanish spoken

LOCATION	Across from Heavenly Valley Ski Resort. From Highway 50, turn on Ski Run Boulevard. Proceed all the way to the top, turn left, go two blocks.
OPEN	All year, except two week closure in late April.
DESCRIPTION	A three-story 1965 European chalet and restaurant furnished with Swiss country antiques.
NO. OF ROOMS	Six rooms with private bathrooms.
RATES	High season rates, Thanskgiving to Easter, for a single or double with private bathroom are $75 to $85, and $145 to $175 for suites. Off season rates for a single or double with private bathroom are $50 to $60, and $85 to $125 for suites. Two night minimum stay on weekends, five day cancellation notice required.
CREDIT CARDS	MC, Visa
BREAKFAST	Continental breakfast served in guestroom includes fresh orange juice, fruit platter, fresh baked muffins and beverages. Other meals available in restaurant.
AMENITIES	TV in rooms, brandy, two suites have saunas in the room, fireplaces in four suites.
RESTRICTIONS	No smoking, no pets.
REVIEWED	*Best Places to Kiss in Northern California, American B&Bs*
MEMBER	California Association of Bed and Breakfast Inns

THE COTTAGE INN

1690 West Lake Boulevard, Tahoe City, CA 96145   916-581-4073
Patty & Terry Giles, Resident Owner

INN AT SUGAR PINES

7123. 4th Avenue, Tahoma, CA 96142   *916-525-1259*
Marilyn & Richard Gould, Resident Owners

LOCATION	Sugar Pines is located on the west shore of Lake Tahoe, twenty miles south on Route 89. Take the Truckee, CA exit. The inn is two blocks off Route 89, 8 miles south of Tahoe City in the village of Tahoma.
OPEN	All year except Thanksgiving, Christmas Eve and Christmas Day.
DESCRIPTION	1969 traditional Tahoe cedar home furnished in English country style.
NO. OF ROOMS	Three rooms with private bathrooms, two rooms share two bathrooms. The Victorian Dormer room has a view of the woods.
RATES	Year round rate for a double room with private bathroom $70, and $60 to $65 for a double room with shared bathroom. Two days cancellation notice required.
CREDIT CARDS	No
BREAKFAST	Full breakfast served in the dining room, on the porch or guestroom includes fresh fruit, homemade rolls and breads, variety of cereals, yogurt, and egg dish and beverages.
AMENITIES	Fresh flowers, chocolates, robes, sauna, evening hors d'oeuvres, beach and dock access and wheelchair access.
RESTRICTIONS	No smoking, children over four years old welcome. Molly McBride, is the Border Terrier.
MEMBER	Professional Association of Innkeepers International

MAYFIELD HOUSE

236 Grove Street, Tahoe City, CA 96145   *916-583-1001*
Bruce Knauss, Resident Owner

LOCATION	From Highway 28, 1-1/2 blocks north of the center of town.
OPEN	All year
DESCRIPTION	A two-story 1932 English Country Tudor with "early Tahoe" furnishings.
NO. OF ROOMS	Six rooms share three bathrooms. Bruce selected the Mayfield room as his best.
RATES	Year round rates are $85 to $95 for a single or a double with shared bathroom and $115 for a suite. There is a minimum stay during high season weekends, June through September and December through April. Cancellation requires two weeks notice and a $10 cancellation fee.
CREDIT CARDS	Amex, MC, Visa
BREAKFAST	Full breakfast served in the dining room, guest room or on the patio includes Portuguese toast, Finnish pancakes, Belgian waffles, crepes and beverages.
AMENITIES	Flowers, robes, phone in hall, TV in master suite, wine, brandy and cheese in the afternoon, collection of books in each room.
RESTRICTIONS	No smoking, no pets, children over 15 are welcome
MEMBER	Professional Association of Innkeepers International

RIVER RANCH LODGE

PO Box 197, Tahoe City, CA 96145 96145   *916-583-4264*
Pete Friedrichson, Resident Owner

ROYAL GORGE'S RAINBOW LODGE

9411 Hampshire Rocks Road, Soda Springs, CA 95728
John Slouber, Resident Owner

916-426-3661
800-500-3871
FAX 916-426-9221

LOCATION	From I-80 take the Rainbow Road exit, turn left and travel one-half mile to lodge.
OPEN	All year
DESCRIPTION	1920s lodge of local granite and handhewn timber. Located in the Sierras by a bend in the Yuba River. Mountain home country-style interior decor.
NO. OF ROOMS	12 rooms with private bathrooms. 19 rooms share four bathrooms.
RATES	Winter Season, November 15 through May 3: singles and doubles with private bath: $99; single with shared bath (sink only) $69; double with shared bath (shower) $85; Bridal and family suites $129. Summer Season, May 2 through November 14: singles and doubles with private bath: $85; single with shared bath (sink only) $59; double with shared bath (shower) $69; Bridal and family suites $110. Minimum stay applies for winter and holiday weekends. Reservation/cancellation policy: Winter-21 days for full refund less $10 cancellation fee; Summer-24 hours for full refund less $10 cancellation fee.
CREDIT CARDS	MC, Visa
BREAKFAST	Full breakfast served in dining room includes a choice of menu items ranging from eggs, French toast, mueslix, oatmeal, pancakes, or half melon with yogurt, plus juice, coffee, and tea. Lunch and dinner are also available.
AMENITIES	TV in bar, large fireplace in guest lounge, garden and deck. Facilities available for meetings, weddings, banquets and parties. Handicapped access.
RESTRICTIONS	No pets.

THE TRAVERSE INN

PO Box 1012, Soda Springs, CA 95728
Wes Ohlsen, Resident Owner

916-426-3010

LAKEPORT

Escape from wine country madness to the western shore of springfed, volcanic Clear Lake—lots of bass, bring rod and reel. The area is also known for its mineral and hot springs, and famous for Barlett Pears. Historic County Courthouse and Museum are worth a visit. So is the Pear Blossom Festival in April, and U.S. Bass Tournament, Boat and Ski Races in August, and Celebrity Pro-Am Bass Tourney in October. North from San Francisco on Highway 101 and 175, and handy to Cow Mountain Recreation Area.

THE FORBESTOWN BED & BREAKFAST INN

825 Forbes Street, Lakeport, CA 95453   707-263-7858
Jack & Nancy Dunne, Resident Owners   FAX 707-263-7878

LOCATION	Downtown Lakeport, one block west of Main Street between 8th and 9th Streets.
OPEN	All year
DESCRIPTION	An 1869 two-story clapboard farmhouse furnished in American oak antiques.
NO. OF ROOMS	One room with a private bathroom, three rooms with shared bathrooms. The Bartlett Suite is the best in the house.
RATES	Year round rates for a single or double with private or shared bathroom are $75 to $110. One week cancellation required.
CREDIT CARDS	Amex, MC, Visa
BREAKFAST	Full breakfast served in the dining room includes fresh fruit, Eggs Benedict, waffles, omelettes, assorted meats, hash browns and beverages. Vegetarian meals are available.
AMENITIES	Flowers, robes, phones, TV, VCR, hot tub and swimming pool, wine and hors d'oeuvres, tea and baked goods, turn down service, bikes, large pool towels.
RESTRICTIONS	No smoking, no pets, children over 12 years old welcome, maximum stay is 10 days. Rusty is the resident Poodle.
REVIEWED	*California Country Inns and Itineraries, The Tastes of California Wine Country, Annual Directory of American and Canadian B & Bs*
MEMBER	California Association of Bed and Breakfast Inns
KUDOS/COMMENTS	"Great full breakfast, warm hospitality and comfort."

THE WOODEN BRIDGE B&B

1441 Oakwood Court, Lakeport, CA 95453   707-263-9125
Don and Ginny Carmody, Resident Owners

LOCATION	From north Highway 29, exit at Park Way Hill Road. Turn left over freeway to Hill Road. Turn left on Hill Road and go three quarter miles to the B&B.
OPEN	All year, except Christmas and New Year's Day.
DESCRIPTION	1991 English manor with country French decors and located on five oak-covered acres.
NO. OF ROOMS	Two rooms with private bathrooms.
RATES	Year round rate for a double with private bathroom is $115. Two night minimum stay on holiday weekends. Cancellation policy requires 72 hours notice for refund.
CREDIT CARDS	No credit cards accepted.
BREAKFAST	Full breakfast served in the dining room includes fritatta or egg puff, juice and fresh fruit, homemade bread and pastries.
AMENITIES	Robes, bicycles, stocked refrigerator, afternoon refreshments.
RESTRICTIONS	No smoking, no pets, children aren't encouraged.
MEMBER	California Association of Bed and Breakfast Inns

LEWISTON

A fishing paradise on Lake Lewiston, and great base camp for access into the stunning Trinity Alps Wilderness and Trinity Lake. And make time for a tour of the Trinity River Fish Hatchery (salmon and steelhead) just south of the dam. Northwest of Redding via Highway 299 and Road 105.

OLD LEWISTON INN

Deadwood Road, Historic District, Lewiston, CA 96052   916-778-3354
Connor & Mary Nixon, Resident Owners   800-286-4441
Spanish spoken   FAX 916-778-0309

LOCATION	From Highway 299 take Lewiston exit and go four mile to Lewiston Valley, turn right on Turnpike Road for 1/4 mile to Historic District and take first right on Deadwood Road.
OPEN	All year
DESCRIPTION	An 1875 "49er" mining town style inn with mining era antiques. Listed on the National and State Historic Register
NO. OF ROOMS	Seven rooms with private bathrooms. Connor thinks French Gulch is the best room.
RATES	Year round rates for a double with a private bathroom are $75 and that includes tax. There is a minimum stay on holidays and cancellation requires seven days notice except for emergencies.
CREDIT CARDS	MC, Visa
BREAKFAST	Full breakfast is served in the main dining room or on the decks and includes cereal, juice, fresh fruit, French toast, two eggs and four strips of bacon. Box lunches are available when ordered in advance.
AMENITIES	Cable TV, hot tub by the river, hiking and biking maps, flyfishing instruction and guide services, handicapped access, all rooms with decks overlooking the river.
RESTRICTIONS	No smoking, Sparkie the dog is the English Pointer.
REVIEWED	*Northern California's Best Inns & Resorts, Great Getaways.*

LITTLE RIVER

Don't miss this place. This is picture-postcard New England, founded as a lumber town by serttlers from Maine. A good reason to be here is Van Damme State Park, one of the finer things along this stretch of the coast. Most notable: the 2-1/2-mile Fern Canyon Trail and the fairy-like Pygmy Forest, where rhododendrons dwarf the trees! On the rugged northcentral coast, just south of Mendocino. Divers love it here, too.

GLENDEVEN

8221 North Highway 1, Little River, CA 95456   707-937-0083
Jan & Jane deVries, Resident Owner

KUDOS/COMMENTS   "One of the finest inns on the Medocino coast. Decor, privacy, spacious rooms."

HERITAGE HOUSE

5200 North Highway 1, Little River, CA 95456   707-937-5885
Gay & R.J. Jones, Resident Owners   800-235-5885
                                                      FAX 707-937-0318

LOCATION	Five miles south of Mendocino on the ocean side of Highway 1.
OPEN	Open President's Day weekend in February to January 2 of the following year.
DESCRIPTION	New England country inn, built in 1877, is surrounded by 37 acres of landscaped grounds overlooking the Pacific Ocean.
NO. OF ROOMS	74 rooms with private bathrooms. R.J. recommends Carousel 4.
RATES	High season rates, mid-April through October, are $150 to $330 for a single, $170 to $330 for a double. Off season rates are $125 to $278 for a single, $145 to $298 for a double. Package rates available for Christmas and New Year's. There is a minimum stay over Thanksgiving, Christmas and New Year's, and a cancellation policy of 72 hours in advance and a $10 fee.
CREDIT CARDS	MC, Visa
BREAKFAST	Full country breakfast and dinner are include in the rates and served in the dining rooms. Lunch is also available.
AMENITIES	Some rooms include fireplaces, jacuzzis, robes. and wet bars, most have ocean views. In-room coffee service. Piano music in lounge on weekends. Four dining rooms have ocean views. Retail shops and nursery and the movie "Same Time Next Year " was filmed here.
RESTRICTIONS	No smoking in dining rooms, no pets. Resident critters include wild cats and Muscovi quackless ducks...ducks that should be seen, not heard...TI
REVIEWED	*Karen Brown's California Country Inns & Itineraries, Bed and Breakfast in California, Recommeded Country Inns West Coast, Best Places to Kiss in Northern California*
MEMBER	California Lodging Industry Association, Redwood Empire Association

STEVENSWOOD LODGE

8211 North Highway 1, Little River, CA 95456　　　　707-937-2810
Robert & Vera Zimmer, Owners

KUDOS/COMMENTS "Darn near perfect"

LODI

WINE & ROSES COUNTRY INN

2505 West Turner Road, Lodi, CA 95242　　　　209-334-6988
Kris Cromwell, Resident Owner　　　　FAX 209-334-6570

LOWER LAKE

The southernmost town near Clear Lake's shore is worth a stop. From here can be reached Anderson Marsh State Historic Park and its John Still Anderson Ranch House (the park's headquarters). Anyone with an archaeological bent will love this area. Check out the Blackberry Festival in August, and wineries anytime. Take the scenic route north through Napa Valley on Highway 29.

BIG CANYON INN

11750 Big Canyon Road, Lower Lake, CA 95457　　　　　　707-928-5631
John and Helen Wiegand, Resident Owners
German spoken

LOCATION	From Lower Lake head north on Highway 20 one mile, turn left on Seigler Canyon Road. Go 5 miles, turn left on Big Canyon Road, go .2 miles, turn left, go .3 miles, turn right, go .2 miles, driveway is on the left.
OPEN	All year
DESCRIPTION	Two-story host home on 12 wooded acres.
NO. OF ROOMS	Two rooms with private bathrooms.
RATES	Year round rate for a single or double with private bathroom is $65. Cancellation requires 24 hours notice.
CREDIT CARDS	No
BREAKFAST	Continental breakfast served in your room includes fruit and pastry.
RESTRICTIONS	No smoking, no pets, children are welcome.
REVIEWED	*Bed and Breakfast Homes Directory*

LOYALTON

CLOVER VALLEY MILL HOUSE

Railroad Avenue & Mill Street, Loyalton, CA 96118　　　　916-993-4819
Leslie Hernandez-Black

KUDOS/COMMENTS　"A special inn that we run away to whenever we can."

MAMMOTH LAKES

One of the state's best four-season reacreation/resort areas. Here are the Pacific Crest Trail, Devils Postpile National Monument, Rainbow Falls, geothermal springs (Hot Creek is an area tradition for soaking the bod), and endless lakes. As for skiing, Mammoth Mountain has no equal for the longest season or the best snow. [This is an unpaid, first-hand testimonial . . . Ed.] Significant events: Festival of Performing Arts, and Jazz Jubilee in July–August; Mammoth Mountain Motocross and Oktoberfest in September; Festival of Lights in December. North of Bishop via Highway 395 and just southeast of Yellowstone.

SNOW GOOSE INN

---

57 Forest Trail, Mammoth Lakes, CA 93546　　　　　　　　619-934-2260
Bob & Carol Roster, Resident Owners　　　　　　　　　　800-874-7368
　　　　　　　　　　　　　　　　　　　　　　　　　　FAX 619-934-5655

LOCATION	From Highway 395 exit on Highway 203 to Mammoth Lakes. In town, go through one traffic light and turn right on Forest Trail. The inn is 1/2 block on the left.
OPEN	All year
DESCRIPTION	A two-story 1969 mountain lodge with antique and European furnishings.
NO. OF ROOMS	Nineteen rooms with private bathrooms.
RATES	High season, mid-November to mid-April, rates are $68 to $98 for a single or a double with a with private bathroom, and suites are $148 to $168. Low season, mid-April to mid-November, rates are $48 to $68 for a single or a double with private bathroom, and suites are $88 to $93. There is a three day minimum stay on holiday weekends.
CREDIT CARDS	Discover, MC, Visa
BREAKFAST	Full breakfast served in the dining room includes fresh baked muffins, coffee cakes, fresh fruit, fritatas, quiche and beverages.
AMENITIES	Hot tub, evening appetizers and wine, telephone, TV in rooms.
RESTRICTIONS	No smoking, no pets. The resident cat is called Mama.
MEMBER	California Association of Bed & Breakfast Innkeepers
RATED	AAA 2 Diamonds, Mobil 2 Stars

THE WHITE HORSE INN

2180 Old Mammoth Road, Mammoth Lakes, CA 93546   *619-924-3656*
Lynn Criss, Manager   *800-982-5657*
Some Spanish, French spoken

LOCATION	From Highway 395, take Mammoth Lakes/Highway 203 exit. Follow Highway 203 to first signal in town (Old Mammoth Road). Turn left, follow for almost 3 miles to 2180 Old Mammoth Road, inn is on the right.
OPEN	All year
DESCRIPTION	1963 two-story contomporary inn located in the trees.
NO. OF ROOMS	Three rooms with private bathroms, two rooms shared one bathroom. The Emporer's Room is the best in the house.
RATES	High season rates mid-November through April for a single or double with private bathroom are $100 to $150, and $150 for two bedroom/one bath suite, $600 for entire inn. Off season rates May through mid-November are $65 to $105, $120 for suites, and $500 for the entire inn. Deposit is forfeited if reservation is cancelled within 30 days, unless room is rebooked.
CREDIT CARDS	Amex, MC, Diners Club, Visa, Discover
BREAKFAST	Full breakfast served in the dining room includes fresh fruit, fresh baked goods, omelettes, waffles, souffles and fresh ground coffee.
AMENITIES	Afternoon hors d'oeuvres and refreshments, robes in each room, paperback library, TVs/VCRs, movie channel, pool room, kitchen for guests, fireplaces in living rooms, safe for storing valuables.
RESTRICTIONS	No smoking, no pets. Rosie the Australian Shepherd and the cats, Fatso and Thomas are "delightful and friendly, no fleas in the mountains."
REVIEWED	*Fodor's Eastern Sierra B & Bs, AAA Bed & Breakfast Guide—Southern California*
MEMBER	Professional Association of Innkeepers International

MARIPOSA

The peaceful and woodsy southwestern gateway into Yosemite National Park is a nifty surprise. Meander the unmarked ghost towns in the hills nearby, or hang out around the local offerings: Old Mariposa Jail, County Courthouse (check out the second floor), and the excellent State Mining and Mineral Exhibit. Also, wonderful wineries with fine chardonnays, cabernets, and merlots. Why leave? North of Fresno via Hwy. 99 and west of Merced on Hwy. 140. This is almost always open, and will get you to Yosemite Village and Badger Pass Ski Area in Winter. Or plan on the two-week Christmas Heritage Celebration in early December.

BOULDER CREEK BED & BREAKFAST

4572 Ben Hur Road, Mariposa, CA 95338   209-742-7729
Nancy & Michael Habermann, Resident Owners
German spoken

LOCATION	Two miles from Mariposa on Highway 49 south, make a right turn on Ben Hur Road, the host home is a 1/4 mile on the left.
OPEN	All year
DESCRIPTION	A 1988 Swiss Chalet host home with contemporary and antique furnishings.
NO. OF ROOMS	Three rooms with private bathrooms. Try the bridal room.
RATES	Year round rates are $70 to $75 for a single or a double with a private bathroom. The entire host home rents for $225. There is no minimum stay and cancellation requires 72 hours notice with a $10 fee
CREDIT CARDS	MC, Visa
BREAKFAST	Full breakfast is served in the dining room or on the Redwood deck and includes spinach souffle, hot baked bread, orange or banana smoothie, fresh fruit, jam, and coffee.Vegetarians are welcome and special meals are available.
AMENITIES	Spa under a gazebo, flower gardens, boulders and trails, complimentary refreshments.
RESTRICTIONS	No smoking inside, children over 12 are welcome. The outdoor cat is Peggy Sue "who loves to go on the trail out back with the guests."
REVIEWED	*AAA Bed & Breakfast Guide—Northern and Central California, Bed & Breakfast —A Selected Guide, The Best of the Sierra Nevada, The Best of Gold Country*
MEMBER	Yosemite-Mariposa Bed & Breakfast Association

DUBORD'S RESTFUL NEST

4274 Buckeye Creek Road, Mariposa, CA 95338   209-742-7127
Huguette Dubord, Resident Owner   FAX 209-742-6888
French spoken

LOCATION	Near the western edge of Yosemite National Park in Mariposa. Guest will be given specific directions or met if need be.
OPEN	All year
DESCRIPTION	A two-story 1984 country ranch on 11 acres.
NO. OF ROOMS	Three rooms have a private entrance and private bathroom. Huguette recommends the Guest House.
RATES	Year round rates for a double with private bathroom are $75 and $85 for the guesthouse. November through March there is a 12% discount. Minimum two night stay required, two days advance notice for cancellation plus $10 fee.
CREDIT CARDS	Amex, MC, Visa, Discover
BREAKFAST	Full breakfast served in the dining room includes French toast, beignets, casseroles, fancy jello, crepes, quiche, homemade jam and muffins from "the little French lady who is always cooking".
AMENITIES	Private entrances, fishing pond, swimming pool, TV in rooms, phone, snacks, movies.
RESTRICTIONS	No smoking inside, children are welcome. A Labrador and a Poodle love children and are very gentle.
MEMBER	California Association of Bed and Breakfast Inns, Yosemite Bed and Breakfast Association
KUDOS/COMMENTS	"Warm friendly hosts, and nice grounds - good breakfast - Guest house was comfortable."

THE EAGLE'S NEST

6308 Jerseydale Road, Mariposa, CA 95338   209-966-3737
Ted & Carol Galas, Resident Owners

FINCH HAVEN

4605 Triangle Road, Mariposa, CA 95338   209-966-4738
Bruce Fincham, Resident Owners

GRANNY'S GARDEN

7333 Highway 49 North, Mariposa, CA 95338   209-377-8342
David & Dixie Trabucco, Resident Owners

MARIPOSA HOTEL & INN

5029 *Highway 140, Mariposa, CA 95338*   *209-966-4676*
Mac & Lyn Maccarone, Resident Owners
Italian spoken

LOCATION	In the center of town between 5th and 6th Streets.
OPEN	All year
DESCRIPTION	A 1901 two-story restored Gold Country stage stop with "yesteryear decor" that is on both the National and California Historic Registers.
NO. OF ROOMS	Six rooms with private bathrooms. Lyn likes Alice's room.
RATES	High season, April through October, rates are $68 to $95 for a single or a double with private bathroom and low season, November through March, rates are $59 to $85 for a single or a double with a private bathroom. There is a minimum stay on holiday weekends and cancellation requires three days notice.
CREDIT CARDS	Amex, Diners Club, Discover, MC, Visa
BREAKFAST	Continental Plus is served in the dining area of the lobby or the veranda and includes juice, coffee, tea, hot chocolate, muffins, sweet rolls and choice of cereal.
AMENITIES	Cable TV, tape players, radios, clocks, hairdryers, in-room coffee/tea, bird watching, wine tasting, seasonal horse and buggy stop at front door, air conditioning, refreshments.
RESTRICTIONS	Smoking on the veranda only, no pets, children over four are welcome. The resident Toy Poodle is Micki the Bellman who is quiet and sociable...and proud of his name...TI
REVIEWED	*The Definitive California Bed & Breakfast Touring Guide, The Best of the Gold Country, Northern California Best Places, Northern California Handbook.*
MEMBER	Yosemite-Mariposa B&B Association
RATED	AAA 2 Diamonds

MEADOW CREEK RANCH B&B INN

2669 Triangle Road, Mariposa, CA 95338   209-966-3843
Bob & Carol Shockley, Resident Owners
Some Spanish spoken

LOCATION	From Mariposa, 11.5 miles from Highway 140 turn off. Visible from Highway 49 south at corner of Triangle Road.
OPEN	All year
DESCRIPTION	An 1858 two-story ranch house and cottage furnished with American and European antiques.
NO. OF ROOMS	One room has a private bathroom, three rooms share three bathrooms. The Country Cottage, with private bathroom, is a favorite.
RATES	Year round rates for a single or double with a private bathroom are $80 to $85, and $70 to $75 for a single or double with a shared bathroom. No minimum stay, seven day cancellation policy.
CREDIT CARDS	Amex, MC, Visa, Discover
BREAKFAST	Full breakfast served in the dining room includes fresh fruit compote, French toast, ham, fried apples, or various pancakes with bacon and baked eggs.
AMENITIES	Library, old water wheel amd porch.
RESTRICTIONS	No smoking in buildings, no pets, children over 12 years old welcome. Watch for Poopie, the ranch dog and resident cats...Did Poopie have a say about this name...TI
REVIEWED	*Bed and Breakfast California, Best of the Gold Country, Northern California Best Places*
MEMBER	Yosemite/Mariposa Bed and Breakfast Association

OAK MEADOWS, TOO

5263 Highway 140, Mariposa, CA 95338   209-742-6161
Francie Starchman. Resident Owner

THE PELENNOR BED & BREAKFAST

3871 Highway 49 South, Mariposa, CA 95338   *209-966-2832*
Dick & Gwen Foster, Resident Owners

LOCATION	From Mariposa go south on Highway 49 for 5.5 miles, turn right in drive directly across from the Bootjack Volunteer Fire Station and follow signs.
OPEN	All year, but when the Fosters "occasionally go off for a few days," there is no breakfast but a slightly cheaper rate.
DESCRIPTION	A 1986 two-story "box" with "very basic Scottish tartans" interior, on 15 wooded acres.
NO. OF ROOMS	Four rooms share two bathrooms.
RATES	Year round rate for a single with shared bathroom is $35 and a double with a shared bathroom is $45. The entire B&B rents for $140. There is no minimum stay and cancellation requires one day's notice.
CREDIT CARDS	No
BREAKFAST	Full breakfast is served in the main house and includes meat, eggs, english muffin, cereal, fruit, orange juice or other juices, hash browns and beverages.
AMENITIES	Both of the owners play bagpipes which is an acquired taste but one that we approve of...TI, darts and bumper pool in the common area, spa, lap pool and sauna outside, walking and jogging paths.
RESTRICTIONS	Smoking outside only, the resident Scottie is called Angus Dhu and the cat is called Snowy.
REVIEWED	*Yosemite-Mariposa B&B Association*

POPPY HILL

5218 Crystal Aire Drive, Mariposa, CA 95338   *209-742-6273*
Tom & Mary Ellen Kirn, Resident Owners

SCHLAGETER HOUSE

5038 Bullion Street, Mariposa, CA 95338   *209-966-2471*
Roger & Lee McElligott, Resident Owner

SHIRL'S

4870 Triangle Road, Mariposa, CA 95338   209-966-2514
Shirley Fiester, Resident Owner

WINDSOR FARMS B&B

5636 East Whitlock Road, Mariposa, CA 95338   209-966-5592
Donald & Janice Haag, Resident Owner

McCLOUD

STONEY BROOK INN BED & BREAKFAST

309 West Colombero Road, McCloud, CA 96057   916-964-3106
Keith & Shelby Drotar, Managers

MENDOCINO

A town too beautiful for its own good, settled in the 19th century by lumbermen from Maine and noted for its Cape Cod architecture. Dress for the weather and head outdoors to Mendocino Headlands State Park, and the falls in Russian Gulch State Park. There's always beachcombing. In town, the Art Center is the best place to go for cultural events. Doings: Whale Festival in March; ten Heritage Days in May; and a two-week Mendocino (classical) Music Festival in July, outdoors on the Headlands. On the wild and rugged North Coast, halfway between San Francisco and Eureka via scenic Hwy. 1.

1021 MAIN STREET

Main at Evergreen, Mendocino, CA 95460   707-937-5150
Carl Solomon, Resident Owner

AGATE COVE INN

11201 Lansing Street, Mendocino, CA 95460   707-937-0551
Sallie McConnell & Jake Zahavi, Resident Owners   800-527-3111
Spanish, Danish, Hebrew and French spoken   (CA only)

LOCATION	From Highway 1 north at Mendocino take the first Lansing Street exit, the inn is 1/2 mile north.
OPEN	All year
DESCRIPTION	An 1863 farmhouse and cottages with country decor on a bluff above the Pacific Ocean.
NO. OF ROOMS	Ten rooms with private bathrooms. Obsidian Cottage at the top of the list.
RATES	High season rates July through October are $89 to $189. Off season rates November through June are $79 to $165. Weekends are always high season rates.There is a two night minimum stay on weekends, three nights on holidays. Cancellation requires seven days notice and a $15 fee.
CREDIT CARDS	Amex, MC, Visa, Discover
BREAKFAST	Full breakfast served in dining room, includes fresh fruit with yogurt, home-made breads, eggs benedict, French toast or omelettes, coffee and tea.
AMENITIES	Fresh flowers in each guest room as well as a decanter of sherry and newspaper delivered each morning. All but one room has TV, fireplaces and decks.
RESTRICTIONS	No smoking, no pets. Resident critters include lovable Wheaton Terriers, Sadie and Willi Wonka, and a tabby cat, Lulu.
MEMBER	Professional Association of Innkeepers International, California Association of Bed and Breakfast Inns
RATED	AAA 2 Diamonds
KUDOS/COMMENTS	"Compete privacy, comfortable rooms with wood stoves and a path to the beach right outside your room. . . . Delicious breakfast"

BLAIR HOUSE INN

45110 Little Lake Street, Mendocino, CA 95460   *707-937-1800*
Norm Fluhrer, Manager   *FAX 707-937-2444*

LOCATION	In the heart of Mendocino on the corner of Ford and Little Lake Street, three blocks form the ocean.
OPEN	All year
DESCRIPTION	An 1888 two-story Victorian furnished with antiques and Persian rugs. Jessica Fletcher's home in "Murder She Wrote."
NO. OF ROOMS	Three rooms with private bathrooms and two rooms share one bathroom. Norm's best room is Angela's Suite.
RATES	Year round rates are $85 to $130 for a single or double with private bathroom; $75 to $85 for a single or double with shared bathroom and $115 to $130 for a suite. There is a two day minimum stay on weekends and a three day minimum stay on holiday weekends. Cancellation requires five days notice.
CREDIT CARDS	MC, Visa
BREAKFAST	Continental breakfast is served at the Mendocino Bakery down the street. The Inn gives each person a $3.50 ticket to use at the bakery.
AMENITIES	Complimentary bottle of wine
RESTRICTIONS	No smoking
MEMBER	Professional Association of Innkeepers International

BREWERY GULCH INN

9350 North Coast Highway 1, Mendocino, CA 95460   707-937-4752
Authur Ciancutti, Resident Owner

LOCATION	One mile south of town.
OPEN	All year
DESCRIPTION	An 1862 country inn with gardens and Victorian furnishings.
NO. OF ROOMS	Three rooms with private bathrooms and two rooms share two bathrooms. Linda the manager suggests the Garden Room.
RATES	High season, May through October, rates are $85 to $110 for a single or a double with a private bathroom, $110 to $130 for a suite. Low season, November through April (excluding holidays), rates are $75 to $95 for a single or a double, $95 to $115 for a suite. There is a two night minimum stay on the weekends and cancellation requires five days notice.
CREDIT CARDS	MC, Visa
BREAKFAST	Full breakfast is served in the dining room and includes quiche and scones, banana pancakes, fruit, orange juice and coffee.
AMENITIES	Wine and port on Saturday night, limited handicapped access.
RESTRICTIONS	No smoking except on the outside porch, children over 15 are welcome. The resident dog is Cindy and the Manx cat is Mickey.
REVIEWED	*America's Wonderful Little Hotels & Inns, The Best Places to Kiss in Northern California*

THE HEADLANDS INN

Corner of Howard & Albion Streets, Mendocino, CA 95460   707-937-4431
David & Sharon Hyman, Resident Owners

LOCATION	Turn into the village of Mendocino at the stop light (Little Lake Road), go west two blocks and turn left onto Howard and go two blocks to the corner of Howard and Albion.
OPEN	All year
DESCRIPTION	A three-story 1868 New England Victorian Salt Box furnished with "casual" antiques.
NO. OF ROOMS	Six rooms with private bathrooms. Try the Strauss room.
RATES	Year round rates are $85 to $180 for a single or double with a private bathroom. There is a two night minimum stay on the weekends and three and four night minimum stay on holiday weekends. Cancellation requires seven days notice, 14 for holidays.
CREDIT CARDS	No
BREAKFAST	Full breakfast served in guestroom includes a hot entree that changes daily, fresh baked bread, fresh fruit and choice of beverage.
AMENITIES	Afternoon tea with mineral waters, cookies, nuts, breads, fresh cut flowers, some rooms have robes, feather beds, down comforters, European reading pillows, woodburning fireplaces in rooms, phone, fresh fruit and candy in parlor. English garden and ocean views.
RESTRICTIONS	No smoking, no pets, children over 12 are welcome.
REVIEWED	*50 Romantic Getaways, Best Places to Kiss in Northern California, California Country Inns and Iteneraries, Bed & Breakfast California, Country Inns West Coast, Country Inns and Back Roads.*
MEMBER	California Association of Bed & Breakfast Inns, California Lodging Industry Association

JOHN DOUGHERTY HOUSE

571 Ukiah Street, Mendocino, CA 95460   707-937-5266
David & Marion Wells, Resident Owners

LOCATION	Take Mendocino exit from Highway 1. In the center of town
OPEN	All year
DESCRIPTION	An 1867 two-story Salt box furnished with Early American antiques.
NO. OF ROOMS	Six rooms with private bathrooms. Check out the Captain's Room.
RATES	Year round rates for a single or double with private bathroom $95-$165. Minimum stay on weekends, seven day cancellation policy.
CREDIT CARDS	MC, Visa, Discover
BREAKFAST	Full breakfast served buffet style includes various items that change daily, plus homemade scones and fresh local fruit.
AMENITIES	Color TV, refrigerators, ocean view verandas, English garden.
RESTRICTIONS	No smoking, no pets, children over 12 years old welcome. Three cats roam the gardens, Basil, Coriander and Tristan.

JOSHUA GRINDLE INN

44800 Little Lake Road, Mendocino, CA 95460   707-937-4143
Arlene & Jim Moorehead, Resident Owner   800-474-6353

LOCATION	At the edge of the village on Little Lake Road at Highway 1.
OPEN	All year
DESCRIPTION	An 1879 two-story New England farmhouse with an eclectic mix of early American and Shaker furnishings
NO. OF ROOMS	Ten rooms with private bathrooms. Pick the Grindle Room.
RATES	Year round rates are $90 to $155 for a single or double with a private bathroom. There is a two night minimum stay on weekends and cancellation requires seven days notice and a $10 fee.
CREDIT CARDS	Amex, MC, Visa
BREAKFAST	Full breakfast is served in the dining rooms and includes frittata, quiche or oven baked omelett, muffins, scones, or fresh seasonal fruit, yogurt, granola, cold cereals and beverages.
AMENITIES	Fresh fruit bowl, cream sherry and mineral water in the parlor, complimentary of bottle wine when you mention this book by title.
RESTRICTIONS	No smoking, no pets. The resident cat Sadie "loves our guests."
REVIEWED	*Weekends for Two in Northern California, Fifty Romantic Getaways, Karen Brown's California Country Inns & Itineraries, America's Wonder Little Hotels & Inns, Northern California Best Places*
MEMBER	Professional Association of Innkeepers International, California Association of Bed & Breakfast Inns
RATED	Mobil 2 Stars
KUDOS/COMMENTS	"A very nice inn."..."The best in Mendocino, comfortable, not intrusive"

MACCALLUM HOUSE

45020 Albion Street, Mendocino, CA 95460   707-937-0289
Nick Redding, Manager

MENDOCINO FARMHOUSE

43410 Comptche-Ukiah Road, Mendocino, CA 95460   707-937-0241
Margie & Bud Kamb, Resident Owners   FAX 707-937-1086

LOCATION	On Comptche-Ukiah Road 1.5 miles from Highway 1. Two miles from village of Mendocino.
OPEN	All year
DESCRIPTION	1976 two-story country farmhouse in a redwood forest with antique furnishings.
NO. OF ROOMS	Five rooms with private bathrooms. Margie recommends John's room or the Cedar room.
RATES	High season rates, May through September for a single or a double with private bathroom are $85 to $115. Off season rates, October through March, are $5 to $10 less. Two night minimum on weekends, three nights on holidays. Seven day cancellation policy.
CREDIT CARDS	MC, Visa
BREAKFAST	Full breakfast served in the dining room varies daily
AMENITIES	Fireplaces, pond, beach mats, piano, snacks fresh flowers, in-room refrigerators and coffeemakers and picnic baskets on request.
RESTRICTIONS	No smoking, no pets. Numerous dogs and cats: Lab/Retrievers, Molly and Sidney, and kitties, Tinker and Bubba...Bubba the cat...great name...TI
REVIEWED	*Karen Brown's California Country Inns and Itineraries, Country Inns and Backroads, Fodor's Bed and Breakfasts—West Coast*
MEMBER	Professional Association of Innkeepers International, California Association of Bed and Breakfast Inns

MENDOCINO VILLAGE INN

44860 Main Street, Mendocino, CA 95460   707-937-0246
Bill & Kathleen Erwin, Resident Owners   800-882-7029
French, Spanish and Tagalog spoken.

LOCATION	About a 1/4 mile west of Highway 1, across from the Presbyterion Church
OPEN	All year
DESCRIPTION	An three-story 1892 Queen Anne Victorian on the California Historic Register. Furnished with an eclectic mix of Victorian, early California furnishings.
NO. OF ROOMS	Eleven rooms with private bathrooms, two rooms share one bathroom and the best room is a "toss-up:" 8, 4 or 7.
RATES	Year round rates are $70 to $175 for a single or a double with a private or shared bathroom. There is two night minimum stay on the weekends, three on some holidays. Cancellation requires 72 hours notice and there is a $10 fee.
CREDIT CARDS	No
BREAKFAST	Full breakfast is served in the dining room and includes a souffle, blue cornmeal pancakes, omelette or other hot dish, fresh fruit, homemade baked goods, yogurt and beverages.
AMENITIES	Fresh flowers throughout the inn, sundeck, evening wine and snacks, daily newspaper, guest refrigerator and hadicapped accessible.
RESTRICTIONS	No smoking, no pets, children over 10 are welcome, "shirts and shoes in all common areas please." The there are many outside "panhandler" cats and eight Cockateils who "have a glee club."
REVIEWED	*Best Places to Kiss in Northern California, Fodor's Northern California.*

REED MANOR

44950 Little Lake Road, Mendocino, CA 95460   707-937-5446
Monte Reed, Resident Owner

SEA GULL INN

44960 Albion, Mendocino, CA 95460   707-937-5204
Marlene McIntyre & Bill Yearous, Managers

SEA ROCK BED & BREAKFAST INN

11101 Lansing Street, Mendocino, CA 95460   707-937-0926
Andy & Susie Plocher, Resident Owners
Some Spanish spoken

LOCATION	One half mile north of the village of Mendocino on Lansing Street.
OPEN	All year
DESCRIPTION	1960/1980 country cottages overlooking the ocean. Surrounded by century-old Cypress trees, lawns and gardens.
NO. OF ROOMS	Fourteen cottages with private bathrooms. Cottage #1 comes highly recommended.
RATES	High season rates, March 15 through December, for a cottage with private bathroom are $85 to $130, and $140 to $155 for two bedrooms and kitchens. Off season rates are 25% less midweek. Two night stay required on weekends, three days on holidays, cancellation accepted with two weeks notice with $20 service charge.
CREDIT CARDS	MC, Visa
BREAKFAST	Continental Plus breakfast served in the dining room, outside, or carried back to your cottage includes fruit salad, bagels, muffins, yogurt, breakfast breads and beverages.
AMENITIES	Mountain spring water in all rooms, TV/VCR, flowers, down pillows, comforters and some feather beds, fireplaces, some kitchens and two bedrooms available.
RESTRICTIONS	No smoking, no pets, children welcome.
REVIEWED	*Bed and Breakfast in California, Hidden Coast of California, Fifty Best Places to Kiss in Northern California*

STANFORD INN BY THE SEA

Coast Hwy. & Comptche-Ukiah Rd., Mendocino, CA 95460   707-937-5615
Joan & Jeff Stanford, Resident Owners   800-331-8884
Spanish, Japanese and German spoken   FAX 707-937-0305

LOCATION	South of the village, across Big River Bridge.
OPEN	All year
DESCRIPTION	A 1960-1994 Redwood Lodge that sits in meadow overlooking the ocean and Mendocino. Decorated with Ponderosa Pine and Redwood panelling.
NO. OF ROOMS	Twenty-three rooms with private bathrooms. Try a suite.
RATES	Year round rates are $160 to $190 for a single or a double with private bathroom. The suites are $200 to $255. There is a minimum stay on the weekends and cancellation requires seven days notice.
CREDIT CARDS	Amex, Diners Club, Discover, JCB, MC, Visa
BREAKFAST	Full breakfast served in the lobby includes Champagne, croissants, fritatas, quiches, freshly squeezed orange and grapefruit juice, fruit and granola.
AMENITIES	Hors d'oeuvres, organic vegetables served with juices in the evening, TV, VCRs, robes, refrigerators, woodburning fireplaces, telephones, coffee makers, wine and/or juice fresh flowers, down comforters and meeting facilites for 20 people.
RESTRICTIONS	No smoking. There are 40 resident critters including three dogs, 10 cats, 14 llamas, two horses, two rabbits, six swans and two geese... for the winner of the Northern California B&B Resident Critter Count Contest...TI
REVIEWED	*America's Wonderful Little Hotels & Inns, Weekend for Two in Northern California - 50 Romantic Getaways, Dog Lover's Companion, The Best Places to Kiss in Northern California, Country Inns and Backroads—California*
MEMBER	California Association of Bed & Breakfast Innkeepers, Professional Association of Innkeepers International
RATED	AAA 4 Diamonds

WHITEGATE INN BED & BREAKFAST

499 Howard Street, Mendocino, CA 95460   707-937-4892
George & Carol Bechtoff, Resident Owners   800-531-7282
Spanish spoken   *FAX 707-937-1131*

LOCATION
Turn west off Highway 1 at Little Lake, go to Howard Street and turn left to Ukiah.

OPEN
All year

DESCRIPTION
An 1883 two-story Victorian with guesthouse listed on the National and State Historic Registers. Furnished in French and Victorian antiques.

NO. OF ROOMS
Six rooms with private bathrooms. George recommends the French Rose room as the best in the house.

RATES
High season (June through December) rates for a single or double room with private bathroom $99 to $169, off season or midweek rates $20 less per night. Two night minimum stay on weekends, seven day cancellation policy with a $15 service charge.

CREDIT CARDS
Amex, MC, Visa

BREAKFAST
Full breakfast served in the dining room includes egg souffle, carmel apple French toast, muffins or scones, fresh fruit and beverages.

AMENITIES
Flowers, candy and fruit in rooms, some rooms have ocean views, fireplaces and TV's, English gardens, decks, gazebo, afternoon wine and hors d'oeuvres in the parlor.

RESTRICTIONS
No smoking, no pets, children over 10 years old are welcome, younger ages welcome in the guest house. Two colorful cats, Sienna and Violet, roam the grounds.

REVIEWED
Country Inns and Back Roads, Best Places to Kiss in Northern California, Northern California Weddings in Style, Bed and Breakfast Country Inns

MEMBER
Professional Association of Innkeepers International, California Association of Bed and Breakfast Inns, Mendocino Coast Innkeepers Association

RATED
Mobil 3 Stars

KUDOS/COMMENTS
"Great decor, and breakfast"

MILL VALLEY

This Bay Area residential community lined with BMWs had the good sense to locate at the base of triple-peaked Mount Tamalpais, and in affluent Marin County, where ecological diversity is a pride and joy. In town, visit Old Mill Park and the remains of the old sawmill for which the town was named. The main event is the Mill Valley Film Festival. Mount Tamalpais State Park, six miles west, covers 6,233 acres of coastal hill country, and endless hiking and biking trails wind to the summit. Cross the Golden Gate Bridge onto Highway 1.

MOUNTAIN HOME INN

810 Panoramic Highway, Mill Valley, CA 94941   415-381-9000
Lynn Saggese, Manager   FAX 415-381-3615
Spanish spoken

LOCATION	Heading north on Highway 101, take the Stinson Beach exit. After 2/3 mile turn left at the light, staying on Highway 1. After 2.6 miles turn right onto Panoramic Highway (signs say Mt. Tamalpais). Go .8 miles, at a four way intersection, take the high road, Panoramic. After 1.8 miles the inn is on the right.
OPEN	All year
DESCRIPTION	A three-story 1985 rustic inn with spactacular views and "rustic-elegant" furnishings.
NO. OF ROOMS	Ten rooms with private bathrooms. Lynn suggest deluxe room #1.
RATES	Year round rates are $131 to $215 for a single or double with a private bathroom. There is no minimum stay and a five day cancellation policy.
CREDIT CARDS	MC, Visa
BREAKFAST	Full breakfast is served in the dining room and includes a choice of spinach and mushroom omelette, Fench toast, eggs any style and muffins, yogurt and fruit. Lunch and dinner are also available.
AMENITIES	Phones in rooms, meeting facilities, handicapped acces, decks.
RESTRICTIONS	No smoking in 50% of the rooms, no pets.

MOKELUMNE HILL

It's only a block long, but remains of the once-bawdy and very rich Gold Rush town are still in evidence. On the Mokelumne River and handy to Pardee Reservoir, southeast of Sacramento via Highway 16 and 49.

HOTEL LEGER

8304 Main Street, Mokelumne Hill, CA 95245   *209-286-1401*
Marci Biagi & Joseph Rohde, Resident Owners   *FAX 209-286-1931*
Spanish and some German spoken

LOCATION	On Highway 49, midway between Jackson and San Andreas turn north on Main Street, 1/4 mile on the left.
OPEN	All year except for the first two weeks of January.
DESCRIPTION	A two-story 1852 hotel with "Rhylite Tuff" architecture that includes the old Calaveras Courthouse building and gold rush/Victorian interior. The hotel is on the State Historic Register.
NO. OF ROOMS	Seven rooms with private bathrooms and six rooms share six bathrooms. Try to get rooms 1, 2 or 13.
RATES	Year round rates are $60 to $90. There is a minimum stay on holiday weekends; cancellation requires seven days notice and a $10 cancellation fee.
CREDIT CARDS	Discover, MC, and Visa
BREAKFAST	Continental Plus is served and dinner is available.
AMENITIES	Swimming pool. The Courtroom hosts theatre performances in the spring and fall and is used for meetings, banquets and parties.
RESTRICTIONS	No smoking and no pets. There are two resident Australian Shepards, Bonnie and Thor and a potbelly pig called Buddy.
MEMBER	Calaveras County Lodging Association

MONTARA

Here the land juts out from the San Mateo Coastline, and the Montara State Beach (among several others) offers great bird- and whale-watching. Beachcombing and walking the sandy-rocky shore are reasons to escape from The City. South of San Francisco on Highway 1.

FARALLONE BED & BREAKFAST

1410 Main Street, Montara, CA 94037   *415-728-8200*
Ruth Johnson, Resident Manager

GOOSE & TURRETS B&B

835 George Street, Montara, CA 94037   *415-728-5451*
Raymond & Emily Hoche-Mong, Resident Owners   *FAX 415-728-0141*
Fluent French and halting Spanish spoken.

LOCATION	In Montara, turn east on 2nd Street, turn right on Main Street, turn left on 3rd Street, go 1/2 mile to the inn on the left (3rd Street changes to Kanoff and then George, "ignore the street signs").
OPEN	All year
DESCRIPTION	A two-story 1908 Italian villa with eclectic furnishings and collections from around the world.
NO. OF ROOMS	Five rooms with private bathrooms. Pick Hummingbird in the winter and Whale in the summer as the best rooms.
RATES	Year round rates are $85 to $110 for a single or a double with a private bathroom. There is no minimum stay and cancellation requires three days notice.
CREDIT CARDS	Amex, Discover, MC, Visa
BREAKFAST	Full breakfast is served in the dining room and changes daily. As an example, it might be smoked salmon and cream cheese on bagel, Scottish oatmeal, crumpets florentine, etc. Special meals available with one weeks notice.
AMENITIES	Down comforters and towel warmers, swing, hammock, bocce ball pista and fountains in the garden, Afternoon tea with savories and sweets. Emily will take guest on walks in the Pescadero Marsh.
RESTRICTIONS	No smoking, no pets. Three geese, Mrs. Goose, Piper and Romeo, "sometimes live up to their reputations."
REVIEWED	America's Wonderful Little Hotels & Inns, Bed & Breakfast California, Northern California Handbook, Bay Area Backroads, Food & Lodging Guide.
MEMBER	Professional Association of Innkeepers International

MONTE RIO

Essentially an old resort town, this is home of the infamous Bohemian Grove, elite all-male playground of San Francisco's Bohemian Club, founded in the 1920s by such literary anarchists as Jack London and Ambrose Bierce. In July, the Bohos arrive by private helicopters, stretch limos, or under cover of the dark of night. Just north of Bodega Bay via Hwy. 1 and 116. It comes to life in a big way on July Fourth, and it's handy to the beach.

HIGHLAND DELL INN

21050 River Boulevard, Monte Rio, CA 95462   707-865-1759
Glenn Dixon & Anthony Patchett, Resident Owners   800-767-1759
                                                  FAX 707-865-2732

LOCATION	From Guerneville take Highway 116 four miles to Monte Rio, left on to Bohemian Highway, across bridge, the first left is River Boulevard.
OPEN	All year except for December 1 through 20.
DESCRIPTION	A 1906-1908 two-story Germanic redwood lodge on the Russian River with period antiques.
NO. OF ROOMS	Eight rooms with private bathrooms and two rooms share one bathroom. Try the Bohemian suite.
RATES	Year round rates are $75 to $120 for a single or a double with a private bathroom, $75 to $85 for a single or a double with a shared bathroom and $160 to $225 for a suite. The entire lodge rents for $1,000. There is a minimum stay on weekends and holidays and cancellation requires 10 days notice, 30 days for holidays.
CREDIT CARDS	Amex, Discover, JCB, MC, Visa
BREAKFAST	Full breakfast is served buffet style in the dining room and includes egg dishes, Dutch babies, French toast, bacon, sausage, fresh fruit, juices, fresh baked coffee cake and croissants. Dinner is available.
AMENITIES	Telephone in rooms, TV/VCR in suites, homemade truffles upon arrival in room, pool, unusual collection of personal amenities and meeting room for up to 20.
RESTRICTIONS	No smoking, pets limited to 35 pounds and certain rooms. The resident golden retriever mix is called Lady who, "smiles upon arrival" Sure...TI
REVIEWED	*Ultimate California, Bed, Breakfast & Bike Northern California, Bed & Breakfasts of Northern California*
MEMBER	California Lodging Industry Association, California Hotel & Motel Association
RATED	Mobil 2 Stars

HOUSE OF A THOUSAND FLOWERS

PO Box 369, Monte Rio, CA 95462   707-632-5571
Dave Silva, Resident Owner

HUCKLEBERRY SPRINGS

PO Box 400, Monte Rio, CA 95462   707-865-2683
Suzanne Greene, Resident Owner   800-822-2683
Spanish, Italian spoken.   FAX 707-865-2683

LOCATION	Take Russian River Resorts exit west from Santa Rosa, travel 23 miles to Monte Rio; left across bridge, then immediate right on Main Street. Travel 1 mile to Tyrone and right for one-half mile up to sign for lodge.
OPEN	March to December 15
DESCRIPTION	1987 contemporary California Country Inn with eclectic furnishings on 56 acres.
NO. OF ROOMS	Six rooms with private baths
RATES	Singles with private bathroom $125; double with private bathroom $145; guesthouses $145; entire B&B $600. Minimum stay required. Reservation/cancellation policy: seven days.
CREDIT CARDS	Amex, MC, Visa
BREAKFAST	Full breakfast served in guestrooms.
AMENITIES	Fresh flowers, hair dryers, hillside spa, pool, deck.
RESTRICTIONS	No smoking, no pets. Children over 15 year of age are welcome. Resident dog and cats and Rocky the Racoon, "who can eat your lunch."
REVIEWED	*Northern California Best Places; Recommended Country Inns: West Coast; The Complete B&B Inns & Guesthouses; The Best B&B and Country Inns West.*
MEMBER	California Association of Bed & Breakfast Inns, Country Inns of Russian River

MORAGA

In the hills behind Oakland are some amazing natural wonders to explore, among them: serene and wonderful Redwood and Chabot Regional Parks and Sibley Volcanic Preserve. Nice.

HALLMAN BED & BREAKFAST

309 Constance Place, Moraga, CA 94556   510-376-4318
Frank & Virginia Hallman, Resident Owners

LOCATION	Five miles south of the Orinda exit off of Highway 24.
OPEN	All year
DESCRIPTION	A 1970 contemporary ranch host home with contemporary furnishings.
NO. OF ROOMS	Two rooms share one bathroom.
RATES	Year round rates are $60 for a single or a double with shared bathroom. If a family takes both rooms the rate is $90. There is no minimum stay and cancellation requires three days notice.
CREDIT CARDS	No
BREAKFAST	Full breakfast is served in the dining room and includes fresh fruit, choice of egg dish or pancakes or French toast, with juice, muffins and coffee.
AMENITIES	TV and private telephone, robes, hot tub and swimming pool.
RESTRICTIONS	No smoking, no pets
REVIEWED	*Bed & Breakfast North America, Annual Directory of American Bed & Breakfasts, Walking From Inn to Inn—San Francisco Bay Area*

MOSS BEACH

Named for the moss that adorns the sea rocks at low tide. A significant reason to be here is James V. Fitzgerald State Park and Marine Reserve. Its 30 acres of tidepools make it one of the state's most diverse intertidal regions. Low tide is the best time to explore. On the San Mateo Coastline, Highway 1.

SEAL COVE INN

221 Cypress Avenue, Moss Beach, CA 94038   415-728-7325
Karen & Rick Herbert, Resident Owners   800-995-9987
Spanish, French and German spoken   FAX 415-728-4116

LOCATION	Six miles north of Half Moon Bay on Highway 1, turn west on Cypress.
OPEN	All year except Christmas week.
DESCRIPTION	A 1991 two-story inn styled after an English country home with a traditional interior of antiques and original art. The Inn sits on a hillside overlooking the ocean.
NO. OF ROOMS	Ten rooms with private bathrooms. Karen recommends the Fitgerald as her best room.
RATES	Year round rates are $165 to $185 for a double with a private bathroom and $250 for a suite. The entire B&B may be rented mid-week. There is a minimum stay on holiday weekends, cancellation requires seven days notice and a $20 cancellation fee. Reservations must be guaranteed with a credit card.
CREDIT CARDS	Amex, Discover, MC and Visa.
BREAKFAST	Full breakfast is served in the dining room and includes fresh fruit, juice and a hot entree that varies daily, e.g., French toast, egg souffle, etc. Guests may option for Continental breakfast in the room.
AMENITIES	Evening buffet of wine and hors d' ourvres. Each room has a refrigerator stocked with wine and sodas, TV & VCR, wood-burning fireplaces, phones and "excellent reading lights." There is a 200 tape free movie library, popcorn, fresh flowers, daily newspapers, turn-down service, evening chocolates, a five to 14 person conference room and one handicapped access guestroom.
RESTRICTIONS	No smoking and no pets.
REVIEWED	*Best of Northern California, Northern California Best Places, America's Wonderful Little Hotels & Inns, Hidden Coast of California, Recommended Country Inns, West Coast, Jan Peverill's Inn Places for Bed & Breakfast, Karen Brown's California Country Inns & Itineraries.*
MEMBER	California Association of Bed & Breakfast Inn
RATED	Mobil 4 Stars
AWARDS	One of the Twelve Best for 1993, Country Inns Magazine.
KUDOS/COMMENTS	"Special breakfast and lots of outside areas to explore." "Lovely location, great service so close to San Francisco."

MOUNT SHASTA

At the foot and always in the shadows of towering Mt. Shasta, the largest volcano (extinct or just dormant?) in the U.S. From here, head to the Sisson Fish Hatchery and Park, and outdoor recreation at Lake Siskiyou. North of Redding via I-5.

DREAM INN

326 Chestnut Street, Mount Shasta, CA 96067   *916-926-1536*
David Ream, Resident Owner   *FAX 916-926-1536*
Spanish spoken

LOCATION	From Interstate 5, take Mount Shasta Central exit. Head "mountain bound" on Lake Street, turn left on Chestnut, inn is five doors down on your left.
OPEN	All year
DESCRIPTION	Two-story restored 1904 Victorian with family antiques and original wainscoting.
NO. OF ROOMS	One room with private bathroom, four rooms share two bathrooms.
RATES	Year round rates are $60 to $80.
CREDIT CARDS	Amex, MC, Visa
BREAKFAST	Full breakfast served in the dining room includes juices, granola, pancakes, waffles, eggs, hashbrowns breads coffee and tea.
AMENITIES	Front porch complete with classic swing and rocking chairs, back patio with lily pond, fireplaces.
RESTRICTIONS	No smoking, no pets. Be sure to pet the Black Lab, Noel.
MEMBER	American Bed and Breakfast Association, California Association of Bed and Breakfast Inns

MOUNT SHASTA RANCH
BED & BREAKFAST

1008 W. A. Barr Road, Mount Shasta, CA 96067   916-926-3870
Bill & Mary Larsen, Resident Owners   FAX 916-926-6882

LOCATION	Southwest 1.5 miles from Mt. Shasta City, off Interstate 5. Follow signs to Lake Siskiyou. The inn is on the corner of Ream Avenue and W.A. Barr Road.
OPEN	All year
DESCRIPTION	A two-story 1923 ranch with Dutch gambrel roof, carriage house and cottage with Victorian furnishings.
NO. OF ROOMS	Four rooms with private bathrooms and five rooms share five bathrooms and two bedroom cottage.
RATES	Year round rates are $70 to $80 for a single or a double with a private bathroom. A single or a double with a shared bathroom is $50 to $60 and the cottage rents for $95 to $110. There is a minimum stay on holidays and summer weekends and cancellation requires 72 hours notice.
CREDIT CARDS	Amex, Discover, MC, Visa
BREAKFAST	Full country style breakfast served in the dining room includes juice, fresh fruit, entree, meat, breads and beverages.
AMENITIES	Drinks and snacks, game room with piano, ping-pong and pool tables, outside spa, robes available for spa, TV, meeting room in dining room.
RESTRICTIONS	No smoking. The resident critters include a parrot named Ahab who "talks a lot", and three dogs, Mah Lee, Mokie and Lady.
REVIEWED	*Bed, Breakfast & Bike Northern California*
KUDOS/COMMENTS	"Spacious, beautiful views, sumptuous breakfasts, gracious hosts."

WARD'S BIG FOOT RANCH

1530 Hill Road, Mount Shasta, CA 96067   916-926-5170
Phil & Barbara Ward, Resident Owners   800-926-1272

LOCATION	Two miles from downtown Mount Shasta. Take Central Mount Shasta exit, go west .5 mile, turn north on North Old Stage Road, exactly one mile from the Fish Hatchery turn left (west), go .3 mile to Ward's, on the left on Hill Road.
OPEN	All year
DESCRIPTION	1960 Ranch style home with country English, French and some antiques furnishings.
NO. OF ROOMS	Two rooms with private bathrooms.
RATES	Year round rates for a single or double with private bathroom are $55 to $90. Two days cancellation notice required for full refund.
CREDIT CARDS	No
BREAKFAST	Full breakfast served in the dining room includes fruit, meat, eggs, pancakes or popovers, Dutch babies and beverages.
AMENITIES	Flowers, robes, phone available, hot tub on deck, baby grand piano and stereo in living room, cheese and crackers, horse boarding by arrangement.
RESTRICTIONS	Smoking allowed outside, no pets. Resident friendly pets of all sizes include Bobbin the llama, Jasper the donkey, two Goldens, Buffer and Baron and a "Happy" Cockapoo.
REVIEWED	*Best Places to Stay in California, Northern California Guide, Bed and Breakfast Homes Directory*
MEMBER	International Bed and Breakfast Exchange, California Association of Bed and Breakfast Inns
KUDOS/COMMENTS	"Super setting that is peaceful with a creek meandering through the property and super Mt. Shasta view."..."Great hosts, nice cottage for romantic couple, they go out of their way to make the place very comfortable and romantic."..."Friendly hosts in a relaxing, woodsy atmosphere."

MUIR BEACH

THE PELICAN INN

10 Pacific Way, Muir Beach, CA 94965   415-383-6000
Barry Stock, Resident Manager

MURPHYS

This is a laid-back, one-street town in Gold Country, so just sit awhile. Things to do: Oldtimers Museum, the Town Park, wineries, and Mercer Caverns. Southeast of Sacramento via Hwy. 49, on Scenic Hwy. 4.

DUNBAR HOUSE 1880

271 Jones Street, Murphys, CA 95247   209-728-2897
Bob and Barbara Costa, Resident Owners   800-225-3764, ext 321
                                                  FAX 209-728-1451

LOCATION	From Highway 4, turn left on Main Street, the inn is across from the Melliaire Winery.
OPEN	All year
DESCRIPTION	An 1880 two-story, Italianate and English Gardens with country Victorian furninshings on the State Historic Register.
NO. OF ROOMS	Four rooms with private bathrooms. Barbara prefers the Cedar room for special guests.
RATES	Year round rates, are $105 to $135 for a single, $115 to $145 for a double, $155 for the suite. There is a minimum stay on weekends, cancellations requires five days notice.
CREDIT CARDS	Amex, MC, Visa
BREAKFAST	Full gourmet breakfast served in the dining room, guest room, or garden includes freshly ground coffee, teas, fruit with Grand Marnier cream, bacon-artichoke, frittata, lemon scones, orange juice spritzer.
AMENITIES	Fresh flowers, fireplaces, Jacuzzi spa, TV/VCRs, classic video library, refrigerators stocked with complimentary wine, phones, hair dryers, afternoon appetizer buffet, down comforters, air conditioning and woodburning stoves.
RESTRICTIONS	No smoking, no pets, children over 10 years of age welcome. Smiling Cocker Spaniel, Cody.
REVIEWED	*Northern California Best Places, Karen Brown's California Country Inns and Itineraries, Country Inns and Back Roads, The Best Places to Kiss in Northern California, Bed and Breakfast California, The Non-Smokers Guide to B&Bs*
MEMBER	Professional Association of Innkeepers International, American Bed and Breakfast Association, California Association of Bed and Breakfast Inns
RATED	ABBA 3 Crowns

MURPHYS HISTORIC HOTEL & LODGE

457 Main Street, Murphys, CA 95247   *209-728-3444*
Michael Lane, Manager   *800-532-7684*
Spanish, French and German spoken (varies).   *FAX 209-728-1590*

LOCATION   Eighty-five miles south of Sacramento via Highways 49 and 4.

OPEN   All year

DESCRIPTION   An 1856 Gold Rush hotel that is on both the National and California
                    Historic Registers. It was just renovated and includes antique
                    furnishings.

NO. OF ROOMS   Twenty rooms with private bathrooms and nine rooms share four
                    bathrooms. Michael recommends the US Grant Suite.

RATES   Year round rates are $70 to $85 for a single or a double with a private or
                    a shared bathroom and $90 to $105 for a suite. There is a minimum stay
                    on holiday weekends and cancellation requires 24 hours notice.

CREDIT CARDS   Amex, Diners Club, Discover, MC, Visa

BREAKFAST   Continental breakfast is served in the dining room and includes fresh
                    fruit tray, home baked items, cereals and beverages. Full breakfast,
                    lunch and dinner are also available.

AMENITIES   Meeting and banquet facilities for 100, telephones, TV, special programs
                    throughout the year such as wild game feeds...We need a report back on
                    "wild game feeds", this being Murphys, we had some image of all the
                    local wildlife lined-up for dinner...TI

RESTRICTIONS   No smoking in dining room, no pets.

MEMBER   California Hotel-Motel Association, California Lodging Industry
                    Association

THE REDBUD INN

402 Main Street, Murphys, CA 95247　　　　　　　　209-728-8533
Jan & Steve Drammer, Resident Owners　　　　　　　800-827-8533
German and Spanish spoken　　　　　　　　　　FAX 209-728-9123

LOCATION	Nine miles east of Angels Camp on Highway 4, left on Main Street in Murphys.
OPEN	All year
DESCRIPTION	A two-story 1993 Country Victorian with Country Victorian and eclectic, upscale furnishings.
NO. OF ROOMS	Thirteen rooms with private bathrooms. Jan's best room is the Anniversary Suite.
RATES	Year round rates for a single or double with private bathroom are $90 to $155. The suite is $225 for the first night and $100 per consecutive night thereafter. There is a minimum stay on holiday weekends and cancellation requires three days notice.
CREDIT CARDS	Amex, Discover, MC, Visa
BREAKFAST	Full breakfast served in the dining room includes fresh fruit, orange juice, various breads, muffins, pastries, cereals, yogurt and daily hot entree such as "crab quiche with hollandaise, yesterday". Catered meals are available in the conference room.
AMENITIES	Wine and hors d' oeuvres, NO TV or phones in rooms, horse and buggy tours, wine tasting, massage therapy, eight rooms with balconies, two with fireplaces, three with woodstoves, three with Jacuzzi tubs, one handicapped accessible, conference room for 29, "handsome, clever manager, patient owner-innkeeper and husband with beard."
RESTRICTIONS	No smoking, no pets, children over 21 are welcome, however one room or suite is available for families with small children.
REVIEWED	*California Tourism Guide, Guide to California Bed & Breakfast Inns, Historic Inns of California's Gold Country Cookbook and Guide.*
MEMBER	California Association of Bed & Breakfast Inn, Professional Association of Innkeepers International
KUDOS/COMMENTS	"Delightful."

MYERS FLAT

MYERS COUNTRY INN

12913 Avenue of the Giants, Myers Flat, CA 95554　　　　707-943-3259
John Moschetti & Theresa Jones, Resident Managers

NAPA

Wine Country starts here, at the southeast end of the fertile Napa Valley and just north of the Bay Area, from which hordes of wine tasters slosh forward. Once a silver lode, it's now the county's agricultural hub. But Victorians still stand in the old neighborhoods, and the Opera House is a restored showpiece. There's always action and special events at the Town Center, and major local events include the Chili Ball and Cookoff, and County Fair in July; and Concours d'Elegance in June. The town's pleasant Veterans Park on the Napa River is refreshing, or opt for Lake Berryessa for water recreation. From the Bay Area, try to avoid the valley's "wine spine," Hwy. 29, especially on weekends.

ARBOR GUEST HOUSE

1436 G Street, Napa, CA 94559   707-252-8144
Bruce and Rosemary Logan, Resident Owners

LOCATION	Take the Lincoln Avenue exit off Highway 29 in Napa. Go east until the second signal. Turn right onto Jefferson Street and go three short blocks to G Street. Turn right, the inn is two blocks on the right.
OPEN	All year
DESCRIPTION	1906 two-story Colonial and carriage house.
NO. OF ROOMS	Five rooms with private bathrooms. Winter Haven and Autumn Harvest rooms are "a toss-up" for best in the house.
RATES	High season rates, April through November, for a single or double with private bathroom are $85 to $165, and suites are $145 to $165. Off season rates, December through March, for all rooms are $75 to $135. Two night minimum stay on weekends and holidays. Cancellation policy requires 72 hours advance notice.
CREDIT CARDS	MC, Visa
BREAKFAST	Full gourmet breakfast served in the dining room, Carriage House room, guestrooms or on five garden patio areas includes fresh fruits, crustless quiche, French toast, chicken sausages, muffins, croissants scones coffee and tea,.
AMENITIES	Fireplaces, spa tubs, TV on request, handicapped room available.
RESTRICTIONS	No smoking, no pets, children over 10 years old are welcome.
REVIEWED	*Bed and Breakfast California, Napa-Sonoma Book*
MEMBER	Professional Association of Innkeepers International, Bed and Breakfast Inns of Napa Valley

BEAZLEY HOUSE

1910 First Street, Napa, CA 94559   707-257-1649
Jim & Carol Beazley, Resident Owners   800-559-1649
Spanish and German spoken   *FAX 707-257-1518*

LOCATION	Take the Central Napa exit from Highway 29, follow the road to the right and take a left on Second Street. Go 3/10s of a mile to Warren and turn left to First Street.
OPEN	All year
DESCRIPTION	A three-story 1902 Colonial Revival country inn and carriage house decorated with period antiques.
NO. OF ROOMS	There are 11 rooms with private bathrooms. Jim suggests the west loft as his best room.
RATES	Year round rates are $92.50 to $160 for a single with private bathroom, $105 to $185 for a double with a private bathroom and $160 to $185 for a suite. There is a minimum stay on the weekend and cancellation requires seven days notice.
CREDIT CARDS	Amex, MC, Visa
BREAKFAST	Full breakfast is served in the dining room and includes a hot dish such as quiche, five fruits, baked breads, muffins, juice, coffee and tea. Guest may take trays back to the room.
AMENITIES	Six rooms have fireplaces, five rooms have spas. One room has handicapped access and there is meeting space for up to 20 people.
RESTRICTIONS	No smoking and no pets. The resident cat who goes by the name of Mister does "owl and cigar store Indian imitations (honest!)" We would like a report back on this please...TI
MEMBER	Californian Association of Bed & Breakfast Inns, Professional Association of Innkeepers International.
RATED	Mobil 3 Stars

BLUE VIOLET MANSION

443 Brown Street, Napa, CA 94559   707-253-2583
Bob & Kathy Morris, Resident Owners   1-800-799-2583
                                                                        FAX 707-257-8205

LOCATION	Highway 29 north to Imola exit, right two stop lights, left on Coombs going north 1/2 mile, right on Laurel Street one block east, left on Brown Street, center of the block, in historic Old Town.
OPEN	All year
DESCRIPTION	A two-story 1886 Queen Anne Victorian with Victorian furnishings, on the National Historic Register.
NO. OF ROOMS	Eight rooms with private bathrooms. Pick the Blue Violet room.
RATES	High season, April through December, rates are $115 to $195 and the suite is $185 to $260 and can accommodate to four people. There is a 10% mid-week discount and low season rates are 20% lower on the weekend and 40% lower mid-week. There is a minimum stay and cancellation requires 10 days notice.
CREDIT CARDS	Amex, MC, Visa, JCB
BREAKFAST	Full breakfast is served in the dining room or guest room and includes freshly ground coffee, fruit juice, cakes, beverages and a main course such as quiche, French toast or waffles. Candlelight champagne dinners available.
AMENITIES	Three rooms with spas, two with balconies, five with fireplaces. All rooms have robes, iron, ironing board, silver wine goblets and books, TV in Sunroom.. Dessert buffet in the evenings, wine at check-in, concierge and garden gazebo.
RESTRICTIONS	No smoking, no pets, children welcome in the suite.
REVIEWED	*AAA Bed & Breakfast Guide—Northern California, 50 Most Romantic Inns in Northern California, Best Places to Kiss in Northern California*
MEMBER	California Association of Bed & Breakfast Inns, Bed & Breakfast Inns of Napa, Bed & Breakfast Inns of Napa Valley
AWARDS	Napa County Landmarks Award of Merit for HistoricPreservation 1993.
KUDOS/COMMENTS	"Beautifully restored mansion with all the little extra touches and warm, wonderful host and hostess."

THE CANDLELIGHT INN

1045 Easum Drive, Napa, CA 94558　　　　　　　　707-257-3717
Heather Kartes, Resident Owner

CEDAR GABLES INN

486 Coombs Street, Napa, CA 94559　　　　　　　　707-224-7969
Margaret and Craig Snasdell, Resident Owner　　FAX 707-224-4838

LOCATION	Four blocks south of downtown Napa on the corner of Oak and Coombs streets.
OPEN	All year, closed December 22 through December 27.
DESCRIPTION	A three-story 1892 English Country Manor that was designed by English architect Ernest Coxhead. Decorated with Victorian antiques.
NO. OF ROOMS	Six rooms with private bathrooms. Choose the Churchill Chamber with whirlpool tub and fireplace.
RATES	High season, April 15 to November 15, rates are $89 to $149 for a single or double with a private bathroom. Low season, November 16 to April 14, rates are $79 to $149 for a single or a double with a private bathroom. There is no minimum stay and cancellation requires seven days notice.
CREDIT CARDS	Amex. MC, Visa
BREAKFAST	Full breakfast is served in the dining room or sunroom and includes muffins & scones, fresh fruit and an entree such as French toast with sausage, fritata, crepes and belgian waffles plus beverages.
AMENITIES	Fireplace and whirlpool tubs in two rooms. Fresh flowers in common areas and guest rooms, wine, hors d' oeuvres each evening at the social hour. Large family room with fireplace and TV also serves as a small meeting room.
RESTRICTIONS	No smoking, no pets. The outside cat and dog are called Brandy and Krista respectively.
REVIEWED	*American and Canadian B&B Directory*
MEMBER	California Association of Bed & Breakfast Inns, Professional Association of Innkeepers International
AWARDS	1992 Award of Merit from the Napa County Landmarks Inc.
KUDOS/COMMENTS	"Great old house, hospitality is superb."

CHURCHILL MANOR B&B

485 Brown Street, Napa, CA 94559   *707-253-7733*
Joanna Guidotti & Brian Jensen, Resident Owners   *FAX 707-253-8836*
Spanish spoken

LOCATION	Beautiful downtown Napa at the corner of Oak and Brown
OPEN	All year
DESCRIPTION	A three-story 1889 Second Empire Mansion with Victorian furnishings and original carved redwood columns.
NO. OF ROOMS	Ten rooms with private bathrooms. Joanna thinks Edward's Room is her best.
RATES	Year round rates are $75 to $145 for a single or a double with a private bathroom. The entire inn rents for $1,090. There is two-night minimum stay when a Saturday is involved and cancellation requires five days notice.
CREDIT CARDS	Amex, Discover, MC, Visa
BREAKFAST	Full breakfast is served in the dining room or on the veranda and includes fresh fruits, home-made nut-breads & muffins, croissants, made-to-order omelettes or french toast and fresh ground coffee.
AMENITIES	Fresh flowers in the common areas and guest rooms, cookies & refreshments at check-in, two hour wine and cheese reception in the evening, tandem bicycles, grand piano and facilites for weddings, games, TV/VCR in common room.
RESTRICTIONS	No smoking, no pets, children over 12 are welcome. Ziggy the dog tolerates Zoe and Blackie who "are known to prowl the roof-line at night on search of cat-loving guests with open windows."
REVIEWED	*America's Woinderful Little Hotels & Inns, The Best Places to Stay in California, Best Places to Kiss in Northern California, 50 Most Romantic Getaways*
MEMBER	Professional Association of Innkeepers International, American Bed & Breakfast Association, Napa Bed & Breakfast Inns
RATED	ABBA 3 Crowns

COUNTRY GARDEN INN

1815 Silverado Trail, Napa, CA 94558 707-255-1197
Lisa & George Smith, Resident Owners FAX 707-255-3112

LOCATION	From Highway 29 south, take Trancas east to fork in the road signposted 121. Take the right hand fork signposted to Napa, the inn is 3/4 of a mile on the right.
OPEN	All year
DESCRIPTION	An 1850 carriage house with English country pine antique furnishing.
NO. OF ROOMS	Ten rooms with private bathrooms. Lisa likes a room called Hedgerow.
RATES	High season, April through November, rates are $115 to $130 for a single or a double with private bathroom, the suite is $175 to $195. Low season, December through March, rates are $110 to $125 for a single or a double with a private bathroom, the suite is $170 to $195. Weekday rates are lower. There is a two day minimum stay on weekends and cancellation requires 72 hours notice and 10% fee.
CREDIT CARDS	MC, Visa
BREAKFAST	Full breakfast is served in the dining room and includes fruit, homemade coffee cake, scones, hot entree such as buttermilk French toast with fresh strawberries and beverages.
AMENITIES	Large aviary with over 40 species of birds, ask about "Toot and Carmen", afternoon tea, happy hour with international cheese desserts.
RESTRICTIONS	No smoking, no pets, children over 16 are welcome. The outdoor cat is called Grey Cat and the dogs are Missee and Amber.
REVIEWED	*The Mobil Travel Guide, Country Inns of America: California, Recommended Country Inns—West Coast*
MEMBER	Professional Association of Innkeepers International, California Association of Bed & Breakfast Inns
RATED	Mobil 3 Stars

CROSSROADS INN

6380 Silverado Trail, Napa, CA 94558 707-944-0646
Nancy & Sam Scott, Resident Owners

THE ELM HOUSE

800 California Boulevard, Napa, CA 94559   *707-255-1831*
Christopher Green, Resident Manager   *800-788-4356*
French, Spanish and some Arabic spoken   *FAX 707-255-8609*

LOCATION	In Napa.
OPEN	All year
DESCRIPTION	A 1987 Queen Anne with French country furnishings.
NO. OF ROOMS	Sixteen rooms with private bathrooms. Christopher suggests room 207 as his best.
RATES	High season, April through October, rates are $90 to $145 for a single or a double with a private bathroom and $120 to $165 for a suite. Low season, November through March, rates are $70 to $110 for a single or a double with a private bathroom and suites are $100 to $140. There is no minimum stay and cancellation requires 72 hours notice.
CREDIT CARDS	Amex, MC, Visa
BREAKFAST	Continental Plus is served in the dining room and includes fresh fruits in season, hot scones, muffins and croissants, bananna bread, hard cooked eggs and beverages. Arrangements can be made for catered meals.
AMENITIES	Cable TV, telephones, honor bar, refrigerator, one handicapped access room, hot tub on private patio.
RESTRICTIONS	No pets. Max is the dog, he's Italian.
MEMBER	California Lodging Industry Association

HENNESSEY HOUSE

1727 Main Street, Napa, CA 94559   707-226-3774
Andrea Lamar, Lauriann Delay, Resident Owners   FAX 707-226-2975
Spanish

LOCATION	North on Highway 29, take Lincoln Avenue East exit. After two lights, turn right on Main Street, go up six blocks on the right.
OPEN	All year
DESCRIPTION	An 1889 Queen Anne Victorian, listed on the National Historic Register, was refurbished in the early '80s. Repainted in five color "painted ladies" style to highlight original architectural details.
NO. OF ROOMS	Nine rooms with private bathrooms, one room with shared bathroom. Try the Bridal Suite, even if you don't qualify.
RATES	High season rates, May through November, for double with private bathroom are $100 to $130, the Carriage House is $130 to $155. Off season rates, December thorugh April, about 20% less. Two night minimum if staying over Saturday, 24 hour cancellation policy, $15 fee.
CREDIT CARDS	Amex, MC, Visa
BREAKFAST	Full hot breakfast served in the dining room includes pancakes, quiche, huevos rancheros, polenta, juice and fruit, granola, yogurt and beverages.
AMENITIES	Sherry in rooms, sauna, some rooms have whirlpool tubs, fireplaces, parlor with TV and fireplace, weekend wine and hors d'oeuvres.
RESTRICTIONS	No smoking, no pets, children welcome. The Russian Blue kitty is called Ralphina.
REVIEWED	*Best Places to Kiss in the Northwest, Wine Country Access*
MEMBER	American Bed and Breakfast Association

HILLVIEW COUNTRY INN

1205 Hillview Lane, Napa, CA 94558   707-224-5004
Al & Susie Hasenpusch, Resident Owners   FAX 707-224-6422

LOCATION	Take Highway 29 north. Turn left at Darms Lane, then trun right on Solano Avenue. Go about 1/2 block and turn left at the Hillview Country Inn gate.
OPEN	All year
DESCRIPTION	Newly remodeled two-story country farmhouse built in 1800's.
NO. OF ROOMS	Four bedrooms with private bathrooms. Sample the Vineyard Room.
RATES	High season, May through September, rates for a double with private bathroom are $150 to $175, entire inn rents for $625. Off season, October through January, rates for a double with private bathroom are $125 to $150, entire inn rents for $525. Two night minimum stay on weekends, cancellation policy requires five days notice and $15 charge per night.
CREDIT CARDS	Amex, MC, Visa, Diners Club, Discover
BREAKFAST	Full country breakfast is served in the dining room.
AMENITIES	Pool, vineyard views, dessert wines and brandy, hors d'oeurves, some TV's and fireplaces in rooms, meeting facilities.
RESTRICTIONS	No smoking, children over eight years old are welcome. Big Cat and Little Cat are the resident pets.
MEMBER	Napa Convention and Visitors Bureau, Napa Valley Tourist Bureau

INN ON RANDOLPH

411 Randolph, Napa, CA 94559   707-257-2886
Deborah Coffee, Resident Owner   FAX 707-257-8756
English only, "just ask my college Spanish teacher."

LOCATION	Within blocks of downtown Napa.
OPEN	All year
DESCRIPTION	A two-story 1860 Gothic Revival inn with a blend of antiques and comfortable furniture.
NO. OF ROOMS	Five rooms with private bathrooms. Deborah suggest a room called Autumn.
RATES	High season, May 15 to November 15, rates are $104 to $169 for a single or a double with a private bathroom, $144 to $159 for a suite. Low season, November 16 through May 14, rates are $84 to $149 for a single or a double with private bathroom, $124 to $139 for a suite and the entire inn rents for $565 to $740 depending on season. There is no minimum stay and cancellation requires ten days notice.
CREDIT CARDS	Amex, MC, Visa
BREAKFAST	Full breakfast is served in the dining room, sun room or garden deck and is varied with "a southern accent" and always includes fresh fruit, freshly baked breads, a hot entree and usually a side dish. Special meals and picnic baskets are available.
AMENITIES	Two rooms with fireplaces, two person tubs and balconies, in room telephone jacks, baby grand in dining room, refreshment bar and refrigerator, small meeting facilities, wine, champagne and in-room massage available.
RESTRICTIONS	No smoking inside, no pets.
REVIEWED	Opened June 1994.
MEMBER	Professional Association of Innkeepers International, Bed & Breakfast Innkeepers of Napa Valley

LA BELLE EPOQUE

1386 Calistoga Avenue, Napa, CA 94559 707-257-2161
Merlin & Claudia Wedepohl, Resident Owners 800-238-8070
FAX 707-226-6314

LOCATION	Take the First Street exit from Highway 29, go right to 2nd Street, left on 2nd to Jefferson, left on Jefferson to Calistoga, right one block on Calistoga to Seminary.
OPEN	All year
DESCRIPTION	A two-story 1893 Queen Anne Victorian with stained glass, crafted interiors and Victorian furnishings.
NO. OF ROOMS	Six rooms with private bathrooms. Claudia suggests the Victorian Garden as her best room.
RATES	High season, April through November and low season weekends, the rates are $110 to $145 for a single or a double with a private bathroom. Low season, December through March and week days November through July, the rates are $95 to $125. There is a minimum stay on weekends from April 1 through November 30 and cancellation requires five days notice.
CREDIT CARDS	Amex, Discover, MC, Visa
BREAKFAST	Full breakfast is served in the dining room or on the sun porch.
AMENITIES	TV, VCR, board games, evening wine and hors d'oeuvres served in the wine tasting room, square grand piano in dining room, fresh flowers in guestrooms, air conditioning, sherry in each guestroom, fireplaces, in-house massage.
RESTRICTIONS	No smoking, no pets, children over 10 are welcome. The silver tabby cat is called Samantha.
REVIEWED	*Bed & Breakfast California, Best Places to Kiss in Northern California, The Napa-Sonoma Book, Best of Wine Country, California B&B Inns, Bed & Breakfast in California*
MEMBER	American Bed & Breakfast Association, Napa Bed & Breakfast Inns
RATED	ABBA, A

LA RESIDENCE COUNTRY INN

4066 St. Helena Highway, Napa, CA 94558 707-253-0337
David Jackson & Craig Claussen, Resident Owners

THE NAPA INN

1137 Warren Street, Napa, CA 95449   707-257-1444
Dennis and Alicia Mahoney, Resident Owners   800-435-1144

LOCATION	Exit 1st Street off Highway 29. Turn left on California, right on Clay, left on Warren.
OPEN	All year except three-day Christmas holiday.
DESCRIPTION	Turn-of-the-century, three-story Queen Anne Victorian furnished with antiques.
NO. OF ROOMS	Six rooms with private bathrooms. The Grand Suite comes highly recommended.
RATES	High season rates June through November for a single or double with private bathroom $120 to $170 and suites $155 to $170. Off season rates December through May 10-20% less. Two night minimum stay on weekends, seven days notice required for cancellation, or forfeit one night's charges.
CREDIT CARDS	MC, Visa, Discover
BREAKFAST	Full breakfast served in the dining room varies each day and might include quiche, crepes, fruit, bread and beverages.
AMENITIES	Wine, cheese and biscuits, nuts, flowers, light refreshments after 7 p.m.
RESTRICTIONS	No smoking, no pets, children over 14 years old welcome.
MEMBER	Napa Bed and Breakfast Association

OLD WORLD INN

1301 Jefferson Street, Napa, CA 94559   707-257-0112
Diane Dumaine, Resident Owner

LOCATION	From Highway 29 take Lincoln Street exit. Head east, turn right on Jefferson Street.
OPEN	All year, except Christmas Eve and Christmas Day.
DESCRIPTION	1906 two-story Victorian with Scandinavian country decor.
NO. OF ROOMS	Eight rooms with private bathrooms. Diane recommends the Stockholm room.
RATES	Year round rates for a single or double with bathroom are $110 to $145. The entire inn can be rented for $1,010. Minimum two night stay on weekends, April through November. Seven day cancellation policy.
CREDIT CARDS	Amex, MC, Visa, Discover
BREAKFAST	Continental Plus served in the dining room includes hot entree, fresh fruit buffet, breads, muffins, croissants, coffee cake.
AMENITIES	Outdoor spa, wine in room, afternoon tea and cookies, wine and cheese social, evening desserts, parlor with fireplace and classical music.
RESTRICTIONS	No smoking, no pets, two person maximum per room. The resident cat is Kenya.
REVIEWED	*Best Places to Kiss in Northern California, Bed and Breakfast California, Best Places to Stay in Northern California, Country Inns and Backroads, Recommended Country Inns—West Coast*
MEMBER	Professional Association of Innkeepers International, California Association of Bed and Breakfast Inns, Napa Bed and Breakfast Inns
AWARDS	Mobil 2 Stars

STAHLECKER HOUSE

1042 Easum Drive, Napa, CA 94558   707-257-1588
Ethyl Stahlecker, Resident Owner

TALL TIMBERS CHALETS

1012 Darms Lane, Napa, CA 94558   707-252-7810
Mary Montes, Resident Owner

KUDOS/COMMENTS	"Each squeaky clean 1940's cottage is surrounded by fresh flowers and big trees."

TRUBODY RANCH BED & BREAKFAST

5444 St. Helena Highway, Napa, CA 94558   707-255-5907
Jeff & Mary Page, Resident Owners

LOCATION	Six miles north of Highway 29 and Trancas. Turn right on Washington Street, go north .5 mile. Turn right on Trubody Lane.
OPEN	All year, except Thanksgiving and Christmas.
DESCRIPTION	A 1872 Gothic Victorian farmhouse furnished with antiques is on the California State Historic Register. The compound includes 19th century barns, a watertower, blacksmith shop on 127 acre family vineyard.
NO. OF ROOMS	Three rooms with private bathrooms. The top Watertower Room is recommended.
RATES	High season rates, April 15 through November 15, for a single or double room with private bathroom are $115, and $145 to $225 for suites or guesthouses with private bathroom. Entire B&B rents for $115 to $225. Off season rates are 15% less. Minimum stay required during high season weekends.
CREDIT CARDS	Amex, MC, Visa
BREAKFAST	Continental breakfast includes fruit platter, homebaked muffins and coffee cakes and beverages.
AMENITIES	Fresh cut flowers from the garden, 360 degree view of surrounding valley, vinyard walks. Guesthouse has telephone, fireplace and soaking tub.
RESTRICTIONS	No smoking, no pets. Resident pets include two bob-tailed cats, Sparky and Poppy and designer chickens.
MEMBER	Inns of Napa Valley

NEVADA CITY

One of the state's prettiest and best preserved mining towns with lively and sophisticated overtones. Downtown is great to shop till you drop, or rest by Deer Creek in Pioneer Park. To do and see: the Historical Society Museum in Firehouse #1 (includes Donner Party leftovers); the Miners' Foundry Cultural Center; famous two-week Music in the Mountains Summer Festival in June; and Constitution Weekend in September offers Civil War Battles, and continuous fun entertainment. Handy to Englebright Lake State Recreation Area, and Malakoff Diggings State Historic Park (a ghostly legacy of hydraulic mining). From Sacramento, 64 miles northeast via I-80 and Hwy. 40. Or cruise the new Yuba-Donner Byway.

DEER CREEK INN

116 Nevada Street, Nevada City, CA 95959	*916-265-0363*
Chuck & Elaine Matroni, Resident Owners	*800-655-0363*
Italian spoken	*FAX 916-265-0980*

LOCATION	Located in "Gold Country", California. Take Freeway 49 north, exit at Broad Street, Nevada City. Inn is located at the edge of town.
OPEN	All year
DESCRIPTION	Three-story 1860 Queen Anne Victorian nestled in the trees with porches and verandas overlooking the Deer Creek.
NO. OF ROOMS	Five rooms with private bathrooms. Winifred's Room is the best in the house.
RATES	Year round rates for a single or double with private bathroom are $90 to $135. Two night minimum on holidays and designated weekends, seven day cancellation policy.
CREDIT CARDS	MC, Visa
BREAKFAST	Full breakfast served in the dining room or on the veranda overlooking the creek includes fresh fruit cup, entree choices including Eggs Florentine, onion baked potato, French toast and beverages.
AMENITIES	Wine and hors d'oeuvres each evening, wine or champagne for individual guests on special occasions, brownies/cookies "forever," chocolates and candies "everywhere," fresh flowers in rooms, 30-channel uninterrupted music, cable TV in main parlor only, small meeting facilities.
RESTRICTIONS	No smoking indoors. You will be greeted by Murphy, the Sheltie.
REVIEWED	*Best Places to Kiss in Northern California*
MEMBER	Historical Inns of Grass Valley and Nevada City
AWARDS	Stan Halls Architectural Award, 1993

DOWNEY HOUSE B&B

517 West Broad Street, Nevada City, CA 95959   916-265-2815
Miriam Wright, Manager

FLUME'S END

317 South Pine Street, Nevada City, CA 95959   916-265-9665
Terrianne Straw & Steve Wilson, Resident Owners

LOCATION	Take Interstate 80 east 60 miles to Auburn, then 50 miles to Nevada City. Flume's End is two blocks from center of town on Pine Street.
OPEN	All year
DESCRIPTION	Three-story Victorian mansion built in 1863, surrounded by trees, flowers and a creek.
NO. OF ROOMS	Six rooms with private bathrooms. The Master Room is the best in the house.
RATES	Year round rates for a double with private bathroom are $75 to $135. Two night minimum on weekends and holidays. Cancellation policy in effect.
CREDIT CARDS	MC, Visa
BREAKFAST	Full breakfast of home made breads, granola, fruit, yogurt, hot entree and beverages is served in the dining room or on the terrace.
AMENITIES	Piano and musical instruments, phone and TV in sitting room, games, robes, home baked cookies and fudge, guest refridgerator stocked with beverages and off-street parking.
RESTRICTIONS	No smoking, no pets. Terrianne's two Goldie guidedogs, Roanna and Jamar, share the mansion with guests.
MEMBER	Professional Association of Innkeepers International, California Association Bed and Breakfast Inns, California Lodging Industry Association
KUDOS/COMMENTS	"Very different and pleasant - unique rooms, excellent breakfasts (custom made to order)."

GRANDMERE'S INN

449 Broad Street, Nevada City, CA 95959   916-265-4660
Doug and Geri Boka, Resident Owners

LOCATION	Ask for directions.
OPEN	All year except Christmas Day.
DESCRIPTION	An 1856 two-story Colonial Revival with country furnishings, listed on the National Historic Register.
NO. OF ROOMS	Seven rooms with private bathrooms. Master Suite is the best in the house.
RATES	Year round rates for a single or double with private bathroom are $100 to $150. Seven days cancellation notice required, $10 service charge.
CREDIT CARDS	MC, Visa
BREAKFAST	Full breakfast served in the dining room includes two hot entrees, fruit, croissants or coffee cake and beverages.
AMENITIES	Cookies and soft drinks, bathing accessories, champagne for anniversary couples.
RESTRICTIONS	No smoking, no pets.
MEMBER	Historic Inns of Grass Valley and Nevada City

THE KENDALL HOUSE

534 Spring Street, Nevada City, CA 95959   *916-265-0405*
Jan & Ted Kendall, Resident Owners   *FAX 916-265-6876*

LOCATION	From Highway 49 take Broad Street exit, turn left three blocks through town to Bennett, left on Bennett, right on Spring and one block on left to the inn.
OPEN	All Year
DESCRIPTION	A two-story 1860s California farmhouse with eclectic "but it all works" furnishings.
NO. OF ROOMS	Five rooms with private bathrooms including the "Barn" guest house. Pick the Barn.
RATES	Year round rates are $98 to $115 for a single or a double with private bathroom, the Barn guest house is $150 to $190. There is a two night minimum stay on weekends (April through December) and holidays. Cancellation requires seven days (sometimes 14) and a $15 fee.
CREDIT CARDS	Discover, MC, Visa
BREAKFAST	Full breakfast is served in the dining room and includes juice, fruit plate and entree.
AMENITIES	Swimming pool, wood stove in Barn, air conditioning where needed, cookies, soft drinks and mineral water, multi-level decks, off-street parking and limited handicapped access.
RESTRICTIONS	No smoking, no pets, children over 12 are welcome. The dog is called Kelsey and plays with one of the cats who are called Ginger, Bootsie and Buddy.
REVIEWED	*Northern California Best Places, The Definitive Northern California Bed & Breakfast Touring Guide*
MEMBER	Historic Inns of Grass Valley/Nevada City

THE PARSONAGE B&B

427 Broad Street, Nevada City, CA 95959　　　　　　916-265-9478
Deborah Dane, Resident Owner　　　　　　　　　FAX 916-265-8147

LOCATION	Look for the first white picket fence on the left at the top of Broad Street.
OPEN	All year
DESCRIPTION	A two-story 1865 Cottage Victorian with traditional furnishings and antiques.
NO. OF ROOMS	Six rooms with private bathrooms. The best room is the Victorian.
RATES	Year round rates are $65 to $115 for a single or double with a private bathroom. Mid-week rates a bit less. There is a two night minimum stay if a Saturday or a holiday is included and cancellation requires seven days notice.
CREDIT CARDS	MC, Visa
BREAKFAST	Continental Plus is served in the dining room or guestroom and includes juices, home baked breads, homemade jams, yogurt, cream cheese, fresh fruit platter and beverages.
AMENITIES	Flowers, telephones, TV in rooms.
RESTRICTIONS	No smoking, children over six are welcome.
REVIEWED	*The Best of Northern California*

PIETY HILL INN

523 Sacramento Street, Nevada City, CA 95959　　　　　*916-265-2245*
800-443-2245

LOCATION	Exit Highway 49 at Sacramento Street, turn left, go 1/3 of a mile up hill. Look to your left for the inn behind a white picket fence.
OPEN	All year
DESCRIPTION	1930 English cottages on one acre with huge trees and gardens, decorated with antiques and memorabilia.
NO. OF ROOMS	Nine rooms with private bathrooms. Pick apple blossom.
RATES	Year round rates are $75 for a single or a double with private bathroom, $100 to $135 for suites. There is a minimum stay over Saturdays and cancellation requires seven days notice, fourteen days for holidays.
CREDIT CARDS	Amex, MC, Visa
BREAKFAST	Full breakfast served in the cottages includes homemade muffins, breads, fresh fruit plate, main entree and orange juice. Special meals are available.
AMENITIES	TV, coffee, tea and hot chocolate in the rooms, apple cider, sherry, refrigerators and cooking facilities, one large cottage for meetings, several cottages have handicapped access.
RESTRICTIONS	No smoking, no pets

RED CASTLE INN

109 Prospect Street, Nevada City, CA 95959   916-265-5135
Mary Louise & Conley Weaver, Resident Owners

LOCATION	From Highway 49 East exit on Sacramento Street, turn right onto Adams, left onto Prospect Street, proceed one block to street end. From Highway 20 West turn left onto Coyote Street to Broad, left to Sacramento, right to Adams, left and left onto Prospect to street end.
OPEN	All year
DESCRIPTION	A four-story 1857 brick Gothic Revival mansion listed on the California State Historic Register. Furnished with owner's art collection, period pieces and historic memorabilia.
NO. OF ROOMS	Seven rooms with private bathrooms. Guests' favorite room is the Rose Room.
RATES	Year round rates for a single or double with private bathroom are $95 to $125, and $65 to $75 for a single or double with shared bathroom and suites are $100 to $140. Entire inn rents for $800. Minimum weekend stay April through December requires two nights, cancellation policy requires seven to 30 days advance notice, depending on accommodations.
CREDIT CARDS	MC, Visa
BREAKFAST	Full buffet breakfast served in the foyer includes "original and imaginative five courses." Prix fixe dinner available in 1995.
AMENITIES	Flowers, robes, dream pillows, down comforters, library, classical music, afternoon tea.
RESTRICTIONS	No smoking, no pets, children over six years old welcome. Resident host cats Foxy and Beau "available as lap warmers. They receive almost as much fan mail as we do."
REVIEWED	*Northern California Best Places, Fifty Romantic Getaways, Fodor's B&Bs, Country Inns and Other Weekend Pleasures—California, America's Wonderful Little Hotels and Inns—West Coast, Best Places to Stay in Northern California*
MEMBER	Professional Association of Innkeepers International, American Historic Inns, California Association of Bed and Breakfast Inns, Historic Bed and Breakfast Inns of Grass Valley and Nevada City
RATED	Mobil 1 Star

NEWCASTLE

A suburban town about 15 miles northeast of Sacramento on I-80 and Hwy. 193. Handy to Folsom State Recreation Area.

VICTORIAN MANOR

482 Main Street, Newcastle, CA 95658   *916-663-3009*
Cordy & Ed Sander, Resident Owners

LOCATION	From the east take Newcastle exit off I-80, turn right at the exit, go two blocks to Tin Road, turn right 1/2 block to Main Street.
OPEN	All year
DESCRIPTION	A two-story 1900 Country Victorian with country and Victorian furnishings.
NO. OF ROOMS	One room with private bathroom, three rooms share two bathrooms. Try the Queen Victoria room.
RATES	Year round rates are $65 for a single or double with private bathroom and $52 to $60 for a single or a double with shared bathroom. There is no minimum stay and cancellation requires 72 hours notice.
CREDIT CARDS	Amex, MC, Visa
BREAKFAST	Continental Plus is served in the dining room and includes beverages, fresh fruit, melons and starwberries in season, muffins, croissants, jam and butter.
AMENITIES	Fresh cut roses most of the year, front porch with wicker furniture and gazebo with wicker furniture.
RESTRICTIONS	No smoking, no pets, children over 12 are welcome but must have own room. There are resident cats, "five each and one is totally deaf".
REVIEWED	*California State Automobile Association Bed & Breakfast, Northern and Central California and Nevada.*

NORTH FORK

This little wilderness hideawaay has great access to Bass Lake and the San Joaquin River. Southeast of Yosemite National Park and Oakhurst via Hwy. 41.

YE OLDE SOUTH FORK INN

57665 Road 225, North Fork, CA 93643   209-877-7025
Darrel and Virginia Cochran, Resident Owners

LOCATION	About 30 miles out of Fresno, take Road 200 (O'Neals North Fork turnoff) about 16 miles inland. South Fork is one mile east of North Fork.
OPEN	May 1 through November 1.
DESCRIPTION	A 1925 two-story California chalet furnished with country antiques.
NO. OF ROOMS	Nine rooms share three bathrooms.
RATES	Singles with shared bathroom are $55, doubles with shared bathroom are $65. Family room that sleeps seven is $95. Entire chalet can be rented for $530. Three day minimum on holiday weekends. Two day cancellation policy, $10 fee.
CREDIT CARDS	MC, Visa
BREAKFAST	Continental served in dining room includes juice, fruit, cereals, muffins, coffee, tea and cocoa.
AMENITIES	Large common room with TV, games, toy box, and piano.
RESTRICTIONS	No smoking, no pets.
REVIEWED	*Country Inns of the West Coast, AAA Bed & Breakfast Guide— Northern California*

OAKHURST

The southernmost route into Yosemite starts here, on the scenic stretch of Hwy. 41 northeast of Fresno. Check out Bass Lake for water recreation, and Fresno Flats Historical Park.

CHATEAU DU SUREAU

48688 Victoria Lane, Oakhurst, CA 93644   *209-683-6800*
Erna Kubin-Clanin, Resident Owner   *FAX 209-683-0800*
Spanish, German spoken

LOCATION	Located in the town of Oakhurst, a quarter mile south of the intersection of Highway 49 and Highway 41.
OPEN	Closed from January 1 through January 21.
DESCRIPTION	A two-story French chateau built in 1991 surrounded by gardens.
NO. OF ROOMS	Nine rooms with private bathrooms.
RATES	Year round rates for a double with private bathroom are $260 to $360. Entire chateau rents for $3,600. Two night minimum stay on holidays, cancellation policy requires at least seven days notice for a refund minus 10%.
CREDIT CARDS	Amex, MC, Visa,
BREAKFAST	Full breakfast served in the breakfast room includes fruit frappe, quiche, Black Forest ham, brioche and croissants.
AMENITIES	Flowers, robes, phones, TV available, wine and hors d'oeuvres, pool, slippers, house bar, life-size chess court, fireplaces in rooms, deep soaking tub for two in five rooms.
RESTRICTIONS	No smoking, no pets.
REVIEWED	*Best Places to Kiss in Northern California, Karen Brown's California Country Inns and Itineraries, Country Inns and Back Roads, AAA Bed & Breakfast—Northern and Central California*
MEMBER	Relais and Chateaux
RATED	AAA 4 Diamonds, Mobil 4 Stars

OAKLAND

Redwood and oak-covered hills rise above the city, and the weather is fair year round, even when San Francisco is dreary. This big city across the bay is almost one with Berkeley, and with more than enough scenic, cultural and entertainment offerings to compete with its two neighbors: from the Oakland A's to the Oakland Ballet, and the hills are alive with Redwood and Anthony Chabot Regional Parks. That's just for starters, except for the Oakland Jazz Festival in August.

BEDSIDE MANOR

612 Valle Vista Avenue, Oakland, CA 94610   510-452-4550
Deborah Stevenson, Resident Owner
Spanish spoken

LOCATION	Located near downtown Oakland in the Piedmont Manor district. From 580 Freeway, exit at Grand Avenue. Bedside Manor is two blocks from the freeway near the Rose Garden.
OPEN	All year
DESCRIPTION	A two-story 1924 Moorish inn with hardwood floors and wood and stained glass windows.
NO. OF ROOMS	Two suites with private bathrooms. Deborah recommends the Master Suite.
RATES	Year round rates for either suite with private bathroom are $55 to $65. Special rates are available for long term guests in the Minor Suite. Two night minimum stay required on holidays, no penalty for cancellation.
CREDIT CARDS	No
BREAKFAST	Continental Plus breakfast served in the dining room includes juice, fruit salad, breakfast breads, hot or cold cereal and beverages. Guests are welcome to prepare family meals in the kitchen. Lunches and picnic baskets are available on request.
AMENITIES	Outside deck with a fountain, Master Suite includes phone, sitting room, TV/VCR and small sweets.
RESTRICTIONS	No smoking. Lacy, is a sweet but aging Cocker Spaniel.

DOCKSIDE BOAT & BED

77 Jack London Square, Oakland, CA 94607   510-444-5858
Rob Harris, Resident Owner

TUDOR ROSE BED & BREAKFAST

316 Modoc Avenue, Oakland, CA 94618   510-655-3201
Corinne Edmonson, Resident Owner

WASHINGTON INN

495 10th Street, Oakland, CA 94607   510-452-1776
Philip Paxton, Resident Owner

OCCIDENTAL

INN AT OCCIDENTAL

PO Box 857, Occidental, CA 95465   707-874-1311
Jack Bullard, Resident Owner

OLEMA

The main gateway into the Point Reyes National Seashore boasts a 74,000-acre park of marshes, sandy beaches, dunes and forests. Explore Bear Valley Trail's Fivebrooks Pond, wetlands of Limantour, tidepools and estuaries. Venture out to the Point Reyes Lighthouse and watch for gray whales. On a clear day, look south to the Point Reyes—Farallon Islands National Wildlife Refuge and Marine Sanctuary, now part of UNESCO Biosphere Reserve (for information, call the San Francisco Bay Wildlife Refuge). Make time for the Point Reyes Bird Observatory. Oh, yes—Olema was the epicenter for the 1906 earthquake (just a thought to ponder). From San Francisco, just north on Hwy. 1.

BEAR VALLEY B&B

PO Box 33, Olema, CA 94950   *415-663-1777*
Ron Nowell, Resident Owners

POINT REYES SEASHORE LODGE

10021 Highway 1, Olema, CA 94950   *415-663-9000*
Jeff and Nancy Harriman, Owners   *FAX 415-663-9030*
Spanish and some French spoken

LOCATION	In the center of the small town, one block north of Sir Francis Drake Boulevard.
OPEN	All year
DESCRIPTION	1988 Victorian style lodge. Adjoins Point Reyes National Seashore Park on Olema Creek
NO. OF ROOMS	Twenty two rooms with private bathrooms.
RATES	High season rates, April through October, and all weekends and holidays year round, for single or doubles are $140, suites are $185, guesthouse is $250. Off season singles and doubles are $75 to $95, suites are $140, and guesthouse is $195. Cancellation policy requires five days notice.
CREDIT CARDS	Amex, MC, Visa, Discover
BREAKFAST	Continental Plus served in the dining room or guestrroms include fresh fruit, pastries, cereals, juices and yogurt.
AMENITIES	Wine and champagne, snack baskets, telephones in rooms, antique pool table, library, fireplace, two acres of gardens. Suites include whirlpool tubs, robes, cofeemakers.
RESTRICTIONS	No smoking, no pets.
REVIEWED	*Best Places to Kiss in Northern California*
MEMBER	Professional Association of Innkeepers International, California Association of Bed and Breakfast Innkeepers, California Lodging Industry Association

ORLAND

Handy to Black Butte Lake to the west and Woodson Bridge State Recreation Area due north. Only 10 miles east of Chico via Hwy. 32, and 50 miles south of Redding on the I-5 corridor.

INN AT SHALLOW CREEK FARM

4712 Road DD, Orland, CA 95963   *916-865-4093*
Kurt & Mary Glaeseman, Resident Owners
German, French and Spanish spoken

LOCATION	Take the Chico/Orland exit from I-5. Go west 2.5 miles. Turn right (north) onto Road DD. Proceed .5 mile, cross concrete bridge and take the next driveway on the right.
OPEN	All year
DESCRIPTION	A 1900 two-story country farmhouse and cottage with antique furnishings.
NO. OF ROOMS	Two rooms with private bathrooms and two rooms share one bathroom. Mary suggests the Penfield Suite.
RATES	Year round rates are $65 to $75 for a single or a double with a private bathroom, $55 for a single or a double with a shared bathroom and $75 for the cottage. There is no minimum stay and cancellation requires six days notice.
CREDIT CARDS	MC, Visa
BREAKFAST	Continental Plus is served in the dining room and includes home baked breads and muffins, fresh fruit and juice from the orchard.
AMENITIES	Guest refrigerator, cottage has a fully equipted kitchen and woodburning stove. Phones, books, games, piano and TV in the common room. The hosts are birders.
RESTRICTIONS	No smoking, no pets, the inn is "not particularly suitable for children." The resident calico cats are Monkey Business and Moonshine.
REVIEWED	*Best Places to Stay in Northern California, America's Wonderful Little Hotels & Inns, Northern California Best Places, The Birder's Guide to Bed & Breakfasts*
MEMBER	Professional Association of Innkeepers International

OROVILLE

This foothills Gold Rush town has a wild past and speckled economic history. Now, it's the gateway into Lake Oroville Dam and State Recreation Area. The Feather River Fish Hatchery is great fun to visit, especially during spawning season October–November. And don't miss the Temple of Assorted Dieties, built by the town's Chinese population in 1863. Of interest: Ishi, the last Yahi, was discovered hiding near a local slaughterhosue in 1911. From Chico, 26 miles south on Hwy. 149.

JEAN'S RIVERSIDE BED & BREAKFAST

---

45 Cabana Drive, Oroville, CA 95965　　　　　　　　　　　*916-533-1413*
Jean Pratt, Resident Owner

LOCATION	Entering Oroville, turn left on Oroville Dam Boulevard, immediately cross Feather River, turn right on Middlehoff Lane, within the space of three blocks, "which we don't have, turn right at sign.
OPEN	All year
DESCRIPTION	A two-story 1936 cedar country inn with "upscale" country furnishings on five waterfront acres.
NO. OF ROOMS	Seventeen rooms with private bathrooms. Jean suggests the honeymoon suite.
RATES	Year round rates are $55 to $105 for a single or a double with a private bathroom. Six rooms have a two night minimum stay and cancellation requires one week's notice.
CREDIT CARDS	Diners Club, MC, Visa
BREAKFAST	Full breakfast is served in the dining room and includes fruit of the area, different entree each day and beverages.
AMENITIES	Flowers in room, wine or other refreshment on arrival, TV, phones as requested, fishing, gold panning, horseshoes, ping pong, croquet and serious bird watching.
RESTRICTIONS	No smoking, no pets, children in cottage depending on conversation with parents.
REVIEWED	*Bed & Breakfast Homes Directory, Perfect Places for Special Events and Business Functions*

LAKE OROVILLE BED & BREAKFAST

240 Sunday Drive, Oroville, CA 95916　　　　　916-589-0700
Ronald & Cheryl Damberger, Resident Owners　　800-455-5253
　　　　　　　　　　　　　　　　　　　　　　　　　FAX 916-589-3572

LOCATION
From Route 70 take Oroville Dam Boulevard east 1.7 miles. Turn right at Olive Highway (Route 162), continue 13.5 miles around Lake Oroville. You will have crossed two bridges and seen Foreman Creek Recreation Area sign. Take the next left, Bell Ranch Road, drive .6 mile bearing right to Sunday Drive. Continue three quarter miles to the big yellow house.

OPEN
All year

DESCRIPTION
A 1991 two-story Victorian on 40 acres, furnished with period antiques.

NO. OF ROOMS
Six rooms with private bathrooms. Cheryl recommends the Victorian Room.

RATES
Year round rates for a double room with private bathroom are $65 to $110, entire inn rents for $540. Two night minimum on holiday weekends, five day cancellation policy.

CREDIT CARDS
Amex, MC, Visa, Discover

BREAKFAST
Full breakfast served in the dining room includes fresh-squeezed orange juice, fresh fruit dish, muffins, croissants, 2-3 main entrees served on platters family style and beverages, served on china with crystal and silver. Lunch and dinner available by prior arrangement.

AMENITIES
Telephones, radio with cassettes, TV/VCR upon request, whirlpool tubs in bedrooms, game room with billard table, sodas, snack basket, sunroom with books and reading chairs, 2000 square foot covered porches with private entrance to bedrooms. Meeting, wedding, retreat facilities, children's play room, sitter service, handicapped facility.

RESTRICTIONS
Smoking only on the patio. Two dogs, Abbie and Samantha, and Katrina the cat, grace the inn. "Abbie takes everyone for a walk with Katrina as a tag along. I never realized how much our guests would love our animals."

REVIEWED
Weekends for Two, American Historic Inns, AAA Bed & Breakfast Guide—Northern California.

MEMBER
Professional Association of Innkeepers International, California Association of Bed and Breakfast Inns.

MONTGOMERY INN

1400 Montgomery Street, Oroville, CA 95965　　　　　916-532-1400
June Abts, Resident Owner
Swedish and Spanish spoken

LOCATION	Seven blocks off of Highway 70 toward downtown.
OPEN	All year
DESCRIPTION	A three-story 1904 Victorian with Victorian furnishings.
NO. OF ROOMS	Six rooms with private bathrooms. Pick a Honeymoon Suite.
RATES	Year round rates are $45 to $65 for a single or a double with a private bathroom. There is no minimum stay and cancellation requires one weeks noitice.
CREDIT CARDS	No
BREAKFAST	Full breakfast is served in the dining room and includes fruit, French toast, sausage, cereals and beverages.
AMENITIES	Two rooms have Jacuzzi tubs, cable TV, refrigerator and telephones in the lobby.
RESTRICTIONS	No smoking

PALO ALTO

Stanford University and all things cultural and creative, as well as classy and affluent come together here. Naturally, tour the splendid campus and historic downtown, and check out the Baylands Nature Preserve. Perfectly located at the southwest terminus of San Francisco Bay.

ADELLA VILLA

122 Atherton Avenue, Palo Alto, CA 94027   *415-321-5195*
Tricia Young, Resident Owner
German and Spanish spoken   *FAX 415-325-5121*

LOCATION	From Highway 101 or Highway 280 take Woodside Road exit. (From 101 head west, from 280 head east). Exit at El Camino going south. Go to the fifth stop light and turn right on Atherton Avenue. We are .6 miles up on the right. Look for yellow gate lights after dark.
OPEN	All year
DESCRIPTION	A two-story 1920s Italian villa. Laura Ashley decor and antique furnishings.
NO. OF ROOMS	Five rooms with private bathrooms. The Grey Room is the best in the house.
RATES	Year round rates for a double with private bathroom are $95 to $110. No minimum stay, 72 hours cancellation notice required.
CREDIT CARDS	Amex, MC, Visa, Diners Club
BREAKFAST	Full breakfast served in the dining room includes eggs any style, meats, French toast or pancakes, croissants, assorted breads and beverages.
AMENITIES	Robes, cable TV, VCR, phones with clock radios, hair dryers, sherry, down comforters, individual heaters and electric mattress pads, assorted beverages always available, meeting facilities for ten or less, common room with fireplace.
RESTRICTIONS	No smoking indoors, children over 10 years old welcome. Chat with Mango, the resident parrot.
REVIEWED	*Bed and Breakfast Inns and Guesthouses, Bed & Breakfast Homes Directory*
MEMBER	Professional Association of Innkeepers International, American Bed and Breakfast Associaion
RATED	ABBA 3 Crowns

COWPER INN

705 Cowper Street, Palo Alto, CA 94301   415-327-4475
Peggy & John Woodworth, Resident Owners

HOTAL CALIFORNIA

2431 Ash, Palo Alto, CA 94306   415-322-7666
Warren Wong, Resident Owner

THE VICTORIAN ON LYTTON

555 Lytton Avenue, Palo Alto, CA 94301   415-322-8555
Maxwell & Susan Hall, Resident Owners   FAX 415-322-7141

LOCATION	From San Francisco go south on Highway 101 to University Street exit. Turn west and go about two miles, turn right on Middlefield, turn left on Lytton. Parking in rear.
OPEN	All year
DESCRIPTION	Two-story 1985 Victorian with English decor listed on the National Historic Register. Victorian garden with over 1200 perennials wraps around the building.
NO. OF ROOMS	Ten rooms with private bathrooms. Princess Royal room will make you feel like a queen.
RATES	Year round rates, single/double with private bathroom, are $98 to $200. No minimum stay, 10 day cancellation policy with 10% fee.
CREDIT CARDS	Amex, MC, Visa
BREAKFAST	Continental breakfast served in guestroom includes fresh juice and fruit, homemade muffins and croissants, coffee and tea.
AMENITIES	Flowers, robes, TV, radio, voicemail.
RESTRICTIONS	No smoking, no pets, children over 13 years welcome.
REVIEWED	*Karen Brown's California Country Inns and Itineraries*

PESCADERO

"The fishing place" is off the San Mateo Coast just inland from Highway 1 and Pescadero State Beach. Pescadero Creek runs through it.

HIDDEN FOREST COTTAGE

503 Madrone Butano Canyon, Pescadero, CA 94060   415-879-1046
Robert & Delight Castle, Resident Owners

LOCATION	From Coast Highway 1 travel east on Pescadero Road 2.6 miles, road will fork, stay to the right on Cloverdale Road. Go 3.2 miles and turn left onto Canyon Road. Proceed 2 miles to a locked gate and dial Hidden Forest Cottage number. Proceed on Redwood Road, turn left on Madrone to 503.
OPEN	All year
DESCRIPTION	1984 French Country cottage surrounded by dense redwood forest.
NO. OF ROOMS	One bedroom cottage with living room, kitchen and bathroom.
RATES	Year round rate during the week is $75, and $90 weekends. Two night minimum stay on weekends.
CREDIT CARDS	MC, Visa
BREAKFAST	Breakfast provisions in the cottage include eggs, bacon, sausage, variety of coffee cakes, cereal, fruit, frozen pancakes, waffles, quiches and beverages.
AMENITIES	Flowers, wine, variety of videos and books, wood burning stove, decks, complete privacy.
RESTRICTIONS	No smoking, no pets.

PETALUMA

Chicks and cows are big here—dairy farming and poultry ranching are the major industries. There's more to do than you can shake a feather at: tour the Petaluma River, the cheese factory, and Petaluma Adobe State Historic Park, among other things. On Highway 101 just north of San Francisco.

CAVANAGH INN

10 Keller Street, Petaluma, CA 94952   707-765-4657
Billie Erkel, Resident Owner
Spanish spoken

LOCATION	Traveling north on Highway 101, take Petaluma Boulevard south exit, follow for about 1.5 miles to second signal which is Western Avenue, turn left, go two blocks, turn left onto Keller Street and go 1/2 block.
OPEN	All year
DESCRIPTION	A 1903 Neo-classic Georgian Revival and a 1910 two-story Craftsman. Both buildings have rare redwood heart paneling and are furnished with antiques.
NO. OF ROOMS	Five rooms with private bathrooms and two rooms share one bathroom. Billie suggests the sterling rose room.
RATES	Year round rates are $75 to $115 for a single or a double with a private bathroom and a single or a double with a shared bathroom is $55 to $75. There is no minimum stay and cancellation requires 48 hours notice.
CREDIT CARDS	Amex, MC, Visa
BREAKFAST	Full breakfast served in the dining room or on the deck includes beverages, fresh fruit, egg souffle, chicken-apple sausage and persimmon muffins.
AMENITIES	Whirlpool tub in sterling rose room, turn down service and night trays with homemade cookies, toiletries basket, hot apple cider or cold lemonade, conference room and large garden for weddings.
RESTRICTIONS	No smoking, no pets
REVIEWED	*Karen Brown's California Country Inns & Itineraries, The Definitive California Bed & Breakfast Touring Guide, California Experience - Wine Country and Northern Coast*

PHILO

PHILO POTTERY INN

8550 Route 128, Philo, CA 95466   707-895-3069
Sue & Barry Chiverton, Resident Owners

PLACERVILLE

Once called Hangtown (a frequent activity), this was the historical heart of gold country. Today, it's definitely a growth area. Fun doings include the 60-acre city-owned Gold Bug Mine in Bedford Park and the County Museum; free Jazz in the Plaza concerts from June–September; Pioneer Days Festival in June; County Fair in August; and bring money and a truck to the Mother Lode Antique Show and Sale over Labor Day. Visit the many lcoal wineries, as well as the Spring and Fall Apple and Pear Festivals in nearby Apple Hill. About 30 miles east of Sacramento on Hwy. 50, the straightaway to South Lake Tahoe.

CHICHESTER-MCKEE HOUSE

800 Spring Street, Placerville, CA 95667   916-626-1882
Doreen and Bill Thornhill, Resident Owners   800-831-4008

LOCATION	One and half blocks from historic downtown Placerville, half block north of Highway 50 on Spring Street (Highway 49).
OPEN	All year
DESCRIPTION	1892 two-story Queen Anne Victorian with peroid furnishings, built by local lumber baron D. W. Chichester.
NO. OF ROOMS	Three rooms with private half-bathrooms.
RATES	Year round rates for a single or double with half bathroom are $70 to $85. Entire house, for seven people, rents for $250. Cancellation policy requires five days notice with $8 cancellation fee.
CREDIT CARDS	Amex, MC, Visa, Discover
BREAKFAST	Full breakfast served in the dining room over the gold mine.
AMENITIES	Solarium/conservatory, gardens, air conditioning/heating, robes, fireplaces, soft drinks and "Doreen's Famous Caramel Brownies," ten person meeting facilities available with brunch.
RESTRICTIONS	Smoking restricted to designated areas, no pets. Heidi, a miniature Dachshund, performs math tricks at breakfast...We believe you about this Doreen...field report please...TI
REVIEWED	*Best of the Gold Country, Bed, Breakfast and Bikes—Northern California, Complete Guide to American Bed and Breakfasts, Bed and Breakfast in California, Northern California Best Places*
MEMBER	California Association of Bed and Breakfast Inns, Historic Country Inns of El Dorado County

COMBELLACK-BLAIR HOUSE

3059 Cedar Ravine Road, Placerville, CA 95667   916-622-3764
Al and Rosalie McConnell, Resident Owners
Spanish spoken

LOCATION	Located in downtown Placerville. From Highway 50 turn south on Bedford Street. Go one block, turn left on Main Street. Next street to the right is Cedar Ravine, inn is one block up on the left.
OPEN	All year except Christmas and Mother's Day
DESCRIPTION	A two-story Queen Anne Victorian built in 1895 with extensive gingerbread trim.
NO. OF ROOMS	Two rooms with private bathroom, one room with shared bathroom. Mazzuchi room comes highly recommended.
RATES	Year round rates for a single or double with private bathroom $99, $89 for a single or double with shared bathroom. No minimum stay, one week cancellation required.
CREDIT CARDS	MC, Visa
BREAKFAST	Full breakfast served in the dining room includes fruit, mufins, hot dish and beverages.
AMENITIES	Flowers, wine, iced tea, TVs in rooms.
RESTRICTIONS	No smoking, no pets, children over six years old are welcome. Two resident cats, Crystal and Felix.
REVIEWED	*Painted Ladies Guide to Victorian Bed and Breakfasts*

RIVER ROCK

1756 Georgetown, Placerville, CA 95667   916-622-7640
Dorthy Irvin, Resident Owner

PLEASANTON

PLUM TREE INN

---

262 West Angela, Pleasanton, CA 94566   510-426-9588
Bob & Joan Cordtz, Resident Owners

PLYMOUTH

This may be more grape than gold country, where a dozen fine vintners flourish. Tours and tastings are always available, as are many fun events—Music at the Wineries Festival in May benefits the Amador County Arts Council, Sierra Showcase of Wines in May, Wine Festival in June, Bluegrass Festival in August, and Gold Country Jubilee in September. Thirty-five miles southeast of Sacramento on Hwy. 16 and 49.

AMADOR HARVEST INN

12455 Steiner Road, Plymouth, CA 95669   209-245-5512
Bobbie Deaver, Resident Owner

LOCATION	Five miles southeast of Plymouth off Highway 49. Take E16 exit, go one mile on Steiner Road.
OPEN	All year
DESCRIPTION	1969 ranch country inn surrounded by vineyards and oak trees at the edge of a lake.
NO. OF ROOMS	Four rooms with private bathrooms. The Zinfandel is the best in the house.
RATES	Year round rates for a single or double room with private bathroom are $85 to $95, and $110 for suites. Seven day cancellation notice required.
CREDIT CARDS	MC, Visa
BREAKFAST	Full breakfast served in the dining room includes an egg dish, meat, various breakfast breads and beverages.
AMENITIES	Flowers in rooms, hors d'oeuvres and wine, catch and release fishing in the lake.
RESTRICTIONS	No smoking, no pets.
MEMBER	California Association of Bed and Breakfast Inns, Amador County Bed and Breakfast Association.

POINT REYES STATION

Just outside the southeast end of Tomales Bay, this only slightly yuppie little town is famous for its Pulitzer Prize-winning newspaper, the Point Reyes Light. From here, it's a very short drive to Point Reyes National Seashore. Cross the Golden Gate Bridge and head north on Hwy. 1.

CARRIAGE HOUSE BED & BREAKFAST

325 Mesa Road, Point Reyes Station, CA 94956   *415-663-8627*
Felicity Kirsch, Resident Owner   *FAX 415-663-8431*

LOCATION	Turn right at the west end of town onto Highway 1, then turn left at Mesa Road, go 1/3 mile, turn left down lane at the sign.
OPEN	All year
DESCRIPTION	A 1920 old fashioned country house with country furnishings.
NO. OF ROOMS	Two suites with private bathrooms.
RATES	Year round rates are $130 to $160 for a suite with a private bathroom. The inn (10 people) rents for $350. There is a two night minimum stay on the weekend and cancellation requires seven days notice.
CREDIT CARDS	No
BREAKFAST	Continental Plus is served in the guestrooms and includes fresh squeezed juice, fresh fruit, muffins, cereal, yogurt, tea and coffee.
AMENITIES	Flowers, fireplace, TV, coffee, tea, garden, BBQ, FAX available, breakfast delivered to the suite, babysitting and crib, kitchen or wet bar.
RESTRICTIONS	No smoking, no pets. The resident cats are Mocha and Tuxedo.
MEMBER	California Association of Bed & Breakfast Inns

THE COUNTRY HOUSE

65 Manana Way, Point Reyes Station CA 94956   *415-663-1627*
Ewell McIsaac, Resident Owner
Some French spoken

LOCATION	Manana Way intersects Highway 1 opposite the West Marin School.
OPEN	All year
DESCRIPTION	A ca. 1950 California Ranch guesthouse with a rustic Redwood interior.
NO. OF ROOMS	Three rooms with private bathrooms. The best room is the Sunday best suite.
RATES	Year round rates are $100 "and up". The entire guesthouse rents for $300. There is a minimum stay on the weekends and cancellation requires seven days notice.
CREDIT CARDS	No
BREAKFAST	Full breakfast
AMENITIES	Flowers, piano, children's classic library, fireplaces, 24 foot room for meetings or family gatherings, fireplace.
RESTRICTIONS	No smoking, no pets, children over three are welcome. The resident cat is called Indy.

CRICKETT COTTAGE

PO Box 627, Point Reyes Station, CA 94956   *415-663-9139*
Penny Livingston, Resident Owner

FERRANDO'S HIDEAWAY

12010 Highway 1, Point Reyes Station, CA 94956   *415-663-1966*
Greg and Doris Ferrando, Resident Owners   *800-337-2636*
German Spoken   *FAX 415-666-1825*

LOCATION	One mile north of Point Reyes Station on Highway 1.
OPEN	All year
DESCRIPTION	Two-story 1972 contemporary European home and cottage with country furnishings.
NO. OF ROOMS	Three rooms with private bathrooms. The cottage comes highly recommended.
RATES	Year round rates for a single or double room, or the private cottage are $95 to $120. Two night stay required over Saturday, seven day cancellation notice required.
CREDIT CARDS	No
BREAKFAST	Full breakfast served in the breakfast room includes an egg dish made from eggs from Ferrando's chickens, fresh fruit, muffins, granola, yogurt, cheeses and beverages.
AMENITIES	Outdoor hot tub, TV/VCR in rooms, afternoon beverages, common room with woodstove, private entrances and patio, kitchen in cottage.
RESTRICTIONS	No smoking, no pets.
MEMBER	California Association of Bed and Breakfast Inns, Coastal Lodging - Point Reyes National Seashore
KUDOS/COMMENTS	"Wonderful, clean, gracious accomodations - special hostess."..."Very clean, charming host and hostess, beautiful gardens, restful."

HOLLY TREE INN

3 Silverhills Road, Inverness Park, CA 94956
Tom & Diane Balogh, Resident Owners
Limited French, Spanish spoken

415-663-1554
FAX 415-663-8566

LOCATION	From San Francisco, take Highway 101 north to Larkspur. Exit on Sir Francis Drake Boulevard westbound. At Highway 1 in Olema (45 minutes) head north (right). Take first right on Bear Valley Road, at 1.9 miles turn left on Silver Hills Road at the inn sign.
OPEN	Cottages open all year, inn closed Christmas Eve and Christmas Day.
DESCRIPTION	Built in 1939, this clapboard inn and separate cottages are surrounded by 19 acres of valleys, wooded hillsides and creekside gardens.
NO. OF ROOMS	Four rooms and three cottages with private bathrooms. The best room in the inn is the Laurel Room, the best cottage is the Sea Star.
RATES	Year round rates for a single or double room with private bathroom are $100 to $135, and $165 to $200 for cottages. A two night stay is required on weekends, seven day cancellation notice required with $10 fee.
CREDIT CARDS	MC, Visa
BREAKFAST	Full breakfast served in the dining room or cottage includes quiche, frittata or egg casserole, fresh fruit, scones or pastry, muffins and beverages.
AMENITIES	Garden hot tub, flowers in rooms, robes, telephones in some cottages, private hot tubs in two cottages, massage available, suitable for small meetings or retreats.
RESTRICTIONS	No smoking. Mathilda, a Lab/Weimaramer, and five cats will share the grounds.
REVIEWED	*Hiking from Inn to Inn in California, Country Inns, Lodges and Historic Hotels, Northern California Best Places, Best Places to Kiss in Northern California, America's Wonderful Little Hotels & Inns*
MEMBER	Professional Association of Innkeepers International, California Bed and Breakfast Association, Inns of Point Reyes

JASMINE COTTAGE

PO Box 56, Point Reyes Station, CA 94956   *415-663-1166*
Karen Gray, Resident Owner

KNOB HILL

40 Knob Hill Road, Point Reyes Station, CA 94956   *415-663-1784*
Janet Schlirr, Resident Owner

LOCATION	From Point Reyes Station head north on Highway 1. Turn left on Viento just past the school, Viento turns into Knob Hill.
OPEN	All year
DESCRIPTION	1989 California Redwood cottage.
NO. OF ROOMS	Two rooms with private bathrooms.
RATES	Year round rates for a single or double room with private bathroom are $50 to $105. Minimum two night stay over Saturday, seven day cancellation policy.
BREAKFAST	Continental Plus served in the cottage includes fresh baked goods, fruit, breakfast cheese, yogurts and beverages.
AMENITIES	Flowers, crystal, candles, woodburning stove, access to phone and TV, horse-boarding, barn owls.
RESTRICTIONS	Smoking permitted outside, pets accepted by request. Resident pets include a Yellow Lab Dougal, Patches the cat and many horses.
REVIEWED	*Getting Away for the Weekend*
MEMBER	Coastal Lodging Association

TERRI'S HOMESTAY

83 *Sunnyside Drive, Point Reyes Station, CA 94956*   800-969-1289
Terri Elaine, Resident Owner
Spanish spoken

LOCATION	On the Inverness Ridge via 1.1 miles up steep and winding Drake View Drive in between Inverness and Inverness Park.
OPEN	All year
DESCRIPTION	A 1966 contemporay California host home with Central American furnishings,
NO. OF ROOMS	Two rooms with private bathrooms.
RATES	Year round rates are $95 to $115 for a single or double with a private bathroom. November through March and mid-week rates are lower. There is a minimum stay and cancellation requires seven days notice.
CREDIT CARDS	No
BREAKFAST	"Healthy" Continental Plus is served in the kitchen
AMENITIES	Flowers and robes, hot tub in the garden, large decks, professional massage by appointment.
RESTRICTIONS	No smoking, no pets. The "part-time" resident dogs are Henna and Sadie.
REVIEWED	*Bed & Breakfast Northern & Central California*

THIRTY-NINE CYPRESS

39 Cypress Road, Point Reyes Station, CA 94956   *415-633-1709*
Julia Bartlett, Resident Owner   *FAX 415-663-1709*
French spoken

LOCATION	From Golden Gate Bridge, go nine miles north, turn west on Sir Francis Drake Boulevard. Go 2.5 miles to Route 1, then north 2.3 miles to Mesa Road (on far side of Alliance Gas). Go one mile, then left onto Cypress. In 400 yards on the left, park at end of drive and walk in 100 feet to the inn.
OPEN	All year
DESCRIPTION	1980 contemporary California redwood overlooking a 600-acre cattle ranch with antique and eclectic furnishings.
NO. OF ROOMS	Three rooms with private bathrooms.
RATES	Year round rates for a single or a double with private bathroom are $95 to $125. Entire facility can be rented for $340. Minimum stay on weekends, $20 cancellation fee if less than seven days. Refunds only if room can be re-rented.
CREDIT CARDS	Amex, MC, Visa
BREAKFAST	Full breakfast is served in the dining room and includes orange juice, fruit salad with yogurt, fresh blueberry pan bread, salmon scramble, freshly ground coffee.
AMENITIES	Flowers, robes, outdoor hot tub with 180-degree view, gardens, cozy corner for reading.
RESTRICTIONS	No smoking, children over five years welcome. Australian Cattle dog, Flora Borrealis, is highest scoring cattle dog in obedience in USA. Resca, a Border Collie, rides shotgun. . . .Yahoo!... TI
MEMBER	Professional Association of Innkeepers International, California Association of Bed and Breakfast Inns, Inns of Point Reyes

THE TREE HOUSE

73 Drake Summit, Inverness, CA 94937　　　　　　　*415-663-8720*
Lisa Patsel, Resident Owner　　　　　　　　*FAX 415-663-8720*
Italian spoken

LOCATION	Exactly 1-1/2 mile off main road, three miles from the center of town.
OPEN	All year
DESCRIPTION	A 1975 contemporary host home.
NO. OF ROOMS	Three rooms with private bathrooms. Lisa likes the Queen Quarter.
RATES	Year round rates are $90 to $110 for a single or a double with a private bathroom. There is a mid-week discount and a minimum stay. Cancellation requires five days notice.
CREDIT CARDS	MC, Visa
BREAKFAST	Continental Plus is served in the dining room and includes juices, coffee, fresh seasonal fruit, croissants, muffins, jams, toast, eggs and cheeses.
AMENITIES	Telephones, TV, candy, hot tub in garden, homemade wine and a "fantastic" view.
RESTRICTIONS	No smoking. There are all sorts of resident critters including four cats, three dogs, and two parrots that are named Palla, Bandit, Alexea, Funny Face, Bella, Happy, Cameo, Thalonie and Hope respectively...Thalonie?...TI

WINDSONG COTTAGE

25 McDonald Lane, Pt. Reyes Station, CA 94956　　　　　*415-663-9695*
Anthony Ragona, Resident Owner

LOCATION	One mile north of Point Reyes Station.
OPEN	All year
DESCRIPTION	A 1991 contemporary yurt furnished with some antiques and mostly contemporary furnishings.
NO. OF ROOMS	One room with private bathroom.
RATES	Year round rates for a single or a double are $125. There is a two day minimum stay on the weekend.
CREDIT CARDS	No
BREAKFAST	Full fixings in the stocked kitchen include coffee, tea, local pastries, eggs, milk, cereal, juice, butter and spices "all of high quality".
AMENITIES	Telephone, cable TV, stereo, games, woodstove, private outdoor hot tub, massage by appointment.
RESTRICTIONS	No smoking. There are "three or four cats" on the property.
KUDOS/COMMENTS	"Unique design (yurt), expansive view or Tomales Bay. Mellow innkeeper."

PRINCETON-BY-THE-SEA

This is another seaside charmer with a lovely harbor on the San Mateo Coast just north of Half Moon Bay via Highway 1.

PILLAR POINT INN

380 Capistrano Road, Princeton-by-the-Sea, CA 94018   415-728-7377
Sarah Woodruff, Manager   FAX 415-728-8345
Spanish spoken

LOCATION	Four miles north of Half Moon Bay on Highway 1, turn west onto Capistrano Road at the first stop light. The first building in the right is the Pillar Point Inn.
OPEN	All year
DESCRIPTION	1985 two-story contemporary Cape Cod inn with large bay windows, overlooking the harbor and ocean. Grounds include a topiary and herb garden.
NO. OF ROOMS	Eleven rooms have private bathrooms. Number 10 is recommended.
RATES	Year round rates for doubles with private bathroom are $140 to $175. For June through October weekends, a two night stay is required. Cancellation policy is three days, five days over holidays.
CREDIT CARDS	Amex, MC, Visa
BREAKFAST	Full breakfast served in the dining room and includes homemade granola, locally-grown fruit, fresh yogurt, homebaked breads, egg strata, organic juices, coffee and tea.
AMENITIES	Guestrooms include window seats with ocean views, brass and hand-painted enamel feather beds, concealed refrigerators and fireplaces. First floor rooms have steam baths. Living room snacks include fruit, cookies, candy, port and sherry. Telephones, TVs, VCRs, and radios in rooms. Handicapped access.
RESTRICTIONS	No smoking, no pets.
REVIEWED	*Weekends for Two in Northern California, Best Places to Kiss in Northern California, Best Choices in Northern California*
KUDOS/COMMENTS	"Lovely seaside inn with fireplaces and good seafood nearby."

QUINCY

Here in the far northern reaches of the Sierra Nevada, this little town has a long history of logging and mining. Don't miss the Plumas County Museum, a forested drive to Lake Almanor, or the Beer Festival in June. On Highway 89/70 north of Lake Tahoe.

NEW ENGLAND RANCH

2571 Quincy Junction Road, Quincy, CA 95971   *916-283-2223*
Barbara Scott, Resident Owner   *FAX 916-283-2223*
Spanish "muy poquito" spoken

LOCATION	Three miles from Highway 70 turnoff at Chandler Road to Northeast Ranch Road at intersection of Chandler and Quincy Junction roads.
OPEN	All year, except Thanksgiving and Christmas.
DESCRIPTION	An 1850s two-story Victorian farmhouse and working cattle ranch on 85 acres of pastureland. Decorated with English Country antiques.
NO. OF ROOMS	Three rooms with private bathrooms. Barbara recommends the Greenhorn Room.
RATES	Year round rates for a double room with private bathroom are $75 to $95. Two days cancellation notice required.
CREDIT CARDS	MC, Diners Club, Visa, JCB, Carte Blanche
BREAKFAST	Full breakfast served in the dining room or in the garden in summer includes seasonal fruit, an egg dish, breakfast meat, homemade biscuits, croissants or toast, and beverages. Brunches or dinners are available on request.
AMENITIES	Robes, telephones, llama and horse-boarding, creek swimming or fishing, mountain bikes, picnic lunches, country store, cookies in the evening.
RESTRICTIONS	No smoking in the house, children over five years old are welcome. Resident animals include Pierre the llama, a donkey, Jose "good with people", Ingala an Arabian horse, and three cats, Tess, Mickey and Agnes.
REVIEWED	*Fodor's Bed and Breakfasts, Country Inns and Other Weekend Pleasures—California, AAA Bed & Breakfast —Northern and Central California*
MEMBER	California Association of Bed and Breakfast Inns
KUDOS/COMMENTS	"...rests on 85 acres in a beautiful valley..."

RED BLUFF

Named for the colored sand and gravel cliffs of the surrounding area, it could also be called Red Hot in summer. Horse and cattle sales and roundups in early spring are major events. From here, head out to the Salmon Viewing Plaza at Diversion Dam on the Sacramento River, and the William B. Ide Adobe State Historic Park (remember the Bear Flag Republic?). South of Redding on I-5.

THE FAULKNER HOUSE

1029 Jefferson Street, Red Bluff, CA 96080   916-529-0520
Harvey & Mary Klinger, Resident Owner

KUDOS/COMMENTS   "A nicely decorated Victorian with friendly, knowledgeable hosts."

JARVIS MANSION BED & BREAKFAST

1313 Jackson Street, Red Bluff, CA 96080   916-527-6901
David & Tina Ebert, Resident Owners

LOCATION	From Interstate 5, take the Antelope Boulevard exit and head west, crossing the Sacramento River. Antelope becomes Oak Street, cross railroad tracks and turn right (north) on Jackson Street, go five blocks to the inn.
OPEN	All year
DESCRIPTION	A two-story 1870 Victorian Italianate decorated in period furnishings.
NO. OF ROOMS	Four rooms with private bathrooms. The French Rose room is the best in the house.
RATES	Year round rates for a single or double room with private bathroom are $65 to $90. No minimum stay, 72 hours notice for cancellation.
CREDIT CARDS	MC, Visa
BREAKFAST	Continental Plus breakfast served in the dining room includes seasonal fruit cup, main course, muffins and beverages.
AMENITIES	Wine and hors d'oeuvres at check in, TV, phone available, park-like grounds with gazebo.
RESTRICTIONS	No smoking, no pets, children with prior arrangements. Resident dog, Ebony.
REVIEWED	*AAA Bed & Breakfast Guide—Northern California*

JETER VICTORIAN INN

1107 Jefferson Street, Red Bluff, CA 96080   916-527-7574
Bill and Mary Dunlap

LOCATION	On the corner of Jefferson and Union Streets
OPEN	Open all year
DESCRIPTION	This authentic Victorian inn was built in 1881.
NO. OF ROOMS	Three rooms with private bathrooms, three rooms with shared bathrooms. Try the Imperial Room.
RATES	Year round rates from $65 for shared bathroom to $140 for the Imperial Suite with private bathroom. No minimum stay, 72 hour advance cancellation policy.
CREDIT CARDS	MC, Visa
BREAKFAST	Full breakfast served in the dining room.
AMENITIES	Fresh flowers, robes, TV, hot tub in Imperial Suite. Evening dessert might include wine or champagne, fruit, cookies or candy.
RESTRICTIONS	No smoking, no pets, children over the age of 14 welcome.
REVIEWED	*Bed and Breakfast Country Inns, California Bed and Breakfast Inns*

REDDING

This is the main gateway into the splendors of the Shasta-Trinity National Recreation Area and National Forest. The town itself is on the banks of the Sacramento River and its 14 tributaries, and its restored Victorian neighborhoods make for pleasant strolling. Handy doings: Redding Rodeo Week, and three miles west, the Shasta Dixieland Jazz Festival. Horse lovers can mix with the Mustangs at the Shingletown Wild Horse Sanctuary (this is an up-close experience), about 30 miles southeast of town.

THE CABRAL HOUSE BED & BREAKFAST

1752 Chestnut Street, Redding, CA 96001　　　　　　916-244-3766
Ann & Louie Cabral, Jr., Resident Owners

LOCATION	From I-5 take Cypress exit, right on Pine Street, left on Placer, left on Chestnut. From I-5 south take Central Redding/Eureka Highway 299 West exit, left on Court Street, right on Placer and left on Chestnut.
OPEN	All year
DESCRIPTION	A two-story 1930s host home with art deco "flair" and vintage furnishings.
NO. OF ROOMS	Three rooms with private bathrooms. Ann selected Amelia's room as her best.
RATES	Year round rates are $70 to $115 for a single or a double with private bathroom. There is no minimum stay and cancellation requires seven days notice with a $10 service charge.
CREDIT CARDS	Amex, MC, Visa
BREAKFAST	Full "gourmet" breakfast is served in the dining room or patio and includes a fresh fruit bowl and sauces, oven baked "unusual" entree, homemade scones and breads and coffee.
AMENITIES	Wine and hors d'oeuvres, fresh flowers, phone in common area, "no TV or hot tub."
RESTRICTIONS	No smoking inside, children over 12 are welcome. The resident pets are Prissy the dog and Hannibal and Molly the cats who are in restricted areas of the house.
MEMBER	California Association of Bed & Breakfast Inns, Professional Association of Innkeepers International

PALISADES PARADISE B&B

1200 Palisades Avenue, Redding, CA 96003   *916-223-5305*
Gail Goetz, Resident Owner   *800-382-4648*

LOCATION	From I-5 northbound, take Highway 44 exit to Hilltop, go one mile (road makes a left turn over I-5), make an immediate left on to Palisade Avenue.
OPEN	All year
DESCRIPTION	A 1977 contemporary host home with contemporary mixed with traditional furnishings.
NO. OF ROOMS	Two rooms share 1-1/2 bathrooms. Try the Sunset Suite.
RATES	Year round rates are $55 and $75 for a single with a shared bathroom and $60 and $75 for a double with a shared bathroom. There is no minimum stay and cancellation requires five days notice.
CREDIT CARDS	Amex, MC, Visa
BREAKFAST	Continental Plus is served in the dining room and includes juice, fresh fruit, cereal, pastries, boiled eggs or cheese and beverages.
AMENITIES	Flowers in season, cable TV in rooms, garden spa overlooking river, bird watching, nightly chocolates, refreshments on arrival.
RESTRICTIONS	No smoking. There is an "elderly friendly mutt" called Ebony an "elderly garage cat" called Kitty.
MEMBER	California Association of Bed & Breakfast Innks, Professional Association of Innkeepers International, American Bed & Breakfast Association.
RATED	ABBA 2 Crowns
KUDOS/COMMENTS	"Wonderful setting; pleasant owner - casual newer home - spactacular river view."

REDDING'S BED & BREAKFAST

1094 Palisades Avenue, Redding, CA 96003   *916-222-2494*
Lacy LaMoire, Resident Owner   *FAX 916-224-9375*

LOCATION	Three blocks north of Mt. Shasta Mall take a left on Palisades Avenue to the host home.
OPEN	All year
DESCRIPTION	A two-story 1940 Victorian with country furnishings.
NO. OF ROOMS	One room with private bathroom, two rooms share two bathrooms. Pick the Balcony Room.
RATES	Year round rates are $27.50 to $37.50 for a single with a shared bathroom, $65 to $75 for a double with a shared bathroom and $100 for the "Honeymoon". There is no minimum stay and cancellation requires seven days notice.
CREDIT CARDS	Amex, Discover
BREAKFAST	Full breakfast is served in the guestroom and includes hot apple cobbler, cakes, muffins, fruit bowls or French toast and beverages.
AMENITIES	Fresh roses in rooms, robes and heart shaped Jacuzzi on back deck.
RESTRICTIONS	No smoking, children over six are welcome. The dog is named Betty Boop and the cat is named is Miss Kitty and Miss Kitty "is huge".

TIFFANY HOUSE B&B INN

1510 Barbara Road, Redding, CA 96003   916-244-3225
Arthur & Roberta Dube, Resident Owners

LOCATION	Take Highway 5 through town to Lake Boulevard, left on Lake Boulevard for 3/4 mile to North Market (2nd stop light), left on North Market 1/2 mile to Benton Drive and go 1/2 mile to Barbara Road, right on Barbara and uphill to the inn.
OPEN	All year
DESCRIPTION	A 1939 late Victorian on a hill and nestled under oaks with Victorian interior furnishings.
NO. OF ROOMS	Four rooms with private bathrooms. Roberta likes the Wisteria cottage.
RATES	Year round rates are $65 to $85 for a single or a double with a private bathroom and $125 for the cottage. There is no minimum stay or cancellation policy.
CREDIT CARDS	Amex, MC, Visa
BREAKFAST	Full breakfast is served in the dinning room, country kitchen or gazebo and includes fresh fruit, home baked bread, entree, hot and cold cereals and beverages. Picnic baskets are available by previous order.
AMENITIES	Fresh flowers in room, robes, spa in cottage, hair dryers, TV in drawing room, fireplaces in drawing room and parlor, swimming pool, gazebo and basketball court, very large deck, evening refreshments, cottage is handicapped accessible.
RESTRICTIONS	No smoking, no pets, children welcome. The resident outside cat is called Squeaky.
REVIEWED	*Northern California Best Places, Quick Escapes From San Francisco*
MEMBER	Professional Association of Innkeepers International, California Association of Bed & Breakfast Inns
KUDOS/COMMENTS	" A reputable establishment." ... "wonderful Victorian overlooking city, gracious hosts, excellent food, brsutiful decor."

RUTHEFORD

Winery tours and related activities are the reasons to be here in the heart of Napa County wine country on Highway 29.

RANCHO CAYMUS

1140 Rutheford Road, Rutheford, CA 94573   *707-963-1777*
John Komes, Resident Owner   *800-845-1777*
Spanish, Russian and Hungarian spoken *FAX 707-963-5387*

LOCATION	From the city of Napa, go north on Highway 29 for 18 miles. Turn right at the junction of Highway 128 and go down the road 100 yards. The inn is on the left.
OPEN	All year
DESCRIPTION	A 1985 Southwest hacienda with rustic California furnishings.
NO. OF ROOMS	Twenty-six rooms with private bathrooms. Otto likes room #209.
RATES	High season, April 1 to November 30, rates are $100 to $150 for a single or a double with private bathroom, suites are $200 to $295. Low season, December 1 to March 31, rates are $90 to $135 for a single or a double with private bathroom, suites are $175 to $265. Two night minimum stay on high season weekends, cancellation requires 72 hours notice.
CREDIT CARDS	Amex, MC, Visa
BREAKFAST	Continental Plus is served in the dining room and includes homemade granola and mufffins, fresh fruit and beverages. Lunch and dinner are available for private functions.
AMENITIES	Most of the rooms have fireplaces, five suites include Jacuzzi tubs. Most rooms have TV, telephone, refrigerator and wet bar. Meeting facilities for 50, two handicapped access rooms.
RESTRICTIONS	No pets, children allowed "but not suggested". The resident cat is called Blue Boy and the resident dog, Shorty, "was elected mayor of Rutheford in 1988"...and we thought politics was going to the dogs...TI.
REVIEWED	*Weekends for Two in Northern California, 50 Romantic Getaways, The Definitive California Bed & Breakfast Directory*
MEMBER	California Association of Bed & Breakfast Inns
RATED	AAA 3 Diamonds, Mobil 3 Stars

SACRAMENTO

The state capital since 1854, it has enough cultural offerings to keep you busy. Not to be overlooked is the Capitol building, a splendid example of neo-classic architecture modeled after the nation's Capitol. Other wonders: Old Sacramento, the original gold rush-era town; American River Parkway, an outdoor gem with 23 miles of riverside parkways; and the dreamy, watery world of The Delta explored by houseboat. Very major events include Cinco de Mayo, famous star-studded Sacramento Jazz Jubilee on Memorial Day weekend, the State Fair in August, and Shakespeare in the Park, July–September.

ABIGAIL'S BED & BREAKFAST INN

2120 G Street, Sacramento, CA 95816
Susanne & Ken Ventura, Resident Owners

916-441-5007
800-858-1568
FAX 916-441-0621

LOCATION	Exit H Street from Business 80 loop (east) and cross H Street, turn left on G Street, go eight blocks.
OPEN	All year
DESCRIPTION	A three-story Colonial Revival inn with eclectic and Edwardian furnishings.
NO. OF ROOMS	Five rooms with private bathrooms, by staff vote the Margaret room was selected as the best.
RATES	Year round rates are $79 to $105 for a single with a private bathroom and $95 to $155 for a double with a private bathroom. There is a three night minimum stay on Thanksgiving and Memorial Day weekends. Cancellation requires seven days notice.
CREDIT CARDS	Amex, Diners Club, Discover, MC, Visa
BREAKFAST	Full breakfast is served in the dining room or guestrooms and includes fruit, yogurt, custard "award winning" zucchini-walnut-sour cream pancakes or sundried tomato quiche...How could anything with zucchini in it win an award?...We need a guest report please...TI
AMENITIES	Flowers, robes, telephone, TV, late night snack, early morning coffee on sideboard outside rooms, refrigerator stocked with cold drinks, hot tub in the garden, gazebo.
RESTRICTIONS	No smoking in house, no pets, children over five are welcome. Two cats Sabrina and Abigail,"who if I ask her to say please in almost any language, will sit on her hind legs and rub her ears for cream"...We're not making any of this up...TI
REVIEWED	*Jan Peverille's Inn Places for Bed & Breakfast, The California Bed & Breakfast Book, Bed & Breakfast California, America's Wonderful Little Hotels & Inns, Bay Area Back Roads, Best Places to Stay in California.*
MEMBER	California Association of Bed & Breakfast Inns
KUDOS/COMMENTS	"Nicely kept-up—great breakfast."

AMBER HOUSE BED & BREAKFAST INN

1315 22nd Street, Sacramento, CA 95816	916-444-8085
Michael and Jane Richardson, Resident Owners	800-755-6526
	FAX 916-447-1548

LOCATION	Eight blocks east of the State Capitol, between Capitol Avenue and 22nd Street.
OPEN	All year
DESCRIPTION	Two side-by-side, two-story homes: a 1905 Craftsman and a 1913 Mediterranean, both furnished with antiques.
NO. OF ROOMS	Nine rooms with private bathrooms. The Renoir Room is the best in either house.
RATES	Year round rates for a single or double with a private bathroom are $85 to $195. Both homes rent for $1,295. No minimum stay, cancellation policy requires two days notice for weekdays, seven days notice for weekends.
CREDIT CARDS	Amex, MC, Visa, Diners Club, Discover
BREAKFAST	Full breakfast served in dining room, guestroom or veranda and includes beverages, fruit, a hot entree such as quiche and potatoes with peppers. Breakfast or lunch meeting meals available by prior arrangement.
AMENITIES	Flowers, phones with modem, cable TV, Jacuzzi, VCRs, robes, clock radios with tape players in every room.
RESTRICTIONS	No smoking.
REVIEWED	*Best Places to Kiss in Northern California, Special Places, America's Wonderful Little Hotels and Inns, Recommended Country Inns — West Coast, Northern California Discovery Guide*
MEMBER	American Bed and Breakfast Association, California Association of Bed and Breakfast Inns, Special Places
RATED	ABBA 3 Crowns, Mobil 3 Stars
KUDOS/COMMENTS	"Charming quality B&B—beautifully appointed rooms and bathrooms, friendly staff, yummy breakfast."

HARTLEY HOUSE
BED AND BREAKFAST INN

700 22nd Street, Sacramento, CA 95816   916-447-7829
Randy Hartley, Resident Owner   800-831-5806
Spanish spoken   FAX 916-447-1820

LOCATION	From Interstate 5, take Downtown J Street exit, proceed on J Street to 22nd Street, turn left, to the corner of 22nd Street and G Street.
OPEN	All year
DESCRIPTION	A two-story, 1906 Colonial Revival. Authentic leaded glass and stained glass windows, and historic antiques.
NO. OF ROOMS	Five rooms with private bathrooms. Dover is the best room in the house.
RATES	Year round rates for a single or double with a private bathroom are $79 to $135. Entire inn rents for $600. Minimum stay on holidays and weekends. Cancellation required by noon, one day prior to arrival for full refund.
CREDIT CARDS	Amex, MC, Visa, Diners Club
BREAKFAST	Full breakfast is served in the dining room or the courtyard and includes fresh fruit, egg dish, freshly baked muffins and scones and beverages. Lunch, dinner and special meals available on request.
AMENITIES	Robes, fresh flowers, phones, TV, turn down service, FAX service, meeting facilities, and catering services.
RESTRICTIONS	No smoking except in garden areas, no pets, children over ten years old are welcome.
REVIEWED	*Best Places to Kiss in Northern California, Best Places to Stay in Northern California, AAA Bed & Breakfast Guide—Northern California, Fodor's California*
MEMBER	California Association of Bed and Breakfast Inns

SAN ANDREAS

The Calaveras County Seat is bustling and touristy, and historically colorful. Check out the County Museum, Black Bart's jail cell, the California Cavers, or head out to the New Hogan Reservoir Recreation Area. Southeast of Sacramento on Hwy. 49.

COURTYARD BED & BREAKFAST

334 West St. Charles, San Andreas, CA 95249 209-754-1518
Lucy Thein, Resident Owner

LOCATION	Right in greater downtown San Andreas, population 2,200.
OPEN	All year
DESCRIPTION	A 1920 wood frame host home with a 400-year-old oak tree, gardens and 55 bird houses. The inn has country furnishings.
NO. OF ROOMS	Two rooms with private bathrooms. The best room is the master suite.
RATES	Year round rates for a single or a double are $55 to $75. Cancellation requires 48 hours notice and a $25 fee.
CREDIT CARDS	No
BREAKFAST	Coffee is brought to the room and a full two course breakfast is served in the gardens or breakfast room.
AMENITIES	Redwood hot tub under the trees, hors d'oeuvres served on arrival. The master suite has a fireplace, baby grand piano, stained-glass window over the bathtub and walk-in closet.
RESTRICTIONS	Smoking outside only, children and dogs are welcome.

THE ROBIN'S NEST

247 West St. Charles Street, San Andreas, CA 95249   *209-754-1076*
George and Carolee Jones, Resident Owners

LOCATION	One-half mile west of downtown San Andreas on the south side of Hwy. 49.
OPEN	All year
DESCRIPTION	Restored 1895 Queen Anne Victorian mansion situated on an acre of grass and trees and decorated with antiques. Listed on the State Historic Register and the National List of Historic Places.
NO. OF ROOMS	Seven rooms with private bathrooms; two rooms share one bathroom. Try the Snyder Suite for a special stay.
RATES	April through October and all weekends: singles and doubles with private bathrooms $70 to $95; single and double with shared bathroom $55; entire B&B $725. November through March, Sunday through Thursday: singles and doubles with private bathrooms $55 to $75; single and double with shared bathroom $55; entire B&B $725. Minimum stay required the third weekend of May (Frog Jump). Five days cancellation notice required for full refund.
CREDIT CARDS	Amex, MC, Visa
BREAKFAST	Full breakfast, served in dining room, consists of four courses beginning with cold fruit soup. Includes an entree, such as crab-filled crepes, and ends with dessert.
AMENITIES	Snacks available in the afternoon. Hot tea tray in the evening.
RESTRICTIONS	No smoking inside, no pets. One resident 18-year-old dog, "J.J."
MEMBER	Calaveras County Lodging Association, California Lodging Industry Association

SAN FRANCISCO

First, this is a city of views. Built on 40 hills between the Pacific and the Bay, it's a visual feast that overloads the senses. This cosmopolitan city of many nations has unexpected treasures: the star among them is Golden Gate National Recreation Area, nearly 73,000 acres that sweeps the Marin Headlands and makes it the world's largest urban park. City pleasures: Cable Cars (naturally); endless shopping at S.F. Shopping Center, a 9-story vertical mall; Embarcadero Center, Crocker Galleria, and serious bargains in the SoMa (South of Market) garment district. Among the best events: Yachting Opening Day on the Bay and the S.F. 49ers in Festival staged in Golden Gate Park August–October. And, always cruise the Bay. But understanding the city's neighborhoods (districts) makes all the difference in enjoying this place. Things you will need: time and more time.

ALAMO SQUARE INN

719 Scott Street, San Francisco, CA 94117	*415-922-2055*
Wayne Corn, Resident Owner	

THE AMSTERDAM HOTEL

749 Taylor Street, San Francisco, CA 94108	*415-673-3277*
Kenny Gopal, Manager	

THE ANDREWS HOTEL

624 Post Street, San Francisco, CA 94109	*415-563-6877*
Paula Forselles, Manager	*800-926-3739*
Italian, French and Spanish spoken	*FAX 415-928-6919*

LOCATION	Two blocks west of Union Square at Post and Taylor Streets.
OPEN	All year
DESCRIPTION	A 1905 Queen Anne Hotel.
NO. OF ROOMS	Forty-eight rooms with private bathrooms. Paula likes the petite suite.
RATES	Year round rates are $79 to $119 for a single or a double with a private bathroom. There is no minimum stay and cancellation requires 48 hours notice and seven days for groups that reserve five or more rooms.
CREDIT CARDS	Amex, Diners Club, MC, Visa
BREAKFAST	Continental breakfast is served on buffet tables in the hallway and includes fresh fruit, muffins, rolls, croissants and beverages.
AMENITIES	Telephones, TV, complimentary glass of wine, Italian restaurant on premises and concierge.
RESTRICTIONS	No pets, all rooms are single and double occupancy only, a few rooms can accommodate a third with prior notice only.
REVIEWED	*America's Wonderful Little Hotels & Inns, Frommer's California*
RATED	Mobil 2 Stars

ANNA'S THREE BEARS

114 Divisadero Street, San Francisco, CA 94117   *415-255-3167*
Michael Hofman, Resident Manager   *800-428-8559*
                                                              FAX 415-552-2959

LOCATION	Located in historic Buena Vista Heights, just off Highway 101 exit to Fall Street, which intersects with Divisadero about 6 blocks away. Take Divisadero south to 114.
OPEN	All year
DESCRIPTION	1907 two-story Edwardian Flats architectural style furnished with Victorian and Edwardian antiques.
NO. OF ROOMS	Three Edwardian flats.
RATES	Year round daily rates for a double with private bathroom are $200 to $250, and $1,000 to $1,500 weekly rates. Added charge for extra persons. Two night minimum stay on weekends, seven day cancellation notice required with $20 charge.
CREDIT CARDS	Amex, MC, Visa
BREAKFAST	Continental breakfast including beverages, fresh fruit and pastries will be stocked in suite kitchen.
AMENITIES	Private living room, dining room and stocked kitchen in each flat with fireplaces, private decks, Bay views, phones, cable TV, fax service available.
RESTRICTIONS	No smoking, no pets, children over 10 years old welcome. Trevor the Golden Retriever puppy is the "the best dog in the world."
REVIEWED	*Inn Places, National Trust Guide to Historic Inns and Small Hotels*

Archbishop's Mansion

1000 Fulton Street, San Francisco, CA 94117　　　　　　　*415-563-7872*
Rick Janzier, Manager　　　　　　　　　　　　　　　　　*800-543-5820*
Spanish spoken　　　　　　　　　　　　　　　　　*FAX 415-885-3193*

LOCATION	From Highway 101, take Fell/Laguna exit. Go four blocks on Fell Street to Steiner Street and turn right. Go three blocks to Fulton Street and turn left. Mansion is across the street from Alamo Square Park.
OPEN	All year
DESCRIPTION	A three-story 1904 Second French Empire mansion built "for the Archbishop himself." Filled with antiques and extensive use of exposed Redwood.
NO. OF ROOMS	Fifteen rooms with private bathrooms. Don Giovanni is the best room in the mansion.
RATES	Year round rates for a single or double with a private bathroom are $115 to $189, and $205 to $385 for a suite. Two night minimum stay on weekends, cancellation requires seven days notice.
CREDIT CARDS	Amex, MC, Visa
BREAKFAST	Continental Plus breakfast served in guest room includes fresh orange juice and beverages, muffins and coffee cake, fresh fruit, or granola and yogurt on request.
AMENITIES	Phones and cable TV in all rooms, wine and cheese every afternoon, player piano, VCRs and romantic movies available.
RESTRICTIONS	No smoking in guestrooms, no pets.
REVIEWED	*Country Inns of America, Country Inns and Backroads, West Coast Guide to Bed and Breakfast Inns*
MEMBER	Alamo Square Inn Association
RATED	AAA 3 Diamonds, Mobil 3 Stars

Art Center Bed & Breakfast

1902 Filbert Street, San Francisco, CA 94123　　　　　　*415-567-1526*
George & Helvi Wamsley, Resident Owners

The Bed & Breakfast Inn

4 Charlton Court, San Francisco, CA 94123　　　　　　*415-921-9784*
Francesca Stone, Manager

KUDOS/COMMENTS　"Wonderful location, delightful staff."

BOCK'S BED & BREAKFAST

1448 Willard Street, San Francisco, CA 94117   415-664-6842
Laurie Bock, Resident Owner   FAX 415-664-1109
Smattering of French spoken

LOCATION	Located two blocks from the southeast corner of Golden Gate Park in the Parnassus Heights neighborhood. Nearest major intersection is Parnassus and Stanyan Streets.
OPEN	All year
DESCRIPTION	A 1906 two-story Edwardian restored to include original redwood and mahogany paneling and oak floors.
NO. OF ROOMS	One room with private bathroom, two rooms with shared bathroom.
RATES	Year round rates for single or double room with private bathroom are are $65 to $75, and $40 to $60 for single or double room with shared bathroom. Two night minimum stay required, seven day cancellation requested.
CREDIT CARDS	No
BREAKFAST	Continental Plus breakfast served in the dining room includes fresh fruit, granola, variety of breads and pastries and beverages.
AMENITIES	Decks, private phones, TVs, coffee and tea service in all rooms, guest refrigerator.
RESTRICTIONS	No smoking, no pets, no nude sunbathing on the deck. Rosie, the Scotty dog, will be watching...TI
REVIEWED	*Bed and Breakfast in California, Spartacus Guide, Rough Guide to San Francisco*
MEMBER	Professional Associaion of Innkeepers International

CASA ARGUELLO BED & BREAKFAST

225 Arguello Boulevard, San Francisco, CA 94118   415-752-9482
Emma Baires, Resident Owner

Casita Blanca

330 Edgehill Way, San Francisco, CA 94127   415-564-9339
Joan Bard, Resident Owner   FAX 415-566-4737
Spanish spoken

LOCATION	Twenty minutes drive from San Francisco International Airport. and not far from Golden Gate park. Directions will be sent, "don't despair, as everyone has found us."
OPEN	All year
DESCRIPTION	A 1929 Spanish cottage with contemporary furnishings.
NO. OF ROOMS	One room cottage with private bathroom.
RATES	A single or double with private bathroom is $80 per night with a two night minimum stay.
CREDIT CARDS	No.
BREAKFAST	Continental is served in the cottage.
AMENITIES	Private telephone, TV, fireplace, full kitchen
RESTRICTIONS	No pets. There are two resident Great Pyrenees, Benni and Nana and two cats, Daisey and Oliver.

Chateau Tivoli

1057 Steiner & Golden Gate Avenue,   415-776-5462
San Francisco, CA 94115
Rodney Karr, Resident Owner

CHEZ DUCHENE

1075 Broadway, San Francisco, CA 94133   *415-441-3160*
Jay Duchene, Resident Owner

LOCATION	Top of Russian Hill.
OPEN	All year
DESCRIPTION	A three-story 1906-1908 Victorian host home with "very San Francisco diversity" in furnishings.
NO. OF ROOMS	One room with private bathroom.
RATES	Year round rates are $90 for a single or a double with a two night minimum stay and cancellation requires 48 hours notice.
CREDIT CARDS	No
BREAKFAST	Continental Plus is served in the dining room and includes fresh orange juice, fruit, muffin, pastry, yogurt, cereal and coffee.
AMENITIES	Flowers, candy, view of Nob Hill and Bay Bridge.
RESTRICTIONS	No smoking, no pets
REVIEWED	*Bed & Breakfast USA*

CORNELL HOTEL

715 Bush Street, San Francisco, CA 94108   *415-421-3154*
Claude Lambert, Resident Owner

DOCKSIDE BOAT & BED

Pier 39, San Francisco, CA 94133   *415-392-5526*
Mike Merck, Manager

DOLORES PARK INN

3641 17th Street, San Francisco, CA 94114   *415-621-0482*
Bernie Vielwerth, Resident Owner   *FAX 415-621-0482*
Spanish and German spoken

LOCATION	From San Francisco International Airport take Highway 101 north. Exit at Army Street West, straight to Dolores Street, right on Dolores and turn left on 17th Street. It is one block from the Old Mission Dolores.
OPEN	All year
DESCRIPTION	An 1874 two-story Italianate Victorian with Victorian furnishings. The inn is on the San Francisco Historic Register.
NO. OF ROOMS	One room with private bathroom and four rooms share three bathrooms. Pick the suite.
RATES	Year round rates for a single or double in the suite are $150 and $165 respectively. A single with shared bathroom is $60 and a double with shared bathroom is $90. There is a two night minimum stay and cancellation requires seven days notice.
CREDIT CARDS	MC, Visa
BREAKFAST	Full breakfast served in the dining room includes eggs, toast, muffins and croissants, cheeses, fresh fruit, cereal, juices, tea and coffee.
AMENITIES	TV and clock radio in every room, complimentary afternoon coffee, tea, wine or sherry, free city and Bay Area maps.
RESTRICTIONS	No smoking, no pets, children over 12 are welcome.
REVIEWED	*All American Bed & Breakfast, AAA Bed & Breakfast Guide—Northern California, The Best of San Francisco, San Francisco on a Shoestring, The Rough Guide*

Edward II Bed & Breakfast

3155 Scott Street at Lombard, San Francisco, CA 94123   415-922-3000
Dick Anderton, Resident Manager   800-473-2846
Spanish spoken   FAX 415-931-5784

LOCATION	Ten blocks west of Van Ness Avenue on the corner of Lombard and Scott.
OPEN	All year
DESCRIPTION	A three-story 1915 Edwardian with country furnishings.
NO. OF ROOMS	Nineteen rooms with private bathrooms, 12 rooms share four bathrooms. The Royal Suite was selected as the best room by manager Dick Anderton.
RATES	Year round rates for a single or double with a private bathroom are $89 and a single or a double with shared bathroom is $69. Suites are $150 to $200. There is a two night minimum stay on the weekends, except for rooms with shared bathrooms. Cancellation requires 72 hours notice.
CREDIT CARDS	Amex, MC, Visa
BREAKFAST	Continental breakfast is served in the dining room and includes "the best San Francisco pastries, bagels, english muffins, and beverages."
AMENITIES	Telephone, robes, cable TV in rooms, coffee and tea in the afternoon, sherry in the evening.
RESTRICTIONS	No smoking, no pets, children of any are are welcome, "no whiners."

Golden Gate Hotel

775 Bush Street, San Francisco, CA 94108   415-392-3702
John & Renate Kenaston, Resident Owners

Grove Inn

890 Grove Street, San Francisco, CA 94117   415-929-0780
Klaus Zimmermann, Resident Owner

The Herb'n Inn

PO Box 170106, San Francisco, CA 94117   415-553-8542
Pam & Bruce Brennan, Resident Owner

HILL POINT BED & BREAKFAST

15 Hill Point Avenue, San Francisco, CA 94117
Bob McCormick, Resident Owner
German, French, Italian, Spanish spoken

415-753-0393
FAX 415-753-0738

LOCATION	From Highway 1 (19th Avenue) take Judah Street heading east. Go through UCSF Campus. Hill Point Avenue is the last street on the left before descending down the hill to Stanyan Street.
OPEN	All year
DESCRIPTION	Five 1912 San Francisco Victorians located on a cul-de-sac overlooking Golden Gate Park. Furnishings are both antique and modern.
NO. OF ROOMS	Seven rooms with private bathrooms, eleven rooms share four bathrooms.
RATES	Year round rates for a single or double room with private bathroom are $65 to $73, and $52 to $60 for a single or double room with shared bathroom. Suites are $90 to $195. Cancellation ust be by noon the day of check in.
CREDIT CARDS	Amex, MC, Diners Club, Visa, Discover
BREAKFAST	Continental breakfast served in the dining room includes blueberry muffins, apple turnovers, danish, English muffins, croissants, seasonal fruit and beverages.
AMENITIES	TV, phones, BBQ garden, some rooms have views of Golden Gate Park, ocean and the city.
RESTRICTIONS	No smoking, no pets. Frederick the Great, Elisabeth (the Empress), and Kaiser Franz Jozeph are the resident family of Shih Tzus.
MEMBER	California Lodging Industry Association

HOTEL BOHEME

444 Columbus, San Francisco, CA 94133   415-433-9111
Bruce Abney, Manager

HOTEL DAVID

480 Geary Street, San Francisco, CA 94102   415-771-1600
David, Resident Owner

INN AT UNION SQUARE

440 Post Street, San Francisco, CA 94102   415-397-3510
Brooks Bayly, Manager

INN ON CASTRO

321 Castro Street, San Francisco, CA 94114   415-861-0321
Jan de Gier, Resident Owner

INN SAN FRANCISCO

943 South Van Ness Avenue, San Francisco, CA 94110   415-641-0188
Martin Neely, Resident Owner

JACKSON COURT

2198 Jackson Street, San Francisco, CA 94115   *415-929-7670*
Pat Cremer, Manager   *FAX 415-929-1405*
Spanish spoken

LOCATION	Fifteen minutes west of downtown San Francisco. Five blocks from Van Ness, 2 blocks east of Fillmore, 5 blocks up the hill (south) of Union Street. From the south, take Highway 101 north to Golden Gate Bridge. From the north, take Highway 101 south to Lombard Street, turn right 8 blocks to Jackson and Buchanan.
OPEN	All year
DESCRIPTION	Three-story 1900 brownstone mansion with antique and contemporary furnishings.
NO. OF ROOMS	Ten rooms with private bathrooms. The Library Room is the best in the house.
RATES	Year round rates for a single or double with private bathroom are $108 to $150. Two night minimum on weekends, seven days notice for cancellation.
CREDIT CARDS	Amex, MC, Visa
BREAKFAST	Continental Plus served in the dining room includes fresh fruit salad, cereals, breads, muffins, bagels, croissants or Danish and beverages.
AMENITIES	Flowers, telephones, cable TV in rooms, afternoon refreshments next to the fireplace.
RESTRICTIONS	No smoking, children over 12 years old welcome.
REVIEWED	*America's Wonderful Little Hotels and Inns, Northern California Best Places*
MEMBER	San Francisco Bed and Breakfast Association
RATED	ABBA 3 Crowns

THE MANSIONS HOTEL

2220 Sacramento Street, San Francisco, CA 94115   415-929-9444
Bob Pritiken, Resident Owner

KUDOS/COMMENTS   "Delightful, mysterious, haunted and thoroughly entertaining."

MARINA INN

3110 Octavia Street, San Francisco, CA 94123   415-928-1000
Craig Bell, Manager   800-274-1420
                                                   FAX 415-928-5909

MONTE CRISTO BED AND BREAKFAST

600 Presidio Avenue, San Francisco, CA 94115   415-931-1875
George Yuan, Resident Owner
Spanish, Chinese spoken   FAX 415-931-6005

LOCATION	From San Francisco Airport, take Highway 101 north, exit at 7th Street. Past Market Street to Franklin Street, turn left on Pine Street. Monte Cristo is between Pine and Push Streets on Presidio Avenue.
OPEN	All year
DESCRIPTION	An 1875, two-story Victorian home with English and American furnishings, originally built as a bordello.
NO. OF ROOMS	Eleven rooms with private bathrooms, three rooms share five bathrooms.
RATES	Year round rates for a double with a private bathroom are $78 to $98, and $63 to $73 for a double with a shared bathroom, suites with a private bathroom are $108. Seven day cancellation policy.
CREDIT CARDS	Amex, MC, Visa, Diners Club, Discover
BREAKFAST	Continental Plus served buffet style in the dining room includes fresh orange juice, cereal, breads, blueberry muffins, and a variety of fresh fruit and beverages.
AMENITIES	Robes, tea or wine on arrival, phone, TV and VCR.
RESTRICTIONS	Smoking in designated areas only, no pets, children are welcome.
MEMBER	California Lodging Industry Association

No Name Victorian Bed & Breakfast

847 Fillmore Street, San Francisco CA 94117　　　　　　415-479-1913
Susan & Richard Kreibich, Resident Owners　　　　　　800-452-8249
German and Czechloslovakian spoken　　　　　　FAX 415-921-2273

LOCATION	City center, two miles west of Union Square
OPEN	All year
DESCRIPTION	A three-story 1895 Victorian furnished with antiques and reproductions.
NO. OF ROOMS	Four rooms with private bathrooms and two rooms share one bathroom.
RATES	Year round rates are $75 to $125 for a single or a double with a private bathroom, $65 to $75 for a single or a double with a shared bathroom and $95 to $115 for a suite. There is a two night minimum stay on the weekends and cancellation requires 14 days notice.
CREDIT CARDS	Amex, MC, Visa
BREAKFAST	Full breakfast is served in the dining room and includes waffles, omelettes, cereals, fruits and beverages.
AMENITIES	Complementary wine, fireplaces in most rooms, deck and hot tub.
RESTRICTIONS	No smoking, no pets

The Nob Hill Lambourne

725 Pine Street, San Francisco, CA 94108　　　　　　415-433-2287
Ashley Cole, Manager

NOE'S NEST

3973 23rd Street, San Francisco, CA 94114   *415-821-0751*
Sheila R. Ash, Resident Owner   *FAX 415-821-0723*
French, a little Hebrew and Japanese spoken

LOCATION	Located in the heart of Noe Valley. From airport, take Highway 101 north, exit on Army Street west, take Army to Sanchez, turn right onto Sanchez. Go six blocks, turn left onto 23rd, Noe's Nest is between Sanchez and Noe streets.
OPEN	All year
DESCRIPTION	An 1895 two-story host home has been remodeled to include skylights and decks.
NO. OF ROOMS	Five rooms with private bathrooms.
RATES	High season rates April through mid-December are $75 to $95 for a single or a double and $125 for the penthouse. Off season rates are $65 to $85 for a single or a double and $100 for the penthouse. There is no mimimum stay and cancellation three days notice and a 10% surcharge.
CREDIT CARDS	Amex, MC, Visa
BREAKFAST	Full breakfast served in the kitchen includes fresh squeezed juice, bagels with lox and cream cheese, hot or cold cereal, frittata, muffins, yogurt, coffee and tea.
AMENITIES	Outdoor hot tub, some rooms have decks, fireplace, brass bed or refrigerator. All rooms haveTV/VCR, phone, and fresh flowers. Kitchen, washer and dryer available to guests.
MEMBER	Gay and Lesbian Travel Guide Association

Petite Auberge

863 Bush Street, San Francisco, CA 94108   *415-928-6000*
Celeste Lytle, Manager   *800-365-3004*
French, Spanish spoken   *FAX 415-775-5717*

LOCATION	From Hwy. 101 take Bush Street east. Located between Mason and Taylor, three blocks from Union Square and one block from the cable cars.
OPEN	All year
DESCRIPTION	Early 1900's Baroque Country Inn featuring curved bay windows, parlor with a fireplace and dining room with view of a small courtyard garden. Country French interior decor.
NO. OF ROOMS	Twenty six rooms with private bathrooms.
RATES	Year round rates for doubles with private bathroom $110 to $160; suites $220. Cancellation policy: 24 hours prior to check-in.
CREDIT CARDS	Amex, MC, Visa
BREAKFAST	Full breakfast, served in dining room, includes homemade breads, fresh seasonal fruit, cereals, muffins, hot dish, juices, tea and coffee. Room service option with charge. Afternoon wine and hors d'oeuvres available.
AMENITIES	Terry robes, unlimited coffee, tea and sodas all day, turndown service, newspaper at door, and a large basket of amenities.
RESTRICTIONS	No smoking, no pets.
REVIEWED	*Karen Brown's California Country Inns & Itineraries, Frommer's B&B North America, Best Places to Stay in California*
RATED	AAA 3 Diamonds, Mobil 3 Stars

QUEEN ANNE HOTEL

1590 Sutter Street, San Francisco, CA 94109   415-441-2828
Steven Bobb, Manager   800-227-3970
Spanish, Chinese, German and Greek spoken   FAX 415-775-5212

LOCATION	From Van Ness Avenue (Highway 101) moving from Golden Gate Bridge to downtown San Francisco, turn right on Sutter and go three blocks to Octavia. The hotel is between Octavia and Laguna streets.
OPEN	All year
DESCRIPTION	A four-story 1890 Victorian hotel with Victorian antique furnishings.
NO. OF ROOMS	Forty-nine rooms with private bathrooms. Steven recommends room 414.
RATES	Year round rates are $99 to $150 for a single or a double with private bathroom and $175 to $225 for a suite. There is no minimum stay and cancellation requires 24 hours notice.
CREDIT CARDS	Amex, Diners Club, Discover, JCB, MC, Visa
BREAKFAST	Continental breakfast is served in the dining room.
AMENITIES	Moderate and deluxe rooms have fireplaces, afternoon tea and sherry, complimentary limo to downtown, TV, telephone, meeting facilities for 150 and handicapped access rooms. Non-smoking rooms available.
RESTRICTIONS	Non smoking rooms available.
RATED	AAA 3 Diamonds, Mobil 3 Stars

RED VICTORIAN BED & BREAKFAST

1665 Haight Street, San Francisco, CA 94117   415-864-1978
Sami Sunchild, Resident Owner

SHEEHAN HOTEL

620 Sutter Street, San Francisco, CA 94102   *415-775-6500*
Don Hayden, Resident Manager   *800-848-1529*
French and Spanish spoken   *FAX 415-775-3271*

LOCATION	One block from Powell Street (cable car route), two blocks from Union Square in downtown San Francisco shopping and theatre district. Located at the intersection of Sutter and Mason Streets.
OPEN	All year
DESCRIPTION	Built in 1917, this multi-story Georgian hotel is decorated in European antiques.
NO. OF ROOMS	Fifty four rooms with private bathrooms, 17 rooms with shared bathrooms. The Bridal Suite is the best room in the hotel.
RATES	High season (May 15 through October) rates for a single or double room with private bathroom $60 to $95, $45 to $60 for a single or double with shared bathroom. Low season (November through May 15) rates approximately 15% less. Cancellation requires 24 hours notice.
CREDIT CARDS	Amex, MC, Diners Club, Visa, Discover, JCB
BREAKFAST	Continental breakfast served in the dining room includes homemade muffins, scones, breads and beverages.
AMENITIES	City's largest indoor pool, exercise room, cable TV, direct dial phones, 300 seat theatre, meeting room, beer and wine, afternoon tea, handicapped access.
RESTRICTIONS	No pets.
REVIEWED	*Let's Go USA, San Francisco on a Shoestring, Best Places to Stay in California, The Real Guide*
MEMBER	California Lodging Industry Association, San Francisco Convention and Visitor's Bureau
RATED	Mobil 1 Star

SPENCER HOUSE

1080 Haight Street, San Francisco, CA 94117   *415-626-9205*
Jack & Barbara Chambers, Resident Owners   *FAX 415-626-9230*

LOCATION	Eight blocks east of Golden Gate Park in the Haight-Ashbury neighborhood of San Francisco.
OPEN	All year
DESCRIPTION	An 1887 three-story Queen Anne Victorian mansion, furnished with antiques, handpainted wallpapers and oriental rugs.
NO. OF ROOMS	Six rooms with private bathrooms. The French Room is the best in the house.
RATES	Year round rates for a single or double room with private bathroom are $95 to $155. There is a two-night minimum stay on weekends, five days notice required for cancellation with $10 fee.
CREDIT CARDS	Amex, VC, Visa
BREAKFAST	Full breakfast is served in the grand dining room, and includes fresh orange juice and coffee, eggs ranchero or Belgian waffles with warm strawberries.
AMENITIES	Robes and telephones in rooms, down mattresses, pillows and duvets, anitque linens, antique armoires and beds and decanter of port or sherry.
RESTRICTIONS	No smoking, no pets, children over 10 years old welcome. The resident critters are two American Spaniels, Percy and Perry, Bacchus the Persian cat and Carmen the Macaw.
REVIEWED	*California Country Inns and Itineraries, Country Inns and Back Roads, Best Places to Kiss, Bed and Breakfast in California*
MEMBER	Innkeepers of San Francisco
KUDOS/COMMENTS	"Just outstanding!"

STANYAN PARK HOTEL B&B

750 Stanyan Street, San Francisco, CA 94117   *415-751-1000*
Fred P. Rapp III, CHA   *FAX 415-668-5454*
Spanish spoken

LOCATION	Southwest corner of Golden Gate Park, three miles from downtown San Francisco. Across from Kezar Stadium.
OPEN	All year
DESCRIPTION	Three-story 1904 Queen Anne Victorian. Lobby and dining room on first floor, top two floors for guest rooms. On the State Historic Register.
NO. OF ROOMS	Thirty rooms and six suites with private bathrooms. Fred recommends room 306.
RATES	Year round rates for a single or double are $78 to $96, and suites are $120 to $170. There is no minimum stay and cancellation requires 24 hours notice.
CREDIT CARDS	Amex, MC, Carte Blanche, Diners Club, Visa, Discover
BREAKFAST	Continental breakfast is served in the dining room and includes juice and fresh fruit, assorted breads and pastries and coffee or tea.
AMENITIES	Afternoon tea and cookies in the dining room. All rooms include TV and phones, handicapped rooms available.
RESTRICTIONS	No pets. No smoking in public areas, some guest rooms for smoking.
MEMBER	California Association of Bed and Breakfast Inns
RATED	AAA 3 Diamonds

THE UNION STREET INN

2229 Union Street, San Francisco, CA 94123   *415-346-0424*
Jane Bertorelli & David Coyle, Resident Owners   *FAX 415-922-8046*
Spanish, limited French spoken

LOCATION	Located on Union Street between Steiner and Fillmore Streets in the heart of San Francisco.
OPEN	All year
DESCRIPTION	Two-story 1904 Edwardian/Victorian inn and carriage house furnished with period antiques.
NO. OF ROOMS	Six rooms with private bathrooms. The Carriage House is highly recommended.
RATES	Year round rates for a single or double room with private bathroom, or the carriage house are $125 to $225. Special rates available for four days or longer. Two day minimum stay on weekends, and a very firm seven day cancellation policy.
CREDIT CARDS	Amex, MC, Visa, Discover
BREAKFAST	Full breakfast served in the dining room, the garden, or on the deck inlcudes an egg entree, homemade muffins and breakfast breads, fruit and beverages.
AMENITIES	Flowers, fruit, chocolates, robes, TV, VCR, down comforters, telephones, welcome baskets.
RESTRICTIONS	No smoking, no pets.
MEMBER	California Association of Bed and Breakfast Inns, California Lodging and Industry Association

VICTORIAN INN ON THE PARK

301 Lyon Street, San Francisco, CA 94117　　　　　*415-931-1830*
Lisa & William Benau and　　　　　　　　　　　　*800-435-1967*
Shirley & Paul Weber, Resident Owners　　　　　*FAX 415-931-1830*
Spanish, Italian and Portuguese spoken

LOCATION	From San Francisco Airport take 101 north, exit Fell Street, go one mile west on Fell and turn right on Lyon, adjacent to the Golden Gate Park.
OPEN	All year
DESCRIPTION	A three-story 1897 Queen Anne Victorian with Victorian furnishings and oak paneled dinning room, library and parlor. Listed on the San Francisco Historic Register.
NO. OF ROOMS	Twelve rooms with private bathrooms. Lisa likes the Belevedere Room.
RATES	Year round rates for a single or a double with private bathroom are $99 to $159. The suites range from $159 to $315. There is a two night minimum on weekends and a three night minimum on holiday weekends. Cancellation requires seven days notice.
CREDIT CARDS	Amex, Diner's Club, Discover, JCB, MC, Visa
BREAKFAST	Continental Plus is served in the dining room or guestrooms and includes assorted fruits and cheeses, fresh squeezed orange juice, fresh breads baked daily, croissants, scones and beverages.
AMENITIES	Some rooms have fireplaces, sunken bathtubs and balconies. Wine served daily, decanter of sherry in guest room, parking available and TV and FAX available on request..
RESTRICTIONS	No smoking, no pets
REVIEWED	*Bed & Breakfast Guide — Great American Cities, Country Inns of America — California, Best Places to Kiss in Northern California, San Francisco Access, America's Wonderful Little Hotels and Inns*
MEMBER	Professional Association of Innkeepers International, California Association of Bed & Breakfast Innkeepers.
RATED	Mobil 3 Stars

WASHINGTON SQUARE INN

1660 Stockton Street, San Francisco, CA 94133	*415-981-4220*
Norm and Nan Rosenblatt, Resident Owners	*800-388-0220*
French spoken	*FAX 415-397-7242*

LOCATION	In the heart of North Beach on Washington Square.
OPEN	All year
DESCRIPTION	Two-story 1906 Queen Anne hotel furnished with French and English antiques.
NO. OF ROOMS	Ten rooms with private bathrooms, five rooms with shared bathrooms. Room Seven is the best in the house.
RATES	Year round rates for a single or double with private bathroom are $95 to $180, and $85 to $95 for a single or double with a shared bathroom. Entire inn rents for $1,820. No minimum stay required, cancel by 2 p.m. one day prior to arrival to avoid late charge.
CREDIT CARDS	Amex, MC, Diners Club, Visa, JCB
BREAKFAST	Expanded Continental breakfast served in the dining room or in guestroom includes croissants, muffins, bagels and cream cheese, toast, yogurt, cereal and beverages.
AMENITIES	Flowers, robes, TV, fruit baskets, overnight shoe shine service, concierge, afternoon tea wine, hors d' oeuvres, complimentary valet parking.
RESTRICTIONS	No smoking, no pets.
REVIEWED	*Bed and Breakfast Inns and Guesthouses, Best Places to Kiss in Northern California*
MEMBER	Professional Association of Innkeepers International, American Bed and Breakfast Association, California Association of Bed and Breakfast Inns
RATED	Mobil 3 Stars

WHITE SWAN INN

845 Bush Street, San Francisco, CA 94108	*415-775-1755*
Celeste Lytle, Manager	

SAN GREGORIO

The State Beach is a good reason to visit this tiny hamlet, south of Half Moon Bay and west of Palo Alto on Highway 1 and Highway 84.

RANCHO SAN GREGORIO

5086 La Honda Road, San Gregorio. CA 94074   415-747-0810
Bud & Lee Raynor, Resident Owners   FAX 415-747-0184

LOCATION	Take Highway 1 south 10 miles from Half Moon Bay to Highway 84, go east 5 miles on Highway 84.
OPEN	All year
DESCRIPTION	Two-story 1971 Spanish mission style inn with early California furnishings and Indian quilts and pottery. Located on 15 acres with a creek.
NO. OF ROOMS	Four rooms with private bathrooms. Lee recommends the Corte Madera.
RATES	Year round rates for a single or a double are $85 to $105. The suite is $145. Sunday through Thursday take $15 off the room rate. There is no minimum stay and cancellation requires seven days notice.
CREDIT CARDS	Amex, Discover, MC, Visa
BREAKFAST	Full breakfast is served in the dining room and includes fresh squeezed orange juice, ground coffee, hot entree, e.g., egg dish, meats, pancakes, waffles, homemade muffins and breads. Breakfast incorporates ranch grown products.
AMENITIES	Flowers, robes, hot coffee, chocolate, tea, sodas, candles, homemade cookies and pick your own fruit in season. Meeting facilities are available.
RESTRICTIONS	Limited smoking outside. The resident outdoor critters are Sancho who does creek tours and rock diving (typical Lab behavior, diving after rocks...TI) and two cats, Blackie and Goblin, who ignore Sancho...TI
REVIEWED	*Bed, Breakfast and Bike Northern California, Mobil Travel Guide, Bed & Breakfast in California, America's Wonderful Little Hotels & Inns*
MEMBER	Professional Association of Innkeepers International, California Association of Bed & Breakfast Innkeepers.
RATED	AAA 3 Diamonds, ABBA 2 Crowns, Mobil 2 Stars
KUDOS/COMMENTS	"Charming country inn nestled in an apple orchard."

SAN JOSE

Here in the heart of Silicon Valley, the city is winning visitors and attention with its outstanding new downtown—filled with parks, plazas, cultural centers, sports arena, and historic trolleys. Other things to do and see: events on the San Jose State University campus; the bizzare Winchester Mystery House; Rosicrucean Museum and Planetarium; wineries; and the San Jose Flea Market gives new meaning to shopping.

BRIAR ROSE BED & BREAKFAST INN

897 Jackson Street, San Jose, CA 95112   408-279-5999
James & Cheryl Fuhring, Resident Owners

LOCATION	From Highway 280, take a left on 11th Street and a right on Jackson.
OPEN	All year
DESCRIPTION	A two-story 1875 Victorian farmhouse and two-story Pump House with American Victorian antiques.
NO. OF ROOMS	Three rooms with private bathrooms and two rooms share two bathrooms. Try the cottage.
RATES	Year round rates are $70 to $85 for a single or a double with a private bathroom, $65 for a single or a double with shared bathroom and the Pump House cottage is $125. There is no minimum stay and cancellation requires 48 hours notice.
CREDIT CARDS	Amex, Diners Club, Discover, MC, Visa
BREAKFAST	Full breakfast is served in the dining room and includes crepes or quiche, "or some other gourmet main course", muffins, breads, juice, fruit and "killer spuds".
AMENITIES	Fresh flowers, robes, large wrap-around porch, TV, goodies at night, gardens and meeting facilities.
RESTRICTIONS	No smoking, no pets, children over five are welcome. The dogs are Gertie and Barney and the cats are Ms. Peepers and Wally.
REVIEWED	*The Painted Ladies Guide to Victorian California*

THE HENSLEY HOUSE

456 North Third Street, San Jose, CA 95112 *408-298-3537*
Sharon Layne & Bill Priest, Resident Owners *800-498-3537*
German, Swedish, Finnish, Spanish spoken *FAX 408-298-4676*

LOCATION	Take Highway 101 from San Francisco to Guadalupe Expressway. Exit at Julian Street, turn left under the freeway, turn left onto Third Street, one block to Hensley.
OPEN	All year
DESCRIPTION	A three-story 1884 Queen Anne Victorian, listed on the National and State Historic Registers, with stained glass windows, crystal and brass chandeliers, 12-foot ceilings and sporting a "witchs cap" tower.
NO. OF ROOMS	Five rooms with private bathrooms. Sharon recommends the Judge's Chamber.
RATES	Year round rates for a single or double with private bathroom are $75 to $140. No minimum stay, 48 hour cancellation notice.
CREDIT CARDS	Amex, MC, Diners Club, Visa, Discover
BREAKFAST	Full gourmet breakfast served in the dining room includes fresh juice and fruits, hot entree, muffins, croissants, coffee, expresso and cappuccino. Lunch and dinner also available.
AMENITIES	TV, VCR, phone, jack for computer, air conditioning, flowers, robes, fireplace and grand piano in the living room, tape library, afternoon wine and hors d'oeuvres, high tea at 3 o'clock on Thursday and Saturday, two rooms have whirlpools and one room has a fireplace, meeting facilities.
RESTRICTIONS	No smoking, no pets, children over 12 years old are welcome.
REVIEWED	*Country Inns and Backroads, America's Wonderful Little Hotels and Inns*
MEMBER	Professional Association of Innkeepers International, California Association of Bed and Breakfast Inns
RATED	AAA 3 Diamonds, ABBA 3 Crowns

San Martin

Fine wines are produce here, and fishing and sailing are within easy reach at Coyote Reservoir and Uvas Reserveroir County Park. On Hwy. 101 straightaway south of San Jose.

Country Rose Inn Bed & Breakfast

455-E Fitzgerald Avenue, San Martín, CA 95046　　　　　　408-842-0441
Rose Hernandez, Resident Owner　　　　　　　　　　FAX 408-842-6646
Spanish spoken

LOCATION	From Highway 101 take the northern most Gilroy exit, Masten Avenue and go west. Cross Monterey Road, at this point the street name changes to Fitzgerald. Drive .4 to the first set of mail boxes, go right onto a private lane and travel .3 to the inn.
OPEN	All year
DESCRIPTION	A two-story 1920s Dutch Colonial with a rose motif interior.
NO. OF ROOMS	Five rooms with private bathrooms. Rose recommends the Rambling Rose Suite.
RATES	High season, June through October, rates are $79 to $169 for a double or a single with a private bathroom and $169 to $189 for the suite. Low season, November to May, rates are $69 to $109 for a single or a double with a private bathroom. The suite is $159. There is a minimum stay during festivals and special events and cancellation requires seven days notice and a $10 fee.
CREDIT CARDS	MC, Visa
BREAKFAST	Full breakfast is served in the dining room and includes coffee, juice, fruit and a hot entree with a California platter. There is a $10 charge to be served in the room - by prior arrangement.
AMENITIES	Fresh flowers, dinner and theater reservations, afternoon tea, steam shower, and jetted tub in the suite, woodburning stove, fireplace in parlor and garden room, large common areas and porches, parlor with grand piano.
RESTRICTIONS	No smoking, no pets, children over nine are welcome. The resident cat is called Spunky.
REVIEWED	*Country Inns and Back Roads, Bed & Breakfast California, Best Places to Stay in California, Away for the Weekend, Quick Escapes from San Francisco.*
MEMBER	California Association of Bed & Breakfast Inns

SAN MATEO

This residential city south of San Francisco offers up some goodies. Make time for a day at Coyote Point Museum and Biopark, and Central Park's Japanese Garden. From here there's direct access to Half Moon Bay via Hwy. 92.

THE PALM HOUSE

1216 Palm Avenue, San Mateo, CA 94402   415-573-7256
Alan & Marian Brooks, Resident Owners

LOCATION	Ten miles south of San Francisco International Airport. Go south on Highway 101, exit at Third Avenue West.
OPEN	All year
DESCRIPTION	1902 two-story Craftsman with arts and crafts decor.
NO. OF ROOMS	One room with private bathroom, two rooms share a second bathroom. Room A has the private bathroom.
RATES	Year round rates for Room A with private bathroom are $65 to $70, rooms with shared bathroom are $5 less. Reservations will be guaranteed with $10 deposit.
CREDIT CARDS	No
BREAKFAST	Continental Plus is served in the dining room, solarium or on the veranda includes hot cereal, home baked specialty, fresh fruit and juice, coffee and tea.
AMENITIES	Solarium, sherry or port on arrival.
RESTRICTIONS	No pets. There's a resident canary, Angel and a Weimaraner named Blue.
REVIEWED	*America's Wonderful Little Hotels and Inns, Bed and Breakfast Homes Directory—West Coast*

SAN RAFAEL

The Marin County Seat is noted for its 140-acre Civic Center, Frank Lloyd Wright's last major architectural achievement. Two places to visit: the California Center for Wildlife Rehabilitation, and the Guide Dogs for the Blind campus. North of San Francisco via Hwy. 101.

PANAMA HOTEL

4 Bayview Street, San Rafael, CA 94901   415-457-3993
Dan Miller, Resident Owner   800-899-3993
Spanish, some French spoken

LOCATION	From Highway 101 North take Central San Rafael exit. Go two blocks to Third Street, turn left, go a half mile to B Street, turn left, go five blocks to stop sign, go straight past sign, the hotel is a quarter block down on the right.
OPEN	All year
DESCRIPTION	Two, two-story 1910 vintage Victorian homes connected by a rambling garden patio and restaurant.
NO. OF ROOMS	Nine rooms have private bathrooms and six rooms share two bathrooms. Dan suggests Rosie's Room.
RATES	Year round rates for single or double with private bathroom are $70 to $110, and $45 to $50 for a single or double with shared bathroom. Two night minimum stay on summer weekends, 48 hours cancellation notice required.
CREDIT CARDS	Diners Club, Discover
BREAKFAST	Continental Plus is served in the dining room and includes fruit, scones, muffins, hot & cold cereals, fresh coffee and tea. Lunch and dinner available in the restaurant.
AMENITIES	TVs, telephones, swing music in the dining room on Tuesday nights, room service, Sunday Brunch.
RESTRICTIONS	No smoking, no pets.

Santa Clara

Mission Santa Clara De Asis on the Santa Clara University campus, and Paramount's Great America one-hundred acre amusement park are major offerings here. In the north San Jose suburbs. Pick your route.

Madison Street Inn

1390 Madison Street, Santa Clara, CA 95050
Ralph & Theresa Wigginton, Resident Owners

408-249-5541
800-491-5541
FAX 408-249-6676

LOCATION	From Highway 880 turn north on Bascom Avenue, proceed 1.5 miles to Lewis, turn left and follow Lewis to the intersection of Lewis and Madison.
OPEN	All year
DESCRIPTION	A two-story 1890 Queen Anne Victorian with Victorian furnishings and landscaped gardens.
NO. OF ROOMS	Four rooms with private bathrooms, two rooms share one bathrooms. The Monroe Room is the best in the house.
RATES	Year round rates for a single or double room with private bathroom are $75 to $85, and $60 for a single or double room with shared bathroom. Entire B&B can be rented for $400. Four days notice required for cancellation.
CREDIT CARDS	Amex, MC, Diners Club, Visa, Discover
BREAKFAST	Full breakfast includes eggs benedict, pancakes, omelettes, fresh fruit, breakfast breads and beverages.
AMENITIES	Sherry, fridge packed with sodas, cookies in the evening, fax, phone, dry cleaning picked up, swimming pool and hot tub.
RESTRICTIONS	No smoking, no pets.
MEMBER	California Association of Bed and Breakfast Inns
RATED	Mobil 2 Stars

SANTA CRUZ

First inhabited by the Ohlone and "improved" by Junipero Serra and his missions, today's Santa Cruz is a nice, easy, middle-class tourist and univeristy town that loves its Boardwalk and beaches. And for good reason. Make time for: beautiful, redwood-cloistered University of California campus overlooking the Bay (back to school, anyone?); Natural Bridges State Park for its many tidepools and the mythic Monarch butterflies; and an up-close tour of the seals and sea lions of Año Nuevo State Reserve. Other doings: Monarch Migration Festival and Clam Chowder Cookoff in February; Spring break rites of passage (whenever); and Shakespeare Festival in August. Downtown is still rebuilding from the devastation of the 1989 earthquake, so stick with the beach areas.

CHATEAU VICTORIAN, A BED & BREAKFAST INN

118 First Street, Santa Cruz, CA 95060   *408-458-9458*
Alice June, Resident Owner

LOCATION	Alice will send you instructions.
OPEN	All year
DESCRIPTION	A two-story 1880s Queen Anne Victorian with Victorian furnishings one block from the beach.
NO. OF ROOMS	Seven rooms have private bathrooms.
RATES	Year round rates for a single or a double are $110 to $140. There is no minimum stay and cancellation requires 48 hours notice.
CREDIT CARDS	Amex, MC, Visa
BREAKFAST	Continental Plus is served in the dining room or on the decks or brick patio.
AMENITIES	Evening wine and cheese, queen-sized beds.
RESTRICTIONS	No smoking, no pets, children are not encouraged.
REVIEWED	*Bed & Breakfast in North America, Bed & Breakfast California, Weekend Adventures for City Weary People, Hidden San Francisco and Northern California, American B&B, The Complete B&B Inns and Guesthouses*
MEMBER	Bed & Breakfast Innkeepers of Santa Cruz County.

CLIFF CREST BED & BREAKFAST INN

407 Cliff Street, Santa Cruz, CA 95060　　　　　　408-427-2609
Bruce & Sharon Taylor, Resident Owners

LOCATION	From Highway 17 or 1 northbound take Ocean Street exit and follow to the end. Turn right on San Lorenzo Boulevard and go to the stop light at Riverside, turn left and cross the bridge, immediately turn right on Third Street and go uphill to Cliff Crest, the inn is the second house on the right.
OPEN	All year
DESCRIPTION	An 1887 two-story Queen Anne Victorian with family antiques and stained glass interior. Listed on the California Historic Register.
NO. OF ROOMS	Five rooms with private bathrooms. The best room depends on Sharon's mood...That's what she wrote on her survey...TI
RATES	Year round rates are $85 to $150 for a single or a double with a private bathroom. There is a minimum stay on the weekends and holidays and cancellation requires three days notice.
CREDIT CARDS	Amex, Discover, MC, Visa
BREAKFAST	Full breakfast is served in the dining room or in the garden and includes fresh juice, fresh fruit in season, either egg dish or coffee cake or muffins or French toast or pancakes and sausage.
AMENITIES	Flowers, wine and cheese, soft drinks, lots of books, robes, games and puzzles, telephone in parlor, full candy dishes, TV available, small meeting room and solarium.
RESTRICTIONS	No smoking, no pets, children are discouraged. Harry, Opie and Murphy are the English Bull Terrier, Black Lab mix and tabby, respectively.
REVIEWED	*Bed & Breakfast California: A Selective Guide, Recommended Country Inns—West Coast. Hidden Coast of California, Country Inns and Backroads*
MEMBER	California Association of Bed & Brreakfast Inns, Professional Association of Innkeepers International, Bed & Breakfast Innkeepers of Santa Cruz County
KUDOS/COMMENTS	"One feels at home and significant the moment Sharon or Bruce Taylor answer the phone. A feeling of comfort and belongingness permeates the Inn."...Nice word "belongingness"...TI

THE DARLING HOUSE,
A BED & BREAKFAST INN BY THE SEA

314 West Cliff Drive, Santa Cruz, CA 95060   *408-458-1958*
Darrell & Karen Darling, Resident Owners   *800-458-1958*
Spanish spoken

LOCATION	South on Highway 17 to Highway 1 north (Mission Street), left on Bay, right on West Cliff two blocks, right on Gharkey.
OPEN	All year
DESCRIPTION	A two-story 1860/1910 Spanish Mission Revival with "Prairie School influences" furnished with American antiques.
NO. OF ROOMS	One room with private bathroom, six rooms share three bathrooms. Karen thinks her best room is the Pacific Ocean.
RATES	Year round rates are $150 to $225 for a single or a double with a private bathroom, $60 to $150 for a single or a double with a shared bathroom, the suite rents for $370 and the entire inn rents for $1,150. There is a minimum stay when Saturday or a long weekend is involved and cancellation requires five days notice.
CREDIT CARDS	Amex, Discover, MC, Visa
BREAKFAST	Continental Plus is served in the dining room and includes espresso or capuccino, breads, croissants and fresh fruit, a caterer is on call for special meals.
AMENITIES	Orchids or roses in each room, hot tub spa in garden, telephones in rooms, complimentary gourmet dinner on weekdays September through May.
RESTRICTIONS	No smoking, no pets.
REVIEWED	*Reccomended Country Inns—West Coast, Northern California Best Places, Country Inns, Lodges & Historic Hotels, AAA Bed & Breakfast Guide—Northern California, Northern California Handbook*
MEMBER	California Lodging Industry Association, Santa Cruz County Lodging Association
AWARDS	Santa Cruz Historical Society Landmark Award

INN LAGUNA CREEK

2727 Smith Grade, Santa Cruz, CA 95060   *408-425-0692*
Jim & Gay Holley, Resident Owners

LOCATION	From Santa Cruz north on Highway 1, turn right on Bay, left on High Street (here High St. becomes Empire Grade). Go five miles and turn left on Smith Grade three miles to Inn.
OPEN	All year
DESCRIPTION	1976 contemporary redwood Inn with creek views from every window. All redwood and comfortable country interior decor.
NO. OF ROOMS	Three rooms with private bathrooms. Give the "Topaz" room a try for a special stay.
RATES	May through October: singles and doubles $95; suites $125. November through April: singles and doubles $85; suites $120. Minimum stay of two days on three-day weekends. Reservation/cancellation policy: five days.
CREDIT CARDS	Amex, MC, Visa
BREAKFAST	Full breakfast of homemaade granola, breads, pancakes, egg casserole, juice, coffee, fruit and yogurt served in dining room.
AMENITIES	Plants and flowers, robes, cookies, popcorn and tea. Hot tub on deck beside creek. Sitting room with book and video library, TV/VCR, wet bar and stereo.
RESTRICTIONS	No smoking, no pets. Resident dog, bearded terrier, Kiska and long-haired tiger cat, Red plus birds, racoon and deer.
MEMBER	California Association of Bed & Breakfast Inns

LEMON YELLOW FARM—
THE WAYFARER STATION

111 Vine Hill Road, Santa Cruz, CA 95065   *408-425-5949*
Cecil Carnes, Resident Owner

LOCATION	Two miles south on Vine Hill Road from Highway 17. Fifteen minutes drive north from Santa Cruz.
OPEN	All year
DESCRIPTION	Three classic bungalows built in 1924 located at the base of the Santa Cruz mountains. A country setting with gardens and spacious lawns.
NO. OF ROOMS	Each building has a private bathroom. The original farmhouse building comes highly recommended.
RATES	High season April through October rates for a single or double with private bathroom are $125 to $195. Seven day cancellation notice required.
CREDIT CARDS	No
BREAKFAST	Continental Plus breakfast served in dining room, guestroom or gazebo includes prepared fruit bowl, Swedish oat pancakes and beverages.
AMENITIES	Flowers, robes, wine and hors d'oeuvres, meeting rooms.
RESTRICTIONS	No smoking, no pets. Children over 12 are welcome. Ingrid, the Great Dane, loves company, along with two cats Ajax and Pepper.

PLEASURE POINT INN

3665 East Cliff Drive, Santa Cruz, CA 95062   *408-475-4657*
Barbara & Gary Pasquini, Resident Owners

SANTA ROSA

This sprawling, Bay Area bedroom community with mall madness (at least 20) is part of Wine Country with vineyards worth visiting. In town, head for Railroad Square and Park; Luther Burbank Home and Gardens; and the Church of One Tree. Spring Lake, Lake Ralphine and Annadel State Park are nice oases, or cool off at Charles Schulz's ("Peanuts") ice rink. Main events include Luther Burbank Rose Festival and Parade in May; late summer's Harvest Fair; and the Scottish Gathering and Games over Labor Day (bring kilts).

THE GABLES INN

4257 Petaluma Hill Road, Santa Rosa, CA 95404
Mike & Judy Ogne, Resident Owners

707-585-7777
800-GABLES-N
FAX 707-584-5634

LOCATION	From Highway 101, exit at Rohnert Park Expressway and turn right. Travel 2.5 miles to Petaluma Hill Road. Turn left and travel four miles to Inn.
OPEN	All year
DESCRIPTION	An 1877 Victorian Inn listed on the State and National Historic Registers. A restored Gothic mansion set on 3.5 acres in the cneter of the Wonoma wine country, with a sundeck and a separate Victorian honeymoon cottage.
NO. OF ROOMS	Seven rooms with private bathrooms, the Parlor Suite being the innkeepers favorite.
RATES	Year round rates are singles and doubles $95 to $175. Minimum stays of two nights on weekends, and three nights on holiday weekends are required.
CREDIT CARDS	Amex, Discover, MC, Visa
BREAKFAST	Four-course breakfast is served in the dining room.
AMENITIES	Classical CDs, fresh flowers, casual afternoon refreshments. Full concierge service to arrange for winery tours, dinner, or hot air ballooning. Meeting space for 14 to 16 available. Handicapped access.
RESTRICTIONS	No smoking, no pets. Three resident cats on premises, "Barn Cats 1, 2, and 3."
REVIEWED	*Bed and Breakfast California: A Select Guide; The Best Places to Kiss in Northern California; California Country Inns and Itineraries, Bed and Breakfast Guide: California.*
MEMBER	Wine Country Inns of Sonoma County
KUDOS/COMMENTS	"Beautifully done country mansion. The hospitality of Michael & Judy Ogne insures a memorable stay." ... "It is elegant yet welcoming to weary travelers and they are gracious hosts."

MELITTA STATION INN

5850 Melitta Road, Santa Rosa, CA 95409   707-538-7712
Diane Crandon & Vic Amstadter, Resident Owners

LOCATION	From Highway 101 take Highway 12 exit east in Santa Rosa. Follow Highway 12 (Sonoma Highway) to Melitta Road just past Calistoga Road, turn right on Melitta and go 9/10s of a mile, the inn is on the right, across from Annadel State Park.
OPEN	All Year
DESCRIPTION	An 1880 railroad station furnished with American country and antiques.
NO. OF ROOMS	Four rooms with private bathrooms and two rooms share one bathroom.
RATES	Year round rates for a single or double with a private or shared bathroom are $60 to $90.
CREDIT CARDS	MC, Visa
BREAKFAST	Full breakfast is served in the great room or on the balcony and includes fruit, fresh juice, breads & muffins or cakes and main egg dish plus beverages.
AMENITIES	Fresh flowers in the rooms, wine, cheese and crackers served in the afternoon.
RESTRICTIONS	No smoking, no pets, children over 10 years of age are welcome.
REVIEWED	*Non-Smokers Guide to Bed & Breakfasts, American Historic Bed & Breakfasts, Northern California Best Places*
MEMBER	Wine Country Inns of Sonoma County, B&B Association of Sonoma Valley

PYGMALION HOUSE

331 Orange Street, Santa Rosa, CA 95407   707-526-3407
Lola Wright, Resident Owner

KUDOS/COMMENTS   "Great full breakfast, warm hosts."

VINTNERS INN

4350 Barnes Road, Santa Rosa, CA 95403   *707-575-7350*
John & Francisca Duffy, Resident Owners   *800-421-2584*
Spanish spoken   *FAX 707-575-1426*

LOCATION	From Highway 101 take the River Road Exit, go left on River Road take the first immediate left on Barnes Road.
OPEN	All year
DESCRIPTION	A 1984 European style hotel with French country and pine antique furnishings. Four separate buildings in a 45 acre vineyard.
NO. OF ROOMS	Forty-four rooms with private bathrooms. Try the junior suite upstairs.
RATES	Year round rates are $128 to $168 for a single or a double with a private bathroom. Suites range from $155 to $195. There is a minimum stay from June through October when a Saturday night is included. Cancellation requires 72 hours notice.
CREDIT CARDS	Amex, Diners Club, MC, Visa
BREAKFAST	Continental Plus is served in the dining room and includes homemade breakfast breads, fruits, cereals, yogurt, juices, beverages and waffles. Lunch and dinner are available in the restaurant.
AMENITIES	Sundeck with Jacuzzi, refrigerators, TV, telephone with modem jacks, some rooms have woodburning fireplaces, oversized oval tub/shower, meeting facilities, handicapped access.
RESTRICTIONS	No pets.
REVIEWED	*Away for the Weekend, Northern California Best Places, Zagat Guide, Mobile Travel Guide*
RATED	AAA 4 Diamonds, Mobil 3 Stars

SAUSALITO

This little hillside hamlet is a prime getaway destination from San Francisco. Houses cling precariously to the hills, and Bohemian and marine influences blend nicely between the artists' colony, houseboat community and gorgeous yacht harbor. The entire town is the reason to come here, but in summer weekdays are best—and skip the car and take the ferry. And plan a cruise over to Angel Island State Park.

CASA MADRONA HOTEL

801 Bridgeway, Sausalito, CA 94965   *415-332-0502*
John W. Mans, Resident Owner   *800-567-9524*
Spanish, French, Portugese, Vietnamese spoken   *FAX 415-332-2537*

LOCATION	Downtown Sausalito. Fifteen minute drive from San Francisco across the Golden Gate Bridge or 30 minute ferry ride from San Francisco.
OPEN	All year
DESCRIPTION	An 1885 blend of Victorian hotel and New England style inn listed on the National Historic Register. Surrounded by gardens and bay views.
NO. OF ROOMS	Thirty-four rooms with private bathrooms. The Rose Chalet is the best room in the inn.
RATES	Year round rates for a single or double room with private bathroom are $105 to $245. Two night minimum stay on weekends, 48 hour cancellation required.
CREDIT CARDS	Amex, MC, Diners Club, Visa, Discover
BREAKFAST	Full breakfast served in the dining room includes fresh fruit, toast, homemade muffins and scones, waffles and one hot egg dish. Lunch and dinner available, brunch served on Sunday.
AMENITIES	Five cottages have woodburning stoves, most rooms offer fireplaces, views and decks, wine and cheese social hour every evening, phones, robes, outdoor jacuzzi, wet bar in some rooms, room service available during restaurant hours, valet parking, turndown service, business and concierge services and one handicaaped access room.
RESTRICTIONS	No pets.
REVIEWED	*Weekends for Two in Northern California, Fifty Romantic Getaways, Karen Brown's California Country Inns & Itineraries*
MEMBER	Special Places
RATED	AAA 3 Diamonds, Mobil 3 Stars

SHINGLETOWN

This is the direct gateway into Lassen Volcanic National Park. And (horse lovers take note) it's also site of the Shingletown Wild Horse Sanctuary, a preserve where mustangs get a new lease on life. East of Redding on Highway 44.

WESTON HOUSE

6741 Red Rock Road, Shingletown, CA 96088   916-474-3738
Ivor & Angela Weston, Resident Owners

LOCATION	From Highway 44 east toward Mt. Lassen National Park, travel 26 miles to the sign, turn right on Shingletown Ridge Road, drive 1.2 miles, turn left on Red Rock Road.
OPEN	All year
DESCRIPTION	A two-story 1979 cedar shake country inn with Victorian and eclectic furnishings.
NO. OF ROOMS	Three rooms with private bathrooms and one room shares one bathroom. Angela suggests Helen's Room.
RATES	Year round rates are $75 to $95 for a single or double with a private bathroom. The suite is $105. There is no minimum stay and cancellation requires seven days notice and a $10 fee.
CREDIT CARDS	MC, Visa
BREAKFAST	Full breakfast served in the dining room or on the deck includes fresh fruit, frittatas, casseroles, baked goods and variations on French toast.
AMENITIES	Refreshments upon arrival, use of the pool and outdoor Jacuzzi, gas grill available, TV & VCR in common room, woodburning stoves in all rooms, massage available.
RESTRICTIONS	No smoking, no pets. The resident dog, cat and cockatiel are called Rigger, Arthur and Kiwi.
MEMBER	Professional Association of Innkeepers International
KUDOS/COMMENTS	"A retreat in the foothills near Lassen Park - newer home - very pleasant owners and setting - a great massage is available." ... "Beautiful setting, lovely gardens, tastefully decorated rooms, delicious breakfast and very gracious host and hostess."

SIERRA CITY

BUSCH AND HERINGLAKE COUNTRY INN B&B

PO Box 68, Sierra City, CA 96125   916-862-1501
Carlo Guiffre, Resident Owner

HIGH COUNTRY INN

HCR 2, Box 7, Sierra City, CA 96125   *916-862-1530*
Marlene Cartwright, Resident Owner

SMITH RIVER

This is the last coastal stop before Oregon, and it's actually on the banks of Rowdy Creek. Although the Smith doesn't run through here, it's nearby, and as the state's only undammed river system, it's central to the Smith River National Recreation Area. The town's major events are in July: The Easter in July Lily Festival and the two-mile Smith River Gasquet Raft Race. Pelican State Beach is just up the road. North of Crescent City on Highway 101.

CASA RUBIO

17285 Crissey Road, Smith River, CA 95567   *800-357-6199*
Tony Rubio, Resident Owner
Spanish and some French spoken

LOCATION	Just 800 feet away from the Oregon/California state line, on the beach.
OPEN	All year
DESCRIPTION	A 1940s contemporary beach house with contemporary furnishings
NO. OF ROOMS	Several suites with private bathrooms. Try the upper suite.
RATES	Year round rates are $78 to $88. There is a minimum stay on holiday weekends and cancellation requires seven days notice.
CREDIT CARDS	MC, Visa
BREAKFAST	Continental "do it yourself" breakfast is served in the guestroom and includes muffins, juice and coffee. Dinner is available.
AMENITIES	Fresh flowers, telephones, TV
RESTRICTIONS	No smoking. Lupe the mutt is the resident dog along with a Scottish Fold cat called Cuca.

SOMERSET

It's all alone out here, but handy to Jenkinson Lake and the southwestern edge of El Dorado National Forest. East of Sacramento and southeast of Placerville off Highway 49.

7-UP GUEST RANCH

8060 Fairplay Road, Somerset, CA 95684   916-620-5450
Mike & Alice Chazen, Resident Owners   FAX 916-620-5367

LOCATION	From Placerville, take Highway 49 south 3 miles, turn left on Pleasant Valley Road. Go 7 miles to Bucks Bar Road, 3 miles to E-16, right on E-16, 3 miles and turn left on Fairplay Road, 5 miles to the town of Fairplay, we're up .5 mile on right.
OPEN	All year
DESCRIPTION	1930s restored guest ranch sits on 199 acres and is listed on the National and State Historic Registers.
NO. OF ROOMS	Four rooms with private bathrooms. Try the Buckaroo Four room.
RATES	Year round rates for a single or double with private bathroom are $79 to $89. Entire B&B rents for $355. Seven days advance cancellation notice with a 10% fee.
CREDIT CARDS	MC, Visa, Discover
BREAKFAST	Full ranch style breakfast served in the dining room, vegetarian breakfast available.
RESTRICTIONS	No smoking, no pets, children over 12 welcome. Resident pets include pygmy goats, sheep and wild turkeys.
MEMBER	Historic Country Inns of El Dorado County

FITZPATRICK WINERY & LODGE

7740 Fairplay Road, Somerset, CA 95684   *916-620-3248*
Brian and Diana Fitzpatrick, Resident Owners   *800-245-9166*
FAX 916-620-6838

LOCATION	Get directions ahead of time or call from Placerville.
OPEN	All year
DESCRIPTION	A 1986 white pine log lodge building on 40 acres with country Irish furnishings.
NO. OF ROOMS	Four rooms with private bathrooms. Diana recommends the Log Suite as the best in the house.
RATES	Year round rates for a single or double with private bathroom are $79 to $99. Saturday night stay required on holidays, no refund unless room is rebooked.
CREDIT CARDS	MC, Visa
BREAKFAST	Full breakfast served in the dining room includes cereal, fruit, baked goods, a variety of main dishes and beverages. Plowman's lunch on weekends and special "theme dinners" once a month.
AMENITIES	Hot tub on the deck, beverages, small winery in the cellar, complimentary wine, large great room with fireplace, flowers, candy in room.
RESTRICTIONS	No smoking, no pets. A unique mix of "loving dogs with cats," Golden Retrievers Duffy and Corky, and "too many cats to mention."
MEMBER	California Association of Bed and Breakfast Inns

Sonoma

The birthplace of the state's wind industry has a fascinating history of foreign rule. But Mexican General Mariano Vallejo's legacy is alive and well preserved: the beautiful 8-acre Plaza and adobe buildings that surround it, including Sonoma Mission, are part of Sonoma State Historic Park. May and June are eventful times to be here, and the main event comes in August for the Sonoma County Wine Showcase and Auction. From San Francisco, about 35 miles north on Hwy. 121.

THE HIDDEN OAK INN

214 East Napa Street, Sonoma, CA 95476   707-996-9863
Catherine Crotchett, Resident Owner   FAX 707-996-9863

LOCATION	From the central Plaza in Sonoma, turn right for .2 miles on Napa Street. Hidden Oak is on the left next to the Christian Science Church.
OPEN	All year except Christmas.
DESCRIPTION	A 1913 two-story Craftsman bungalow with antique furnishings that was originally built as a refectory.
NO. OF ROOMS	Four rooms with private bathrooms. The Summer Suite is a new luxury addition.
RATES	Year round rates for a single or double with a private bathroom are $95 to $225. Some weekends require a minimum stay, seven day cancellation required.
CREDIT CARDS	Amex, Discover
BREAKFAST	Full breakfast includes an egg dish, meat, fresh baked breads and muffins, assorted beverages.
AMENITIES	Afternoon refreshments, bicycles, toiletries. The Summer Suite has private patio and fireplace, TV/VCR
RESTRICTIONS	Smoking only on the porch, no pets. Sarah is the resident calico cat.
MEMBER	Professional Association of Innkeepers International, American Bed and Breakfast Association
RATED	ABBA 3 Crowns

MAGLIULO'S BED & BREAKFAST

691 Broadway, Sonoma, CA 95476   707-996-1031
Lori Magliulo, Resident Owner

SONOMA CHALET

18935 Fifth Street West, Sonoma, CA 95476   707-938-3129
Joe Leese, Resident Owner   800-938-3129

LOCATION	At the very north end of Fifth Street West, down the gravel road.
OPEN	All year, except Christmas.
DESCRIPTION	1940 two-story Swiss farmhouse and three country cottages on three acres.
NO. OF ROOMS	Four rooms with private bathrooms, two rooms with shared bathrooms. Check out Sara's cottage.
RATES	High season rate, April through October, for a single or a double with private bathroom, or a suite is $125. A single or a double with shared bathroom is $85. Off season rate, November through March, for a single or a double with private bathroom, or suite is $110, a single or a double with shared bathroom is $75. Two night minimum high season weekends, one week cancellation policy with $10 fee.
CREDIT CARDS	Amex, MC, Visa
BREAKFAST	Continental Plus is served in the dining room or guestroom and includes juice, fresh fruit, granola, cereals, hard-boiled eggs, coffee or tea and pastries.
AMENITIES	Robes, hot tub, bicycles, sun deck, fireplace or woodstoves.
RESTRICTIONS	No smoking in buildings, no pets. Children in cottages by prior arrangement. Array of pets includes pigmy goats, geese, and Petapoo, the Golden Retriever.
REVIEWED	*The Official Bed and Breakfast Guide, Definitive California Bed and Breakfast Touring Guide, AAA Bed & Breakfast Guide—Northern California, Best Places to Kiss in the Bay Area.*
MEMBER	Bed and Breakfast Association of Sonoma Valley

STARWAE INN

21490 Broadway, Sonoma, CA 95476
Janice Crow & John Curry, Resident Owners

707-938-1374
800-793-4792
FAX 707-935-1159

LOCATION	On Highway 12, 2.2 miles south of downtown Sonoma.
OPEN	All year
DESCRIPTION	Two 1930 California stucco cottages on three acres, across from a vineyard. Each cottage is divided into two rooms or suites, each with a private patio and private entrance.
NO. OF ROOMS	Four rooms with private bathrooms.
RATES	High season rates, March 15 through October 31, for single or double with private bathroom are $90 to $130, suites are $110 to $130, entire two bedroom guesthouse $210 to $225. Off season rates, November 1 through March 14, are roughly 10-15% less. Minimum stay is two nights on weekends, three nights on holidays. Cancellation policy requires 72 hour notice.
CREDIT CARDS	MC, Visa
BREAKFAST	Continental Plus served in guestroom includes juice, fresh scones and breads, quiche and coffee..
AMENITIES	Robes, books of art and poetry.
RESTRICTIONS	No smoking, no pets. Birds abound on the property, up to 30 species including hummingbirds, Great Horned owls and woodpeckers.
REVIEWED	AAA Bed & Breakfast Guide—Northern California
MEMBER	Sonoma Valley Bed and Breakfast Association

THISTLE DEW INN

171 West Spain Street, Sonoma, CA 95476   707-938-2909
Larry and Norma Barnett, Resident Owners   800-382-7895
German, French spoken

LOCATION	One half block west of the historic town plaza on West Spain Street.
OPEN	All year
DESCRIPTION	Two 1900 Victorian cottages surrounded by gardens. Furnished with arts and crafts antiques from 1910.
NO. OF ROOMS	Six rooms with private bathrooms, Mimosa is the largest.
RATES	High season rates, April through November, for a single or double room with private bathroom are $100 to $140, and $80 to $120 off season for a single or double room with private bathroom. No minimum stay, 48 hours cancellation required with $10 fee.
CREDIT CARDS	Amex, MC, Visa
BREAKFAST	Full breakfast served in the dining room includes entree cooked to order, fruit, breads, meats and beverages.
AMENITIES	Evening hors d'oeuvres, garden hot tub, fireplaces, private decks, whirlpool tub, fresh flowers, two rooms are handicapped accessible.
RESTRICTIONS	Children over 12 years old are welcome
REVIEWED	Fodor's Bed and Breakfast Guide—California, Bed and Breakfast California, The Napa and Sonoma Book
MEMBER	California Association of Bed and Breakfast Inns

VICTORIAN GARDEN INN

316 East Napa Street, Sonoma, CA 95476
Donna Lewis, Resident Owner
Spanish spoken.

707-996-5339
800-543-5339
FAX 707-996-2446

LOCATION	One and a half blocks from the town square (plaza). Take the Highway 37 exit from Highway 101 north.
OPEN	All year.
DESCRIPTION	An 1870s Victorian farmhouse and cottage with Victorian furnishings and wraparound porch.
NO. OF ROOMS	Three rooms with private bathrooms and one room shares one bathroom. Pick the Woodcutter's Cottage.
RATES	Year round rates are $99 to $139 for a single or a double with a private bathroom, $79 for a single or a double with a shared bathroom and the entire inn rents for $577.50 (including tax). There is a minimum stay when Saturday is involved between April and November and holiday weekends. Cancellation requires seven days notice and there is a $10 fee.
CREDIT CARDS	Amex, Diners Club, MC, Visa
BREAKFAST	Continental Plus is served in the dining room, guest room or outside and includes fresh fruit in season, homemade pastries, granola and beverages. Picnic baskets are available.
AMENITIES	Fresh flowers and terry robes in every room, tea cart with beverages and cookies in the dining room and swimming pool in the back, evening wine and sherry.
RESTRICTIONS	No smoking, no pets, children are not encouraged. Rochelle is the resident cat.
REVIEWED	*Best Places to Kiss in Northern California, Wine Country Access, Country Inns of the Far West, Bed & Breakfast, Inns and Small Hotels*
MEMBER	Professional Association of Innkeepers International, Wine Country Inns

SONORA

Once one of the richest and wildest of "Mother Lodes," this pretty town now relies on lumbering and agriculture. Worth a visit are the Tuolumne County Museum, housed in the former jailhouse, Bradford Street Park, and a walking tour of the many historic adobes and Victorians. From here, scenic Hwy. 108 leads into the Stanislaus National Forest. Sample the good old days during the Mother Lode Roundup Parade and Rodeo in May, and Wild West Days in September. Southeast of Sacramento via Hwy. 16 and 49, and east of Stockton.

BARRETTA GARDENS
BED & BREAKFAST INN

700 South Baretta Street, Sonora, CA 95370　　　　　　　　209-532-6039
Bob & Betty Martin, Resident Owners
Some Spanish understood

LOCATION	One mile from downtown Sonora, off Business Highway 108.
OPEN	All year
DESCRIPTION	A 1903 two-story Victorian with Victorian furnishings.
NO. OF ROOMS	Five rooms with private bathrooms. Try the Dragonfly.
RATES	High season, April through December, rates are $70 to $95 for a single or a double with a private bathroom. Low season, January through March, rates are $60 to $85 for a single or double with a private bathroom. The entire B&B rents for $500. There is a minimum stay on holidays and cancellation requires five days notice.
CREDIT CARDS	Amex, MC, Visa
BREAKFAST	Full breakfast is served in the dining room and includes eggs, quiche, crepes, pastries, fruit and beverages.
AMENITIES	Fresh flowers, one room has a spa for two, sunset view, gardens and facilities for small weddings.
RESTRICTIONS	No pets. The two Labs, Shortcake and Jetta, are "smart, eccentric, humorous and they eat grilled cheese sandwiches and Maine lobsters." We accept everything except for 'smart'...after all they are Labs...TI
REVIEWED	*Best Places in Northern California, Best Places to Kiss in Northern California, Best of the Gold Country, Bed and Breakfast California*

HAMMONS HOUSE INN
BED & BREAKFAST

22963 Robertson Ranch Road, Sonora, CA 95370
Art & Linda Hammons, Resident Owners

209-532-7921
800-432-1135

LOCATION	Eighteen miles from Sonora and 5.5 miles from Twain Harte.
OPEN	All year
DESCRIPTION	A two-story 1985 contemporary ranch and separate two-story bungalow with contemporary furnishings on 6.5 acres.
NO. OF ROOMS	Two rooms with private bathrooms and one room shares one bathroom.
RATES	Year round rates are $70 to $80 for a single or a double with a private or shared bathroom. The bungalow is $110 and $260 for the entire inn. There is no minimum stay and cancellation requires five days notice and a $10 fee.
CREDIT CARDS	Amex, MC, Visa
BREAKFAST	Full breakfast is served in the dining room, guest room or on the deck and includes fruit, meat entree, home baked breads, muffins, cakes. Special and children's meals are available.
AMENITIES	The main house has a fireplace, swimming pool with deck, TV/VCR and stereo. The bungalow has a kitchen, private deck, TV, stereo and BBQ. Located in a meadow with a vegetable garden.
RESTRICTIONS	No smoking, no pets. Katy, who has been in the local paper is an Australian Shepherd and the "Bigbird" Guinea Fowl goes by the name of Stormer.
MEMBER	California Association of Bed & Breakfast Inns, Gold Country Inns of Tuolumme County, Tuolumme County Lodging Association
KUDOS/COMMENTS	"A fine country home on six acres in the sierra foothills near Sonora."

LAVENDER HILL BED & BREAKFAST INN

683 South Barretta Street, Sonora, CA 95370   209-532-9024
Jean & Charlie Marinelli, Resident Owners
Italian spoken

LOCATION	Entering downtown Sonora turn right at the 'T' on to Washington Street, turn left at Church Street, go three blocks to Barretta turn right and go six blocks to the inn.
OPEN	All year, closed December 26th through January 15th.
DESCRIPTION	A 1900 Victorian on a hill with period antiques.
NO. OF ROOMS	Two rooms with private bathrooms and two rooms share one bathroom. Choose the Lavender Room.
RATES	Year round rates are $70 to $80 for a single or a double with a private bathroom and $65 to $70 for a single or a double with a shared bathroom. The entire B&B rents for $295. There is no minimum stay and cancellation requires five days notice.
CREDIT CARDS	Amex, MC, Visa
BREAKFAST	Full breakfast is served in the dining room and includes beverages, fresh fruit plate, main entree such as: casserole, quiche, Fench toast plus breakfast meats. Special meals are available as well as brunch for weddings or anniversaries.
AMENITIES	Refreshments upon arrival and afternoons, fresh flowers, BBQ available, porch swing, pastoral setting with adjoining farm and chickens.
RESTRICTIONS	No smoking, no pets, all children are welcome. The "roving chicken" goes by Cara Cara.
REVIEWED	*California State Auto Association Bed & Breakfasts, Bed & Breakfast in California*
MEMBER	California Association of Bed & Breakfast Inns, Gold Country Inns of Tuolumne County

LLAMAHALL GUEST RANCH

18170 Ward's Ferry Road, Sonora, CA 95370   209-532-7264
Cynthia Hall, Resident Owners

LULU BELLE'S B&B

85 Gold Street, Sonora, CA 95370   209-533-3455
Janet Miller, Resident Owner

KUDOS/COMMENTS	"Friendly, history, comfortable, great breakfast"

Ryan House B&B

153 South Shepherd Street, Sonora, CA 95370   209-533-3445
Nancy and Guy Hoffman, Resident Owners

KUDOS/COMMENTS   "Professional, comfortable & hospitable." ... "All the charm, grace & perfect hospitality you expect from a B&B, as an innkeeper, I was impressed."

Serenity, A Bed & Breakfast Inn

15305 Bear Cub Drive, Sonora, CA 95370   209-533-1441
Fred & Charlotte Hoover, Resident Owners   800-426-1441

LOCATION	From downtown Sonora take business Highway 108 east two miles toward Pinecrest. Continue east one mile to Phoenix Lake Road, turn left and drive three miles to Bear Cub Drive and turn right to the inn.
OPEN	All year
DESCRIPTION	A two-story 1989 Mother Lode Colonial with antiques and reproductions for furnishings and a wrap around veranda overlooking six acres of mixed forest.
NO. OF ROOMS	Four rooms have private bathrooms. Charlotte suggests that you try their room called Violets Are Blue.
RATES	Year round rates are $70 to $110 for a single with private bathroom and $85 to $125 for a double with a private bathroom. There is a minimum stay on holiday weekends and cancellation requires 72 hours notice.
CREDIT CARDS	Amex, Diners Club, MC, Visa
BREAKFAST	Full breakfast is served in the dining room and includes juice, fruit, "artfully presented" entree and choice of beverage. Dietary restrictions respected on request.
AMENITIES	Fireplaces, afternoon refreshments, mobile phone for guest use, library and flowers.
RESTRICTIONS	No smoking, no pets, rooms sleep only one or two people. The 18-year-old Siamese is called Mai Ling.
REVIEWED	*The Best Of Gold Country, Best Places Northern California, The Best Places to Kiss in Northern California, Country Inns & Back Roads— California, Bay Area Back Roads*
MEMBER	California Association of Bed & Breakfast Inns

SOQUEL

This once-booming lumber town is the place to shop for antiques and things of oak. Or head down by the sea in Capitola for September's Begonia Festival, or a day in New Brighton Beach State Park. Just south of Santa Cruz, off Hwy. 1.

BLUE SPRUCE INN

2815 South Main Street, Soquel, CA 95073   408-464-1137
Pat & Tom O'Brien, Resident Owners   800-559-1137
Spanish spoken   FAX 408-475-0608

LOCATION	From Highway 17 exit Highway 1 south toward Monterey, exit "Capitola/Soquel", turn left from exit going under highway to first stop sign on Main Street, turn right to the inn.
OPEN	All year
DESCRIPTION	A two-story 1875/1893 historic Victorian farm and carriage house with country furnishings.
NO. OF ROOMS	Five rooms with private bathrooms. Pat says the carriage house is her best room.
RATES	Year round rates for a single or a double are $85 to $135. The entire B&B rents for the regular rates plus $100. May through October there is a minimum stay on weekends and cancellation requires three days notice.
CREDIT CARDS	Amex, Discover, MC, Visa
BREAKFAST	Full gourmet breakfast is served in the dining room, guestroom or in the garden and includes fresh orange juice, seasonal fruits, homemade muffins or coffee cake, an entree, cold or hot cereals and beverages. Lunch is available for business groups.
AMENITIES	Fresh flowers, robes, telephone and computer service, gas fireplaces and spa tubs in rooms that are decorated around an original piece of art.
RESTRICTIONS	No smoking, no pets. Children over 12 are welcome. Samantha the Black Lab doesn't go inside the inn. "Sam is happy to sit on the porch and enjoy little pats."
REVIEWED	*Best Places to Kiss in Northern California, Country Inns and Other Weekend Pleasures —California, Americas Wonderful Little Hotels & Inns, Northern California Handbook, Hidden Coast of California, Bed, Breakfast & Bike—Northern California*
MEMBER	Professional Association of Innkeepers International, California Association of Bed & Breakfast Inns, Bed & Breakfast Innkeepers of Santa Cruz County
KUDOS/COMMENTS	"Warm hospitality, charming, cozy rooms, most comfortable beds and atmosphere."

SOUTH SAN FRANCISCO

This medium-sized city on the San Francisco Bay shore has direct access to all the wonders of the south bay area. The international airport is an immediate neighbor.

OYSTER POINT MARINA INN

425 Marina Boulevard, South San Francisco, CA 94080   415-737-7633
Douglas Conover, Resident Owner   800-775-7997
French, Spanish, and German spoken   FAX 415-737-0745

LOCATION	On Rte 101 take the Oyster Point Boulevard exit in South San Francisco. Go one-half mile to the water and turn right onto Marina Boulevard.
OPEN	All year
DESCRIPTION	1989 Cape Cod country inn with restaurant situated in a park. Every room has a bay view and a fireplace.
NO. OF ROOMS	Thirty rooms with private bathrooms
RATES	Year round rates are singles $119 to $134, doubles $134 to $149. The entire B&B is available for $2,970. Reservation/cancellation policy: 24 hours.
CREDIT CARDS	Amex, Diners Club, Discover, MC, Visa
BREAKFAST	Continental Plus breakfast served in dining room overlooking the bay includes fresh pastries, muffins, coffee, tea, juices, cereals, fruit, hot oatmeal and boiled eggs.
AMENITIES	Feather beds, aromatherapy baths, infrared sauna, VCRs, 25" TVs in amoires, two phones in every room, refrigerators, and microwave (if requested). Wine, hors d'oeuvres and tea service every day in our living room. Room service every evening from our gourmet restaurant "Pasta Moon." Meeting facilities available. Handicapped access. Shuttle service to and from the San Francisco Airport.
RESTRICTIONS	No pets. Ducks on premises are kept alert by resident cat, "Fishbone!"...Good name for a cat...TI
RATED	AAA 3 Diamonds

ST. HELENA

Let's just say it's small but upscale, and very pretty. Besides the areas 11 wineries, shopping is de regeur (especially for Dansk). Don't miss the Silverado Museum's Robert Louis Stevenson Collection, or Bale Grist Mill State Historic Park (awesome). Bothe-Napa Valley State Park is pleasant. Northeast of San Francisco via Hwy. 29.

AMBROSE BIERCE HOUSE

1515 Main Street, St. Helena, CA 94574   707-963-3003
Jane Hutchings, Resident Owner

LOCATION	From Napa, head north on Highway 29 approximately 15 miles. At the stoplight in St. Helena, the next street is Pine. The inn is the second house on the left after crossing Pine Street, parking in rear.
OPEN	All year
DESCRIPTION	An 1872 two-story Stick Victorian built by author Amborse Bierce and decorated with antiques.
NO. OF ROOMS	Four with private bathrooms. The Ambrose Bierce Suite is recommended by Jane.
RATES	Year round rates for double with private bathroom are $99 to $109, and $139 for suites. Two night minimum stay on weekends, cancellation requires seven days notice.
CREDIT CARDS	No
BREAKFAST	Continental Plus breakfast served in the dining room includes fresh fruit, pastries and beverages.
AMENITIES	Flowers, sherry, concierge service, NO TV or phones in rooms "it's a plus for many people."
RESTRICTIONS	No smoking, no pets, children over 13 years old are welcome. There are two resident cats who patrol the grounds.
REVIEWED	*Napa Valley Access, Northern California Best Places*
KUDOS/COMMENTS	"I recommend it, very nice innkeepers, very good breakfast."

BARRO STATION BED & BREAKFAST

1112 Lodi Lane, St. Helena, CA 94574   707-963-5169
Rich & Tara Minnick, Resident Owners

LOCATION	Two miles north of St. Helena on Highway 29, then right on Lodi Lane, 1/2 mile on left.
OPEN	All year
DESCRIPTION	Two-story farmhouse with southwestern and antique furnishings, vineyard setting
NO. OF ROOMS	Two rooms with private bathrooms. Rich recommends the Vineyard Room.
RATES	Year round rates are $135 to $145 for a single or a double with a private bathroom. There is a two night minimum on weekends and cancellation requires seven days notice with a one night charge for cancellation.
CREDIT CARDS	MC, Visa
BREAKFAST	Continental breakfast is served.
AMENITIES	Flowers, robes and small winery that guest can visit for tasting - no sales.
RESTRICTIONS	Smoking outside only. The resident dog and cat are Brandy and Willy respectively.

BARTELS RANCH & COUNTRY INN

1200 Conn Valley Road, St. Helena, CA 94574   707-963-4001
Jami Bartels, Resident Owner   FAX 707-963-5100
Spanish spoken

LOCATION	Three miles east of St. Helena on Pope Street to Silverado Trail. Pope Street becomes Howell Mountain Road, continue .25 mile to only fork in road and stay right. Exactly 2 miles (Conn Valley Road) to entrance at 1200 Conn Valley Road (left) across bridge .25 mile driveway to top of valley.
OPEN	All year
DESCRIPTION	Built in 1979, this is a sprawling stone and redwood ranch style country inn with antique and eclectic furnishings on 100 acres.
NO. OF ROOMS	Four rooms with private bathrooms. Guests prefer the Heart of the Valley Suite, but Jami loves the Blue Valley Room.
RATES	High season rates mid-June through mid-November for a single or double with private bathroom are $135 to $225, and $275 to $350 for suites. Entire inn rents for $935. Off season rates mid-November through mid-June and midweek rates for a single or double with private bathroom are $95 to $185, and $285 for suites, entire inn rents for $815. Two night minimum on weekends, three nights on holidays, detailed payment and cancellation policy.
CREDIT CARDS	Amex, MC, Visa, Discover
BREAKFAST	Full breakfast is served in the dining room, guestroom or around the pool and includes quiche or frittata, fresh fruit, english muffins, croissants, granola, yogurt compote and beverages. Other meals will be catered on request.
AMENITIES	Swimming pool, robes, flowers,candles, candy, telephones, TV/VCR for movies only, wine and hors d'oeuvres, bicycles, darts, billiards, backgammon, table tennis, microwave, refrigerators and picnic tables. Sundeck by lagoon, fishing in the lake. Two rooms are wheelchair accessible.
RESTRICTIONS	No smoking, no pets, "well mannered children by special arrangement." Variety of resident animals will welcome your company including two horses, Sugar and Irish (one a World Champion), Sheba the German Shepard and two cats, Fluffy and Tuxedo and Bobby the White Dove.
REVIEWED	*Best Places to Stay in California, Bed and Breakfast California, Away for the Weekend, Bed and Breakfast in California, Taste of the Wine Country*
MEMBER	Professional Association of Innkeepers International, California Association of Bed and Breakfast Inns, California Lodging and Industry Association
RATED	ABBA 3 Crowns

Chestelson House

1417 Kearney Street, St. Helena, CA 94574   707-963-2238
Jackie Sweet, Resident Owner

KUDOS/COMMENTS   "Jackie Sweet, who happens to be the best gourmet cook, serves a full breakfast with great style."

Cinnamon Bear Bed & Breakfast

1407 Kearney Street, St. Helena, CA 94574   707-963-4653
Genny Jenkins, Resident Owner
Spanish spoken

LOCATION   From Highway 29 (Main Street) in St.Helena, go to the first stop light and turn left on Adams, go two blocks to the corner of Adams and Kearney.

OPEN   All year

DESCRIPTION   A two-story 1904-1910 Craftsman with 1920s antiques and "some bears". The Inn is on the California Historic Register.

NO. OF ROOMS   Four rooms with private bathrooms. Vanilla is a good choice.

RATES   High season, August through November, rates are $145 to $155 for a single or a double with a private bathroom. Off season, December through July, rates are $95 to $135 for a single or a double with a private bathroom. The entire inn rents for $465 to $525. There is no minimum stay and cancellation requires three days notice with a $15 cancellation fee.

CREDIT CARDS   MC, Visa

BREAKFAST   Full breakfast is served in the dining room and includes health conscious granola and yogurt, juice, egg and cheese quiche, potatoes, meat, fresh fruit and fresh baked goodies.

AMENITIES   Plants and flowers everywhere, bears peek from bookcases, afternoon refreshment, homemade cookies in the evening, board games and puzzles, TV/VCR in parlor.

RESTRICTIONS   Smoking on the porch only, no pets, children over five are welcome.

REVIEWED   *America's Wonderful Little Hotels & Inns, Definative California Bed & Breakfast Touring Guide, Bed & Breakfast North America, Best Places to Kiss in Northern California, Bed & Breakfast Country Inns, National Trust Guide to Historic B&Bs Inns and Guesthouses*

MEMBER   Professional Association of Innkeepers International, California Association of Bed & Breakfast Inns

CREEKSIDE INN

945 Main Street, St. Helena, CA 94574　　　　　　　　*707-963-7244*
Jean Nicholson & Virginia Toogood, Resident Owners

LOCATION	In the heart of St. Helena. Turn left before crossing the bridge into downtown.
OPEN	All year
DESCRIPTION	1947 French Country ranch cottage onWhite Sulphur Creek.
NO. OF ROOMS	Two rooms with a shared bathroom. The Four Poster room comes highly recommended.
RATES	Year round rates for a single or double room with shared bathroom are $85 to $95. Two days notice required for cancellation.
CREDIT CARDS	Amex, MC, Visa
BREAKFAST	Full breakfast served in the dining room includes fruit, waffles, muffins, scones with creme sauce and beverages.
RESTRICTIONS	No smoking, no pets, children over 10 years old welcome.

DEER RUN BED & BREAKFAST

3995 Spring Mountain Road, St. Helena, CA 94574   *707-963-3794*
Tom & Carol Wilson, Resident Owners   *800-843-3408*
                                                      FAX 707-963-4567

LOCATION	Take Highway 29 through St. Helena to second signal light, turn left on Madrona Avenue and go three blocks to Spring Mountain Road, then 4.5 miles to the inn on the left side of the road.
OPEN	All year
DESCRIPTION	A 1929 cedar shingled clapboard home with a carriage house and cottage with a blend of traditional and antique furnishings.
NO. OF ROOMS	Three rooms have private bathrooms.
RATES	Year round rates are $105 to $140 and there is a minimum stay on Friday and Saturday. Cancellation requires 72 hours notice and there is a $10 cancellation fee.
CREDIT CARDS	Amex, MC, Visa
BREAKFAST	Full breakfast is served in the dining room or brought to the guestroom and includes home grown fresh raspberries, homemade breads and muffins, granola, fritatas, coffee and tea.
AMENITIES	TVs, brandy and mints, coffee and tea service in the rooms, robes, flowers, hair dryers.
RESTRICTIONS	No smoking, no pets, children under 12 months are welcome. The resident Lab is Cody and the two cats "who found us" are Teddy and Annie.
REVIEWED	*California B&Bs, Best Places to Stay in California, Frommer's 50 Best B&Bs in North America*
KUDOS/COMMENTS	"Clean, friendly, private retreat."

ERIKA'S HILLSIDE

285 Fawn Park, St. Helena, CA 94574   707-963-2887
Erika Cunningham, Resident Owner

GLASS MOUNTAIN INN

3100 Silverado Trail, St. Helena, CA 94574   707-963-3512
Jerry and Diane Payton, Resident Owners   FAX 707-963-5310
Spanish

LOCATION	One mile north of St. Helena on Silverado Trail.
OPEN	All year
DESCRIPTION	A 1978 two-story Victorian with towers, turrets and stained glass and period furnishings.
NO. OF ROOMS	All rooms have private bathrooms. Diane recommends Private Reserve.
RATES	Year round rates for a single or double room with private bathroom are $100 to $250. Two night minimum stay required on weekends, five day cancellation policy.
CREDIT CARDS	MC, Visa
BREAKFAST	Full "hot and elegant" breakfast served in dining room adjacent to the candelit wine cave.
AMENITIES	TV, phone, air conditioning, champagne, truffles, hot tub, fireplaces, decks, balconies, views, whirlpool Roman soaking tubs.
RESTRICTIONS	No smoking, children over 10 years old welcome.

HARVEST INN

One Main Street, St. Helena, CA 94574   707-963-9463
Jack Medeiros, Manager

HILLTOP HOUSE BED & BREAKFAST

9550 St. Helena Road, St. Helena, CA 94574   707-963-8743
Annette Gevarter, Resident Owner

LOCATION	At the second traffic light on Highway 29 in St. Helena, turn left on Madrona Avenue. Go three blocks to Spring Mountain Road, turn right and go 5.7 miles to Napa County Line. The inn is the first driveway on the left past the county line.
OPEN	All year
DESCRIPTION	A 1980 ranch style inn with a mixture of antiques and traditional furnishings. Located on a ridge between Napa and Sonoma.
NO. OF ROOMS	Four rooms with private bathrooms. Annette recommends the Vista as her best room.
RATES	Year round rates for a single or a double with private bathroom are $115 to $175. The suite is $155 and the entire inn rents for $545 a night. There is a minimum stay on the weekends and cancellation requires five days notice.
CREDIT CARDS	Amex, MC, Visa
BREAKFAST	Full breakfast served in the dining room or on the deck includes homemade breads and muffins, fresh fruit, yogurt, granola, eggs, juice and beverages.
AMENITIES	The view from the deck, hot tub, afternoon refreshments, fresh flowers, ice bucket and glasses, turn-down service, after-dinner sherry and hiking trails.
RESTRICTIONS	No smoking, no pets, children over six are welcome. The resident pets are two dogs, Rachel and Max and the cat, Maude.
REVIEWED	*AAA Bed & Breakfast Guide—California & Nevada, The Official Bed & Breakfast Guide, The Non-Smokers Guide to Bed & Breakfasts, Bed & Breakfast USA, Bed & Breakfast Inns & Guesthouses.*
MEMBER	National Bed & Breakfast Association.

HOTEL ST. HELENA

1309 Main Street, St. Helena, CA 94574   707-963-4388
Floyd Barker, Manager

HYPHEN INN

PO Box 190, St. Helena, CA 94574   707-942-0434
Suzanne Platel, Resident Manager

INK HOUSE B&B

1575 St. Helena Highway, St. Helena, CA 94574   707-963-3890
Ernie Veniegas, Resident Owner

KUDOS/COMMENTS   "Lovely inn, beautifully done, very nice innkeepers, very good breakfast."

JUDY'S BED & BREAKFAST

2036 Madrona, St. Helena, CA 94574   707-963-3081
Judy Sculatti, Resident Owner

JUDY'S RANCH HOUSE

701 Rossi Road, St. Helena, CA 94574   707-963-3081
Larey Sculatti, Resident Owner

La Fleur Bed & Breakfast Inn

1475 Inglewood Avenue, St. Helena, CA 94574   707-963-0233
K. Murphy, Resident Owner
Some Spanish spoken.   FAX 707-963-0233

LOCATION	Two miles north of Rutherford and 1.5 miles south of St. Helena and 1/2 miles west of Highway 29, between the Beacon Gas Station and the Villa Helena Winery.
OPEN	All year except for Thanksgiving and Christmas and maybe January.
DESCRIPTION	A two-story 1882 Queen Anne Victorian with country style furnishings, "My Mother does all the sewing."
NO. OF ROOMS	Seven rooms with private bathrooms.
RATES	Year round weekend rates are $135 to $150 for a single or a double with a private bathroom, weekday rates range from $110 to $125. There is a two night minimum stay on weekends and cancellation requires seven days notice and a 10% charge.
CREDIT CARDS	No
BREAKFAST	Full breakfast is served in the dining room, solarium or back deck and the menu changes daily.
AMENITIES	Private tours of the Villa Helena Winery, Rose garden, guest refrigerator.
RESTRICTIONS	No smoking, no pets, children over 16 are welcome. The Siamese, 'Cat' "is a character."
REVIEWED	AAA Bed & Breakfast Guide—Northern California, Best Places to Kiss in the Bay Area, Getaways for City-Weary People, Wine Country Access

Oliver House Bed & Breakfast

2970 Silverado Trail, St. Helena, CA 94574   707-963-4089
Richard & Clara Oliver, Resident Owners

Prager Winery

1281 Lewelling Lane, St. Helena, CA 94574   707-963-3720
Jim & Imogene Prager, Resident Owner

Rose Garden Inn

1277 South St. Helena Highway, St. Helena, CA 94574   707-963-4417
Joanne Contreras, Resident Owner

RUSTRIDGE RANCH B&B

2910 Lower Chiles Valley Road, St. Helena, CA 94574   *707-965-9353*
Jim & Susan Fresquez, Resident Owners   *FAX 707-965-9263*

LOCATION	Nine miles east of Rutherford (Highway 29 and Highway 128). Take Highway 128 east past Lake Henessey. Turn left on Chiles and Pope Road, proceed 3 miles, turn right on Lower Chiles Valley Road. One mile to driveway.
OPEN	All year
DESCRIPTION	1940s Southwestern Ranch on 442 acres with vineyards and winery.
NO. OF ROOMS	Four rooms with private bathrooms, two rooms share one bathroom. The RustRidge Room is the best in the house.
RATES	Year round weekend rates for a double with private or shared bathroom are $100 to $160, with a 20% midweek discount. Two night minimum stay on weekends.
CREDIT CARDS	Amex, MC, Visa
BREAKFAST	Full breakfast served in the dining room includes traditional offerings plus fresh fruit and beverages. Special meals with advance notice.
AMENITIES	Tennis, water sports, sauna, decks and living room with fireplace.
RESTRICTIONS	No pets, resident critters are "many" cats and horses and Bo and Buster the Yellow Labs.
REVIEWED	*Wine Country Access*
MEMBER	Bed and Breakfast Inns of Napa Valley

SHADY OAKS COUNTRY INN

399 Zinfandel Lane, St. Helena, CA 94574　　　　　　　*707-963-1190*
John & Lisa Wild-Runnells, Resident Owners

LOCATION	Traveling north on Highway 29, turn right on Zinfandel Lane and go 6/10 of a mile. The inn is on the right.
OPEN	All year, closed December 24-25
DESCRIPTION	An 1880s restored winery and 1920s farm house decorated with "unpretentious elegance," on two acres.
NO. OF ROOMS	Four rooms with private bathrooms and one room shares one bathroom. Pick the sunny hideaway.
RATES	High season rates, April through November and all weekends, are $135 to $155 for a single or double with a private bathroom and the suite is $155 to $205 depending on the number of guests. Off season rates, December through March except weekends, are $95 to $125 for a single or double with a private bathroom and the suite is $95 to $125. There is a minimum stay on most weekends (occasional exception) and cancellation requires 10 days notice and a $10 per room cancellation fee.
CREDIT CARDS	No
BREAKFAST	Full breakfast is served in the dining room and includes Champaigne, eggs benedict, belgian waffles, homebaked breads, fresh fruit and beverages, served in garden patio, or main house or in bed.
AMENITIES	Wine and cheese served each evening, croquet, hoseshoes, soft drinks, bottled water, help with winery itineraries (owners are home wine makers).
RESTRICTIONS	No smoking, no pets, children are not encouraged. Roger the Black Lab is often chased by Alexander the 33rd, a four-pound Yorkshire Terrier.

Spanish Villa Inn

474 Glass Mountain Road, St. Helena, CA 94574   707-963-7483
Roy Bissemer, Resident Owner
Spanish, Italian and Portuguse spoken.

LOCATION	A half mile off the Silverado Trail
OPEN	All year.
DESCRIPTION	A 1981 two-story Mediterranean villa with Spanish interior.
NO. OF ROOMS	Three rooms with private bathrooms.
RATES	Seasonal rates are $115 to $135 for a single or double with a private bathroom. There is a minimum stay on the weekend and cancellation requires seven days notice with a cancellation fee of $15.
CREDIT CARDS	No
BREAKFAST	Continental Plus is served in the dining room.
AMENITIES	King sized beds, Tiffany lamps and a rose in each room.
RESTRICTIONS	No smoking, no pets, children are not encouraged.

Villa St. Helena

2727 Sulphur Springs Avenue, St. Helena, CA 94574   707-963-2514
Ralph Cotton, Resident Owner

Vineyard Country Inn

201 Main Street, St. Helena, CA 94574   707-963-1000
Ida & Gene Lubberstfdt, Resident Owners

Wine Country Inn

1152 Lodi Lane, St. Helena, CA 94574   707-963-7077
Jim Smith, Innkeeper   800-473-3463

KUDOS/COMMENTS   "Excellent."

Zinfandel Inn

800 Zinfandel Lane, St. Helena, CA 94574   707-963-3512
Jerry & Diane Payton, Resident Owners

STINSON BEACH

Natural wonders surround this little seaside gem in the Golden Gate National Recreation Area, just south of Point Reyes National Seashore. Check out Audubon Canyon Ranch, a major sanctuary for great blue herons and great egrets.

CASA DEL MAR

37 Belvedere Avenue, Stinson Beach, CA 94970   *415-868-2124*
Rick Klein, Resident Owner   *FAX 415-868-2305*

LOCATION	From San Francisco, take Highway 101 north to the Mill Valley-Stinson Beach exit, Highway 1. Follow the coast to Stinson Beach. As you drive into town, the first building on the right is the firehouse. Turn right onto Belvedere Avenue, Casa del Mar is located 100 yards up the street on the left.
OPEN	All year
DESCRIPTION	A 1989 two-story Mediterranean villa, surrounded by terraced gardens.
NO. OF ROOMS	Six rooms with private bathrooms. Rick gets raves on the Penthouse.
RATES	Year round rates for a single or double with a private bathroom are $94 to $200. Suites are $165 to $200 and the entire villa rents for $1,000. Minimum stay required on weekends, cancellation requires seven days notice with $7 a day service charge.
CREDIT CARDS	Amex, MC, Visa
BREAKFAST	Full breakfast is served in the dining room and includes fresh squeezed juice, yogurt, granola, fresh fruit, huevos rancheros with fresh salsa, apple pancakes and fresh ground coffee.
AMENITIES	Original art collection, fresh flowers, gardens, evening hors d'oeuvres, phone on request.
RESTRICTIONS	No smoking, no pets, children over eight years old are welcome.
REVIEWED	*Best Places to Kiss in Northern California, California Country Inns and Itineraries, Northern California Best Places, Berlitz Traveler's Guide - San Francisco and Northern California*
MEMBER	Professional Association of Innkeepers International, California Lodging Industry Association, Inns of Point Reyes

SUTTER CREEK

Once a lumber mill and supply center during the "Rush," it's now one of the most charming and authentic of the gold rush era towns. Browsing for antiques is a fun pastime, as is Poppy Days in May. But plan to be here in June for the Italian Benevolent Society's annual picnic. About 42 miles southeast of Sacramento via Hwy. 16 and 124.

THE FOXES IN SUTTER CREEK

77 Main Street, Sutter Creek, CA 95685   209-267-5882
Pete & Min Fox, Resident Owners   FAX 209-267-0712

LOCATION	In Sutter Creek at the north end of town on the west side.
OPEN	All year, closed December 24 and 25.
DESCRIPTION	A two-story 1857 Mother Lode Greek Revival with gardens and trees and "comfortable" European antique furnishings and wraparound porch.
NO. OF ROOMS	Seven rooms with private bathrooms. Pick the Honeymoon Suite.
RATES	Year round weekend and holiday rates are $105 to $140 for a single or a double with a private bathroom, and mid-week rates are $90 to $125. There is a two night minimum stay on the weekends and cancellation requires seven days notice with a $10 fee.
CREDIT CARDS	Discover, MC, Visa
BREAKFAST	Full breakfast, cooked to order, served in guestrooms or in gardens. Special meals available according to dietary needs.
AMENITIES	Early coffee, morning newspaper delivered to your door. Woodburning fireplaces in four rooms, air conditioning, covered guest parking, complimentary soft drinks, garden gazebo and common areas
RESTRICTIONS	No smoking, no pets. Rooms and suites accommodate two people only.
REVIEWED	*Best Places to Stay in California, The Best Places to Kiss in Northern California, Bed and Breakfast California, Recommended Country Inns—West Coast, America's Wonderful Little Hotels and Inns, Karen Brown's California Country Inns & Itineraries*
MEMBER	Bed and Breakfast Inns of Amador County, California Association of Bed and Breakfast Inns, California Lodging Industry of Association.
RATED	Mobil 3 Stars
KUDOS/COMMENTS	". . . great inn, terrific innkeepers. . ."

GOLD QUARTZ INN

15 Bryson Drive, Sutter Creek, CA 95685   209-267-9155
Wendy Woolrich, Manager   800-752-8738

GREY GABLES INN

161 Hanford Street, Sutter Creek, CA 95685　　　　209-267-1039
Roger & Sue Garlick, Managers

THE HANFORD HOUSE

61 Hanford Street, Sutter Creek, CA 95685　　　　209-267-0747
Jim & Lucille Jacobus, Resident Owners

LOCATION	In the center of town, Main Street becomes Hanford Street.
OPEN	All year
DESCRIPTION	Two-story brick built around a 1920s cottage with early California antiques.
NO. OF ROOMS	Eight rooms with private bathrooms. Lucille suggest the suite.
RATES	Year round rates are $60 to $110 for a single or a double with a private bathroom. The entire B&B rents for $750. Rates are significantly lower Sunday through Thursday. There is a two-night minimum stay on weekends and cancellation requires seven days notice.
CREDIT CARDS	Discover, MC, Visa
BREAKFAST	Continental Plus is served in the dining room and includes a buffet of fruit, cheeses, cereals, granola, yogurts, juices, muffins and beverages.
AMENITIES	Wine and hors d'oeuvres, soft drinks, iced tea. Cookies available all the time. Daily newspaper under each door. Meeting facilites and handicapped accessible. Off-street parking, rooftop deck, patio two parlors and guest phone.
RESTRICTIONS	No smoking, no pets. The resident mixed terrier-poodle called Nui who "...is nutty, he barks when our guest leave, not when they arrive".
MEMBER	California Association of Bed & Breakfast Inns, California Lodging Industry Association, Amador County Bed & Breakfast Association
RATED	Mobil 2 Stars

SUTTER CREEK INN

75 Main Street, Sutter Creek, CA 95685　　　　209-267-5606
Jane Way, Resident Owner

TOMALES

TOMALES COUNTRY INN

25 Valley Street, Tomales, CA 94971　　　　707-878-2041
Laura Hoffman, Innkeeper

TRINIDAD

This tiny coastal village has one of the most splendid harbors on the West Coast, and trolling for salmon is a full-time pursuit. But don't miss the town's massive crab feed in April or May. Check out Memorial Lighthouse and the aquarium, or Patrick's Point State Park and Agate Beach. Just north of Eureka on Highway 101.

THE LOST WHALE INN

3452 Patrick's Point Drive, Trinidad, CA 95570   707-677-3425
Lee Miller & Susanne Lakin, Resident Owners

LOCATION	From Highway 101 north exit at Trinidad and take an immediate right on to Patrick's Point Drive. The inn is four miles north on the left.
OPEN	All year
DESCRIPTION	A two-story 1989 Cape Cod style country inn on four costal acres with its own private beach. The interior is natural wood and lots of windows.
NO. OF ROOMS	Seven rooms with private batrooms.
RATES	High season, May through October, rates are $100 to $140 for a single or double with a private bathroom and the beach guesthouse is $180. Low season, November through April, rates are $85 to $125 for a single or double with private bathroom and the beach guesthouse is $140. There is a minimum stay on the weekends and cancellation between June 15 and September 15 requires seven days notice.
CREDIT CARDS	Amex, Discover, MC, Visa
BREAKFAST	"Outrageously huge country breakfast soon to be in a national cookbook" is served in the dining room...we would like a guest report please...TI
AMENITIES	Ocean view from all rooms, afternoon tea with wine and sherry cake, complimentary sodas, hot tub overlooking the ocean, two mile private beach with "hundreds" of sea lions, chocolates by the bed, flowers, meeting, wedding and reception facilities and playground with playhouse.
RESTRICTIONS	No smoking, no pets, all children welcome. There are three outdoor cats and the Lakins raise pygmy goats at a farm down the street.
REVIEWED	*Bed & Breakfast Guide—California, America's Wonderful Little Hotels & Inns, Driving the Pacific Coast, Karen Brown's California Country Inns & itineraries, Best Places to Stay in California*
RATED	Mobil 4 Stars
KUDOS/COMMENTS	"Clean, very well-run 4 Star B&B"

TRINIDAD BAY BED & BREAKFAST

560 Edwards Street, Trinidad, CA 95570　　　　　707-677-0840
Paul & Carol Kirk, Resident Owners　　　　　FAX 707-677-3360

LOCATION	From Highway 101 take the Trinidad exit, go west and follow Main Street toward the beach. The inn is on the corner across from the Memorial Lighthouse on the bluff.
OPEN	All year except for December and January
DESCRIPTION	A two-story 1950 Cape Cod inn with country and antique furnishings.
NO. OF ROOMS	Four rooms with private bathrooms. Pick the Mauve Fireplace Suite.
RATES	Year round rates are $105 to $125 for a single or double with a private bathroom. The suite is $145 to $155 and the entire inn rents for $530. There is a minimum stay on the weekend and cancellation requires seven days notice with a $15 fee.
CREDIT CARDS	MC, Visa
BREAKFAST	Continental Plus is served in the dining room or guestroom and includes homemade bread, muffins, baked fruit, fresh fruit medley with yogurt, local cheeses and homemade flavored butter.
AMENITIES	All rooms overlook the ocean, self serve snack and beverage area, fireplaces burn after dinner.
RESTRICTIONS	No smoking, no pets, children will need to be old enough to occupy their own room.
REVIEWED	*Bed & Breakfast Guide of California, Karen Brown's California Country Inns & Itineraries, Jerry Graham's Bay Area Backroads, AAA Bed & Breakfast Guide—Northern California, Northern California Bed & Breakfast Guidebook.*

TRUCKEE

RICHARDSON B&B INN

PO Box 2011, Truckee CA 95734　　　　　916-587-5388
Bonnie Richardson, Resident Owner

TUOLUMNE

This pretty mountain town stands out among Gold Country gems. In September, the annual Indian Acorn Festival is held at the Tuolumne Rancheria, one of the last remaining Miwok reservations. Southeast of Sonora off of Highway 108.

OAK HILL RANCH BED & BREAKFAST

18550 Connally Lane, Tuolumne, CA 95379　　　　209-828-4717
Sanford and Jane Grover, Resident Owners
Smatterings of Spanish and Japanese spoken.

LOCATION	Take Road 17E off State Hwy. 108 to Tuolumne. Turn right on Carter Street and go five blocks to Elm. Turn left and travel one block to Apple Colony Road. Turn right and travel five blocks to Connally Lane (private road) to B&B.
OPEN	All year
DESCRIPTION	1980 two-story Country Victorian and cottage built with genuine (collected) Victorian building materials on 56 wooded acres at 3,000 feet elevation.
NO. OF ROOMS	Three rooms with private bathrooms. Two rooms share one bathroom.
RATES	Year round rates for singles and doubles with private baths $80 to $85; singles and doubles with shared bath $70 to $75; suites $145; guesthouse $115; entire B&B $435. A two night minimum stay is required on national holidays. Reservation/cancellation policy: seven days notice; $10 cancellation fee.
CREDIT CARDS	No
BREAKFAST	Full breakfasts, served in dining room, include hot meats, fruit garni and freshly home baked breads, fresh fruit in season, iced juices, and entrees of crepes Normandie, eggs fantasia, Belgian waffles, crustless Swiss quiche, or French toast, plus hot beverages of all kinds. All guests served together at dining table. Picnic lunches available on request, made to order.
AMENITIES	Player piano sing-alongs after breakfast, meeting facilities available for up to 25 persons, two gazebos in the lawn and flower garden., refreshments on arrival and handicapped access.
RESTRICTIONS	No smoking "any smoking must be out-of-doors and away from other guests", no pets. Children over 13 are welcome. One resident cat, Mitzi, "is never allowed inside the buildings, but is cute nonetheless."
REVIEWED	*Bed & Breakfast Guide–California, Bed & Breakfast Homes Directory, Recommended Country Inns of the West Coast, Country Inns of America—California, California Country Inns & Itineraries; Bed & Breakfast California.*
MEMBER	Gold Country Inns of Tuolumne County

UKIAH

Rough-hewn and maybe a little rowdy, "Yu Haia" (Pomo for "deep valley") is a lumber town populated by redwood loggers and other tree-connected folks. The town is graced by the extraordinary Grace Hudson Museum and Sun House. And just down the road, the City of Ten Thousand Buddhas is a world center for Buddhist study. Check out the wineries nearby, and the Mendocino County Wine Auction and Barbeque in June. From San Francisco, take HIghway 101 north through wine country.

OAK KNOLL BED & BREAKFAST

858 Sanel Drive, Ukiah, CA 95482   707-462-8322
Shirley Wadley, Resident Owner

LOCATION	Seven miles south of Ukiah, exit Henry Station Road.
OPEN	All year
DESCRIPTION	A 1979 contemporary redwood host home surrounded by large decks.
NO. OF ROOMS	Two rooms with shared bathroom.
RATES	Year round rates for single or double with shared bathroom $70 to $80.
CREDIT CARDS	No
BREAKFAST	Full breakfast includes fruit, breads, main dish, homemade jellies and beverages.
AMENITIES	Flowers, study-sitting room with phone, radio and wide screenTV/VCR, wine, cheese and crackers in the evening, two fireplaces and piano in common room.
RESTRICTIONS	No smoking, no pets. Resident host pets, Lady the dog, and Cassie the cat.
REVIEWED	*American and Canadian Bed and Breakfasts, Bed & Breakfast Home Directory*

SANFORD HOUSE B&B

306 Pine Street, Ukiah, CA 95482   707-462-1653
Dorsey & Bob Manogue, Resident Owners

VICHY HOT SPRINGS RESORT B&B

2605 Vichy Springs Road, Ukiah, CA 95482   707-462-9515
Gilbert & Marjorie Ashoff, Resident Owners   FAX 707-462-9516

LOCATION	From Highway 101 take Vichy Springs Road exit and travel three miles east to the resort.
OPEN	All year
DESCRIPTION	Several California Craftsman buildings from the mid-1800s on 700 acres decorated with chintz (waverley) and hardwood floors. Listed on the California Historic Register.
NO. OF ROOMS	Fourteen rooms with private bathrooms. Pick a cottage.
RATES	Year round rates are $85 to $160 for a single or a double with a private bathroom. A suite is $150 to $160. There is two night minimum during holiday periods and cancellation requires four days notice.
CREDIT CARDS	Just about everything.
BREAKFAST	Full breakfast served in the dining room includes coffee, orange juice, fresh fruit, sweet rolls, hard boiled eggs, bagels and cream cheese. Lunch and dinner are available and special meals can be catered.
AMENITIES	Flowers and phones in rooms, olympic sized mineral pool, hot tub, naturally carbonated warm mineral baths, water fall, massage available.
RESTRICTIONS	No smoking indoors, no pets. The resident Queensland Blue Heelers are Sheila and Basil who, "chase deer so flowers can survive."
REVIEWED	*The Official B&B Guide, The National Trust Guide to Historic B&Bs, Inns and Guesthouses, Bed & Breakfast Guesthouses & Inns of America, North American B&B Directory, The Best B&Bs & Country Inns*
MEMBER	American Historic Inns
RATED	AAA 2 Diamonds

VOLCANO

Set in a deep, crater-like valley, it's almost a ghost town (pop. 100 more or less), but alive with history. The Volcano Theatre Company performs year-round, and Chow'se Indian Grinding Rock State Historic Park should not be missed. In spring, Daffodil Hill is a blooming feast. Southeast of Sacramento off Highway 88.

ST. GEORGE HOTEL

Two Main Street, Volcano, CA 95689   209-296-4458
Marlene & Chuck Inman, Resident Owners

LOCATION	"Volcano has four blocks - we are one of them."
OPEN	From mid-February to Christmas, closed Monday after breakfast and reopens for dinner Wednesday.
DESCRIPTION	A three-story Gold Rush hotel with original furnishings that is on both the National and California Historic Registers.
NO. OF ROOMS	Six rooms with private bathrooms and 14 rooms share four bathrooms. Try the Dogtown Room.
RATES	Year round rates are $88 for a single with private bathroom, $117 to $123 for a double with private bathroom, $62 to $83 for a single with shared bathroom and $112 to $117 for a double with shared bathroom. There is a minimum stay on Thanksgiving weekend and cancellation requires 48 hours notice.
CREDIT CARDS	Amex, Diner's Club, Discover, MC, Visa
BREAKFAST	Full breakfast served in the dining room includes ham or bacon, scrambled eggs, blueberry banana pancakes, juice and coffee. Dinner is include in the price of the room.
AMENITIES	Full bar, sometimes with live bluegrass music, fireplace in the lounge and dinner/meeting facilities.
RESTRICTIONS	No smoking, children under 12 in the annex only.

VOLCANO INN

16114 Jerome Street, Volcano, CA 95689   209-296-4959
Jane Norcross/Baird, Resident Owner

WALNUT CREEK

From this large suburban city northeast of Oakland, Mt. Diablo State Park is easily accessible. In town, children will enjoy the live animals at Lindsay Museum.

THE MANSION AT LAKEWOOD

1056 Hacienda Drive, Walnut Creek, CA 94598 510-945-3600
Sharyn and Mike McCoy, Resident Owners 800-477-7898
FAX 510-945-3608

LOCATION	Take Highway 24 from San Francisco to Ygnacio Valley Road exit. Head north to 7th signal, turn right onto Homestead, go 3 blocks and turn left on Hacienda Drive. Look for white iron gates at the end.
OPEN	All year
DESCRIPTION	An 1860 two-story Victorian country estate surrounded by three acres of gardens.
NO. OF ROOMS	Seven rooms with private bathrooms. Try the Estate Suite for a treat.
RATES	Year round rates for a single or double with private bathroom are $135 to $195 and $225 to $300 for suites. Cancellation requires 72 hours notice and $10 fee. Inquire about special corporate rates.
CREDIT CARDS	Amex, MC, Visa, Discover
BREAKFAST	Continental Plus served dining room, guestroom or terrace includes "elegant and romantic dishes" such as heart shaped waffles, quiches, baked eggs, fruit compotes and beverages.
AMENITIES	Wildflowers and fresh fruit from the garden, hot cider in winter, old fashioned lemonade in summer, TV/VCR in the library, woodburning fireplaces, private phones, Egyptian cotton towels and robes, down pillows and comforters, AM/FM/tape players in rooms, meeting facilities, handicapped access.
RESTRICTIONS	No smoking, no pets, children over 10 years of age welcome. Seymour is the "outdoor kitty."
REVIEWED	*Best Places to Kiss in Northern California*
MEMBER	American Bed and Breakfast Association, California Association of Bed and Breakfast Inns
RATED	ABBA 3 Crowns
KUDOS/COMMENTS	"Quiet elegance in an urban setting."

WATSONVILLE

DUNMOVIN

1006 Hecker Pass Road, Watsonville, CA 95076 408-722-2810
Don & Ruth Wakefield, Resident Owners

WESTPORT

The little coastal lumber mill town north of Fort Bragg is at the end of a long and beautiful northbound stretch of state parks and beaches. The Westport–Union Landing State Beach here is perfect.

BOWEN'S PELICAN LODGE & INN

38921 North Highway 1, Westport, CA 95488   707-964-5588
Velma Bowen, Resident Owner

DEHAVEN VALLEY FARM COUNTRY INN

39247 North Highway 1, Westport, CA 95488   707-961-1660
Jim & Kathleen Tobin, Resident Owners   FAX 707-961-1677
Some Spanish spoken   F

LOCATION	On Highway 1, north of Westport Village 1.7 miles.
OPEN	Open February 1 through January 1, closed the week prior to Christmas.
DESCRIPTION	An 1875 two-story Victorian farmhouse on 20 coastal acres of meadows and farmland. Early American furnishings.
NO. OF ROOMS	Six rooms with private bathrooms, two rooms with shared bathroom. The Eagle's Nest is the best in the house.
RATES	Year round rates for a single or double room with private bathroom are $95 to $125, and $85 to $90 for a single or double room with shared bathroom. Weekends in August and holidays require minimum stay, 72 hour cancellation policy.
CREDIT CARDS	Amex, MC, Visa
BREAKFAST	Full breakfast served in the dining room includes fruit course, entree includes egg dish or waffles, pancakes, strata and beverages. Vegetarians and diet restrictions easily accommodated with prior notice.
AMENITIES	Flowers, cookies, sherry, hot tub on the hill, phones, tidepools nearby and blackberry picking.
RESTRICTIONS	No smoking, no pets. Farm animals including Martine and Margarita the llamas. "Our sheep, Starbuck, who thinks he's a horse and our goats, Al and Al2, who are our dogs. . ."
REVIEWED	*Northern Califonia Best Places, AAA Bed & Breakfast Guide—Northern California, Weekend Adventures for City Weary People, Complete Guide to American Bed and Breakfast, Feather Beds and Flapjacks, Recommended Country Inns—West Coast*
MEMBER	Professional Association Innkeepers International, California Association of Bed and Breakfast Inns

HOWARD CREEK RANCH

40501 North Highway 1, Westport, CA 95488   707-964-6725
Charles & Sally Grigg, Resident Owners
German, Spanish, Dutch, Italian spoken   FAX 707-964-6725

LOCATION	Three miles north of Westport on Highway 1, at milepost 80.49.
OPEN	All year
DESCRIPTION	An 1871 two-story Victorian farmhouse bordered by 40 acres of ocean beaches. Furnished with 1880 antiques and listed on the County Historic Register.
NO. OF ROOMS	Nine rooms with private bathrooms, one room with shared bathroom.
RATES	Year round rates for a double or single with a private or shared bathroom are $55 to $145. Two night minimum stay required on some weekends and holidays, one week advance cancellation required.
CREDIT CARDS	Amex, MC, Visa
BREAKFAST	Full breakfast served in the dining room includes strawberry/banana hot cakes, omelettes with garden tomatoes, scallions, and cheese, baked apples with granola and French whipped cream, sausage, fresh fruit and beverages.
AMENITIES	Hot tub and sauna on the hill, massage, flower gardens, horse and wagon rides, farm animals, private decks and balconies, skylights, fireplaces/woodstoves, piano and guitar, great books.
RESTRICTIONS	Smoking outside only, pets OK by prior arrangement. Children are welcome, in fact, "we love babies." Standard farm animals include cows, Percheron horses, dogs and cats.
REVIEWED	Best Places to Stay in California, Northern California Best Places, Fodor's Travel Guide - California, Bed and Breakfast North America, Feather Beds and Flapjacks
MEMBER	Professional Association of Innkeepers International, California Association of Bed and Breakfast Inns, Mendocino Coast Innkeepers Association

WHITETHORN

SHELTER COVE B&B

148 Dolphin Drive, Whitethorn, CA 95589   707-986-7161
Don Sack, Manager

WILLOW CREEK

PEACH TREE INN

201 Enchanted Springs Lane, Willow Creek, CA 95573   916-629-2969
Les & Diane Christian, Resident Owners

WINDSOR

Here in the heart of Sonoma County, the grapes reign, just south of Healdsburg on Highway 101.

COUNTRY MEADOW INN

11360 Old Redwood Highway, Windsor, CA 95492   707-431-1276
Susan Hardesty, Resident Owner   800-238-1728

LOCATION	Traveling north on Highway 101, take Healdsburg Avenue exit and turn left on Old Redwood Highway. Continue south for two miles. The inn is just after the Rodney Strong and Piper Sonoma Wineries.
OPEN	All year, closed Thanksgiving and Christmas days.
DESCRIPTION	An 1890 two-story Queen Anne Victorian on six acres of gardens with country and antique furnishings.
NO. OF ROOMS	Five rooms with private bathrooms. Susan suggests the Garden Suite.
RATES	Year round rates vary widely between the rooms and are $65 to $165 for a single or a double with a private bathroom. There is a two night minimum stay on the weekends.
CREDIT CARDS	MC, Visa
BREAKFAST	Full breakfast is served in the dining room and includes fruit dish (fresh and baked), farm fresh egg dish or pancakes, fresh baked muffins, bread and coffe and tea.
AMENITIES	Swiming pool and tennis court, fresh flowers in rooms, rooms with whirlpool tub, fireplaces, one handicapped access room and afternoon refreshments.
RESTRICTIONS	No smoking, no pets. Simon and Sheila are the resident Cocker Spaniels, there are also chickens, ducks and a turkey.
REVIEWED	*Weekends for Two in Northern California, 50 Romantic Getaways*

YOSEMITE

In the exquisite Yosemite Valley of Yosemite National Park. From here all its wonders are within reach, especially Yosemite and Bridal Veil Falls and the Visitor Center. From Merced, take Highway 140 east.

WALDSCHLOSS BED & BREAKFAST

7486 Henness Circle, Yosemite West,   209-372-4958
Yosemite National Park, CA 95389
John & Betty Clark, Resident Owners
Limited German spoken

LOCATION	Fifteen miles from the valley floor...get a good map from the folks at the park entrance...TI
OPEN	March 1 through November 30
DESCRIPTION	A 1982 mountain host home decorated with traditional furnishings and family antiques.
NO. OF ROOMS	Two rooms with private bathrooms.
RATES	Year round rates for a double or a single with private bathroom are $78 to $88. The entire B&B rents for $166 a night. There is no minimum stay and cancellation requires seven days notice.
CREDIT CARDS	MC, Visa
BREAKFAST	Full breakfast served in the dining room includes juice, fresh fruit, breakfast meat, egg dish or entree such as pancakes, French toast, omelettes, coffee cake and torte.
AMENITIES	Afternoon refreshments, fireplace and decks, starry nights at 6400 feet, TV in rooms, nearby walking trails.
RESTRICTIONS	No smoking, no pets, children over 12 are welcome.
REVIEWED	*California Bed & Breakfast Homes Directory*
MEMBER	Professional Association of Innkeepers international

YOUNTVILLE

The first vineyard in the Napa Valley was planted here in 1830, thanks to George Yount. Fine wineries have since proliferated to include the famous $42 million Domaine Chandon facility. The tiny town has gone upscale—shopping centers around the Vintage 1870 complex housed in an old winery, and hot air balloons are the primary "way to go" here. Or just picnic in lovely City Park. Just north of Napa via (preferably not) Hwy. 29 from the Bay Area.

BORDEAUX HOUSE

6600 Washington Street, Yountville, CA 94599　　　707-944-2855
Jean Lunney, Resident Owner　　　800-677-6370

BURGUNDY HOUSE

6711 Washington Street, Yountville, CA 94599　　　707-944-0889
Deanna Roque, Resident Owner

LOCATION	Yountville exit off Highway 29 directly to Washington Street.
OPEN	All year
DESCRIPTION	Two-story 1893 French Country inn constructed from river rock and field stone. On both the National and State Historic Registers.
NO. OF ROOMS	Six rooms with private bathrooms.
RATES	High season rates, April through November, are $115 to $125 for a single or double with private bathroom. Off season rates, December through March, are $90 to $100 for a single or double with private bathroom. Minimum two night stay on weekends, cancellation policy requires seven days notice and $15 cancellation charge.
CREDIT CARDS	MC, Visa
BREAKFAST	Full breakfast is served in the "distillery" or garden includes juice and fruit platter, cereals, pastries, hot casserole, coffee and tea.
AMENITIES	Fresh flowers, decanter of local white wine in room.
RESTRICTIONS	No smoking, no pets, children over 12 years of age are welcome.
REVIEWED	*Historic Bed and Breakfast Inns, AAA Bed & Breakfast Guide— California*

MAISON FLEURIE

6529 Yount Street, Yountville, CA 94599   707-944-2056
Roger Asbiu, Manager   FAX 707-944-9342

LOCATION	Take the Yountville exit from Highway 29. Turn right at the end of the ramp, then left onto Washington. When the road forks, stay right on Yount. The inn is on the left.
OPEN	All year
DESCRIPTION	Three 1880s French Country brick buildings on landscaped grounds.
NO. OF ROOMS	Thirteen rooms with private bathrooms. Number Ten tops the hit parade.
RATES	High season, April through October, rates for a double with private bathroom are $110 to $125, and $175 to $190 for deluxe rooms. Off season, November through March, Sunday through Thursday, rates for a double with private bathroom are $95 to $110, and $150 to $165 for deluxe rooms. No minimum stay, two day cancellation policy.
CREDIT CARDS	Amex, MC, Visa
BREAKFAST	Full breakfast is served either in the dining room or in your guest room includes homebaked bread and rolls, hot dish, fresh fruit, cereals and beverages.
AMENITIES	Morning paper, bicycles, afternoon tea, concierge and turndown service, phones, outdoor spa and swimming pool, beach towels, terry robes.
RESTRICTIONS	No smoking, no pets.

OLEANDER HOUSE

7433 St. Helena Highway, Yountville, CA 94599   707-944-8315
John & Louise Packard, Resident Owner

THE SYBRON HOUSE

7400 St. Helena Highway, Yountville, CA 94599
Cheryl Maddox, Resident Owner
Spanish

707-944-2785
800-944-2785
FAX 707-944-9418

LOCATION	Located 1.5 miles north of Yountville. Across the street from Mustard's Grill on the east side of Highway 29 (St. Helena Highway).
OPEN	February 1 through November 30.
DESCRIPTION	Built in 1978, this Victorian Country Inn with country and antique furnishings overlooks the Napa Valley.
NO. OF ROOMS	Four rooms with private bathrooms. Try the Honeymoon Suite even if you don't qualify.
RATES	Year round rates for a single or double with private bathroom are $120 to $160. Two night minimum stay on weekends, three nights on holidays, seven day cancellation notice required.
CREDIT CARDS	MC, Visa
BREAKFAST	Full breakfast served in the dining room includes "homemade and healthy" freshly baked items, seasonal fruit, fresh-squeezed orange juice and "great coffee."
AMENITIES	Cheese and crackers in the early evening, fresh flowers, hot tub on outside deck, grand piano, private tennis court, library, sunroom and balcony.
RESTRICTIONS	No smoking, no pets, children under six are not encouraged.
MEMBER	Professional Association of Innkeepers International, California Association of Bed and Breakfast Inns, Bed and Breakfast Inns of the Napa Valley
KUDOS/COMMENTS	". . .great views, beautifully kept . . ."

THE WEBBER PLACE

6610 Webber Street, Yountville, CA 94599
Diane Bartholomew, Resident Owner

707-944-8384

YUBA CITY

It h as its own claim to fame (no ribald jokes will be printed in this guide), to wit: Prunes. Two-thirds of the nation's prunes are grown and processed here. The Prune Festival in September celebrates their yummyness and variety of uses. Most surprising is the large Sikh community that has settled here. The Tierra Buena Temple is absolutely a must visit (permission required), and check out the Punjab Bazaar for a fast glimpse of India. Most significant is the town's access to the Sutter Buttes, the world's smallest mountain range. North of Sacramento about 50 miles via Hwy. 99. On the Feather River.

HARKEY HOUSE B&B

212 C Street, Yuba City, CA 95991　　　　　　　　　　*916-674-1942*
Robert Jones, Resident Owner

MOORE MANSION INN

560 Cooper Avenue, Yuba City, CA 95991　　　　　　*916-674-8559*
Peggy Gehert, Resident Owner　　　　　　　　　　*FAX 916-674-8559*

LOCATION	From Highway 99 go east on Bridge Street for 3/4 of a mile. The inn is on the southwest corner of Bridge and Cooper Streets. And if you have a Global Positioning System (GPS) Peggy claims that her place is north 39/07.6 and west 121/36.5. Someone check this out please...Peggy was probably holding the GPS upside down...TI
OPEN	All year
DESCRIPTION	A 1925 two-story Craftsman with comfortable furnishings and some antiques.
NO. OF ROOMS	Five rooms with private bathrooms. Try the Feather River, if Peggy can find it for you.
RATES	Year round rates are $65 to $85 for a single or double with a private bathroom. The entire inn rents for $675. There is no minimum stay or cancellation policy.
CREDIT CARDS	MC, Visa
BREAKFAST	Full breakfast served in the dining room, rose garden or patio includes fresh fruits in season, juice, breads cereal and a hot entree.
AMENITIES	Air conditioning, fireplace, game room, roses, large double hammock in the back yard, telephone and FAX available.
RESTRICTIONS	No smoking, no pets, "children over one day are welcome."
MEMBER	California Association of Bed & Breakfast Inns

BED & BREAKFAST INDEX

ORDERING INFORMATION

If you would like additional copies of this book or other books in the series, please contact your local bookseller and give them all the information listed with each title. If the bookseller doesn't have the book in stock, she or he can get it for you in about a week to ten days.

THE ROCKY MOUNTAIN SERIES

Absolutely Every Bed & Breakfast in Arizona (*Almost)*, Second Edition, ISBN 1-882092-12-0, $15.95.

Absolutely Every Bed & Breakfast in California, Monterey to San Diego (*Almost)*, ISBN 1-882092-10-4, $15.95.

Absolutely Every Bed & Breakfast in Northern California, (*Almost)*, ISBN 1-882092-13-1, $16.95.

Absolutely Every Bed & Breakfast in Colorado (*Almost)*, Third Edition, ISBN 1-882092-11-2, $16.95.

Absolutely Every Bed & Breakfast in New Mexico (*Almost)*, ISBN 1-882092-07-4, $12.95.

Absolutely Every Bed & Breakfast in Texas (*Almost)*, Toni Knapp, editor, ISBN 1-882092-09-0, $15.95.